Cognitive Ecopoetics

Environmental Cultures Series

Bloomsbury's *Environmental Cultures* series makes available to students and scholars at all levels the latest cutting-edge research on the diverse ways in which culture has responded to the age of environmental crisis. Publishing ambitious and innovative literary ecocriticism that crosses disciplines, national boundaries, and media, books in the series explore and test the challenges of ecocriticism to conventional forms of cultural study.

Titles available

Bodies of Water, Astrida Neimanis
Cities and Wetlands, Rod Giblett
Civil Rights and the Environment in African-American Literature, 1895–1941, John Claborn
Climate Change Scepticism, Greg Garrard, George Handley, Axel Goodbody, and Stephanie Posthumus
Climate Crisis and the 21st-Century British Novel, Astrid Bracke
Colonialism, Culture, Whales, Graham Huggan

Ecocriticism and Italy, Serenella Iovino
Fuel, Heidi C. M. Scott
Literature as Cultural Ecology, Hubert Zapf
Nerd Ecology, Anthony Lioi
The New Nature Writing, Jos Smith
The New Poetics of Climate Change, Matthew Griffiths
This Contentious Storm, Jennifer Mae Hamilton
Climate Change Scepticism, Greg Garrard, Axel Goodbody, George B. Handley, and Stephanie Posthumus

Forthcoming Titles

Reclaiming Romanticism, Kate Rigby
Ecospectrality, Laura White
Radical Animism, Jemma Deer
Cognitive Ecopoetics, Sharon Lattig
Eco-Digital Art, Lisa FitzGerald
Environmental Cultures in Soviet East Europe, Anna Barcz
Weathering Shakespeare, Evelyn O'Malley
Imagining the Plains of Latin America, Axel Pérez Trujillo Diniz
Ecocriticism and Turkey, Meliz Ergin

Cognitive Ecopoetics

A New Theory of Lyric

Sharon Lattig

BLOOMSBURY ACADEMIC
LONDON • NEW YORK • OXFORD • NEW DELHI • SYDNEY

BLOOMSBURY ACADEMIC
Bloomsbury Publishing Plc
50 Bedford Square, London, WC1B 3DP, UK
1385 Broadway, New York, NY 10018, USA
29 Earlsfort Terrace, Dublin 2, Ireland

BLOOMSBURY, BLOOMSBURY ACADEMIC, and the Diana logo are trademarks of Bloomsbury Publishing Plc

First published in Great Britain 2021
This paperback edition published in 2022

Cover design: Burge Agency
Cover image: Shutterstock

A catalogue record for this book is available from the British Library.

A catalog record for this book is available from the Library of Congress.

ISBN: HB: 978-1-3500-6925-1
PB: 978-1-3501-8613-2
ePDF: 978-1-3500-6926-8
eBook: 978-1-3500-6927-5

Series: Environmental Cultures

Typeset by Newgen KnowledgeWorks Pvt. Ltd., Chennai, India

To find out more about our authors and books visit www.bloomsbury.com and sign up for our newsletters.

For Beth and for Deb
Three sisters, always

Contents

Acknowledgments

I would like to offer gratitude to Greg Garrard, Richard Kerridge, David Avital, Ben Doyle, Mary Newell, Joan Richardson, Jonathan Levitt, the late Joshua Wallman, Joshua Wilner, Devin Zuber, Victoria N. Alexander, Donald C. Freeman, Margaret Freeman, Peter Schneck, Peter Stockwell, the late Walter J. Freeman, Max Gabrielson, Ann Lauterbach, Bruce Clarke, Clara Herberg, Lucy Brown, and especially Sophie Roberts.

Portions of the Introduction and Chapters 2 and 3 appeared in "Perception and the Lyric: The Emerging Mind of the Poem." *Contemporary Stylistics*. Ed. Marina Lambrou and Peter Stockwell. London: Continuum, 2007. 168–79. Reprinted with the permission of Continuum Publishing, an imprint of Bloomsbury Publishing Plc.

Portions of Chapter 4 appeared in "The Perception of Metaphor and the Metaphor of Perception," published in *Intertexts*, Vol. 9, No. 1 (Spring 2005): 23–42. Reprinted with the permission of Texas Tech University Press.

Portions of Chapter 4 appeared in "Vatic Craft: The Science and Poetics of Perception," published in *Challenging the Boundaries*. Ed. Işil Baş and Donald C. Freeman. Amsterdam: Rodopi, 2007. 69–94. Reprinted with the permission of Brill | Rodopi.

Introduction: The Region of the Song

Not Chaos, not
The darkest pit of lowest Erebus,
Nor aught of blinder vacancy, scooped out
By help of dreams can breed such fear and awe
As fall upon us often when we look
Into our Minds, into the Mind of Man
My haunt, and the main region of my song.

—William Wordsworth

Prologue: An Ecopoetics

This book arises at the confluence of three distinct tributaries: ecopoetics, cognitive poetics, and the theory of the lyric. Common to many advocates and practitioners of ecopoetry is the view that it might serve to negotiate a relationship with the physical world, nudging its makers and hearers alike into alignment with "nature," the definition of which is then contested. The belief is not simply a Romantic holdover, or Jonathan Bate's notion of the poem as a park in which we may "accommodate ourselves to a mode of dwelling that is not alienated" (10), for it is shared, for instance, by Olsonian poetics bent on undoing the subject. In fact, the aim of reconciliation with a physical reality reaches an extreme when it is framed as ecological: "For ecopoetics reflects yet another in a series of human decenterings, as from an ecological perspective, the self dissolves into the gene pool and the species into the ecosystem" (Reilly 257). As it is sensed—and, further, as it is enabled linguistically—a poetic forging and foregrounding of connection must be effected in part cognitively. Glossed over within the brief history of ecopoetics is the salient fact that in experiencing both "nature" and poetry, we engage with environments through cognitive processes that shoulder ecological import because they are at base physical. I have thus set out to ground the integration poetry offers (and at times frustrates) in the mental and neuronal faculty embedding humans in their environments—that of perception. Once one regards poetry as ecologically cognitive, as enabled by—and reflective of—a perceptually derived condition of embeddedness, one might enlighten the age-old question of genre: the third stream emptying into this watersmeet is that of lyric genre theory, the troubled status of which is in consequence assuaged.

The intuition that lyric poetry not only discloses or heightens perceptions but also derives expressly from them is a time-honored one echoing within ecopoetics. Leonard Scigaj observes early on that "ecopoets and environmental poets are much more concerned with affirming the integrity of the lived body of quotidian, prereflective experience as the base of all thinking" (11), describing a level of experience that must embroil the sensory if it is to be a basis for thought. But rather than regarding the poem as an expression of the contents of perception, the present work implicates the faculty's physical dynamics, along with the structures permitting them, to argue for the homologous relationship of poem to embedded cognitive activity. This understanding in turn allows one to theorize the elusive genre of lyric poetry, to account for its sundry and seemingly irreconcilable features, which come to cohere when the lyric poem is regarded as a recapitulation of an organism's negotiation of an environment, one that is, in accordance with the redefined term "cognitive," fundamentally perceptual. In other words, I shall argue that all lyric poetry is "eco" poetry, at least to some degree.

To fly an "eco" banner, then, poetry need not address (in either sense of the word) nonhuman nature; in fact, "nature" here takes on the scope Emerson reserved for it when he opined, "Nature who made the mason, made the house" ("Nature" 1844 548). Adopted by many ecopoets and critics, this encompassing definition incorporates "environments that have undergone radical anthropogenic transformation" (Keller 3), those that are degraded or autonomously rebounding ("Third landscapes" is the concept Jonathan Skinner alights upon ["Thoughts" 22–3]) and those that are circumscribed, personal, constructed—environments framed as an object of desire or a Keastian urn. "Nature" becomes that which is available to an organism to perceive—and by extension to act into—the physical environment complementing the organism as well as the process of its perceiving (the "cognitive environment," if you will). Given this definition, inclusive at the same time it is delimited and contingent, I am interested in the contents of poems only to the extent that they self-reflexively acknowledge—and thereby reinforce—such a fundamental form of engagement. If perception and poetry each negotiates embeddedness, each also disembeds, for duality, alienation, the "interfering ego" emerge as the apparent ends of the very process that counters them. Much ecopoetry strives to suppress this emergence (as other poetry champions it), but both the embedding activity and the apparent emergence from embeddedness characteristic of perception signify ecologically. In laying bare this tension endemic to lyric poetry, this work validates the suspicion that has haunted so many that poetry surfs the currents of perception and enhances it.

In grounding the lyric poem in perception, my theory is allied with the foundational claim within ecopoetics that poetry must mirror ecological processes.[1] In revealing the manner in which it does so, I explain how poetry about the natural world enhances one's sense of connection to it: enacting the poem strengthens said connection in offering up a means of connecting, prompting a linguistic experience of embedding perceptual activity. To the extent that this engagement is efficacious in a far-reaching sense in contexts beyond the poetic, whether by healing psychic wounds (a function Bate ascribes to nature poetry early on) or by inciting activism (an efficacy Terry Gifford attributes to poetry's posing of questions to be answered by other endeavors (8), John Felstiner to its potential to lure one to practical response (13–14), and I to the pragmatic nature of poetry and perception both), all the better.

An Indefinite Genre

From lyric's inception as a critical and a categorical term in the West, the poetry it aspires to affiliate has chafed at the bit of definition. Contrary to a prevailing assumption, the foundational, classical attempts to codify genre in effect omit the lyric altogether. Plato's attitude toward the category, if he meant to impart one, is divisive and ultimately latent. When he refers to it, he does so only obliquely in his classification of direct (dramatic), indirect (narrative), and mixed (epic) telling ("Republic" III 394c). The express topic of his "Republic" is in fact *diegesis*, an order under which he lumps the "elegiac poetry" of the dithyramb with narrative tales of heroism, but not the lyric per se.[2] Aristotle's view, if he promulgated one, is not extant, although his discussion of lyric is sometimes presumed to have been among a missing portion of the *Poetics* or even, as Gérard Genette points out, a part of the treatise's subject matter.[3] Genette is quick to remind us that the genre that is, with epic and drama, a member of a classical triumvirate is a belated construction of the neoclassical age grandfathered into the venerable schema with all of the ambiguity and the conviction myth-making affords (3–8).

This is not to say that an awareness of lyric as an especial type of poetry, and hence literature, is not long-standing. The idea of lyric is as ancient as it is capacious, and it preexists modernity as a concept even if its assumption into the official triadic schema does not. The retrospective invention of a lineage for the term in order to account for certain types of poems is symptomatic of at least three facts surrounding its treatment. First, in comparison with other genre concepts, the lyric had, as far as we know, received scant consideration, and the consideration it did receive remains more or less obscure. Second, at some point the lack of attention was thought flagrant enough to warrant redressing within the contexts from which it was apparently omitted. Third, in order to remedy the omission, the critical imagination was willing to forego empirical rigor and to content itself with an aura of mystique,[4] a trend that, with rare exceptions, has been reversed only recently, in the salvo of criticism that has emerged since the inception of the present line of work.

The subsequent history of lyric inquiry is fraught with tensions between continuity and revision, loosenings and retrenchments, enlargements and salvagings. Beginning with Plato's however unintentional extrication of standard elegiac poetry from the remainder of the genre—implicitly substandard nonelegiac lyrics—the category has been ranked, reconceived, flanked by epic and drama, and, by fits and starts, described. Yet its contours remain nebulous, shrouded in the trappings of legend, undefined—to some indefinable—a rubric without a chapter. The critical quagmire surrounding the lyric results in part from the doubly centric nature of a category that must somehow revolve around the separate poles of musicality, first as a literal and then as a vestigial presence, and what is usually deemed to be a Romantic notion of self or subjective expression. Clearly, neither of these customary understandings tolerates broad application to the poetry, nor do any of the minor and contradictory characteristics a core body of criticism has assigned to the genre, including brevity, unity, and fictionality.

Neither is the poetry any less slippery than the theories that attempt to fix it. Speculatively the oldest genre and perhaps actually so, the extant body of lyrics and lyrical poems is still more remote than the understanding of lyric as such. This far-ranging, eclectic assemblage compasses the traditions of the Anglo-Saxon riddle, the Pindaric victory ode, the medieval Arabic "lament for lost cities," the Japanese *tanka*, and the love song of the Provencal courtier. The subgenres and poetic forms populating the genre, including the complaint, the ode, the elegy, the song, the sonetta, the sonnet, the riddle, and the charm, are a group that, superficially at least, is anything but homogenous. Yet this malleable category is distinguished. If they do not easily bear the strictures of definition, lyric poems remain enduringly recognizable as such. Despite the advent of a Romantic hegemony and the castigations and disinheritings of the twentieth century, the poetry "lyric" describes will not tolerate the term's disposal in either its nominal or adjectival form. Lyrics continue to surface, to be aired, and it is in that airing, in their vital, ephemeral dissemination, that lyric depths remain audible. We hear, in the melodies and in the discords of the poetry, remembered echoes and hauntingly pertinent refrains.

As a discipline, literary studies tends to suspect definitions, especially those whose purview is thought too sweeping and those that must be agile enough to withstand retrospective application. In the latter case, it is maintained, the act of reviewing perforce brings interceding developments to bear. By way of example, although the Anglo-Saxon tradition produced a solid body of lyric poems, the Old English lexicon contains no one word that corresponds to a modern understanding of the lyric genre. Viewing the attempt to define as one that confines and thereby curbs innovation, of inclusion and, conversely, exclusion, we eschew the categorical, imagining we do a political service in rebelling against what must be at best imprecise and at worst oppressive constraints. Yet the aversion to the use of category as a literary tool is not a general one, but is rather based on a perceived problem of referential breadth. All but the most dedicated post-structuralists are perfectly comfortable installing, for instance, a particular metaphor as a full-fledged member of the subcategory metaphor and the category figure, or trope. Marginal members are often in dispute because they may be read literally or metaphorically, in which case they are simply awarded dual citizenship within classes alleged to be either alternative or coextensive. The concept and the act of categorization are not called into question with the same consistent resolve.

Is it that we are at our ease as long as the literary work as a whole is not labeled and in our minds reduced? The present moment is heir to a kind of literary folk wisdom that advises with all the conviction of unexamined belief that our terms are indefinable, and the most renitent are those denoting genre. Motives fueling the perpetuation of this truism range from the frustration that no doubt prompted Frye's tongue-in-cheek throwing up of the hands in describing lyric as "anything you can reasonably get uncut into an anthology" ("Approaching" 31) to Marjorie Perloff's absolutist polemic: "No definition of the lyric poem or of the novel can, in short, be wholly transhistorical" (18):

> It seems in any case impossible to talk about something called "the lyric" as if the genre were a timeless and stable product to which various theoretical paradigms can be "applied" so as to tease out new meanings. … Form, to adapt Robert

> Creeley's well-known injunction, is *never* more than the extension of culture. (29) (emphasis added)

Perloff does not marshal absolutes naively: her etiological bias is cultural, and it is avowedly a bias. She begins the volume *Poetic License* by conceding the irony that the two prevailing attitudes toward poetry—the humanist's claim to its universal relevance based on the singularity of human nature and the relativist's insistence on its cultural genesis—are equally essentialist, "at least in practice" (2). I would suggest that the qualifier "in practice" be stricken. Her stance essentializes to the extent that it assumes its own objectivity and overarching truth value: in determining exclusive significance for cultural difference, it is as reductive as any undisguised universalizing tack.

Perloff's conclusion that art and artifacts are solely the products of cultural influence has the support of legions. But surely we have moved beyond the use of humanism as a straw man and the literally pointless (in the mathematical sense) oscillation between essentialisms that strands the discipline on the horns of a dilemma. Relativism follows from the acknowledgment of diversity as certainly as the consistency against which it must be defined. In the wake of the twentieth century, perspectives that attempt to comprehend this art form—one that remains to varying degrees culturally marginal despite insistence on its uniquely cultural significance—shall we say comprehensively, are overdue. The need to defend this oddly defenseless genre presses when that comprehensive understanding is cast in broadly human terms. One thinks of the controversy over Oren Izenberg's recent book *Being Numerous*, which responds to the trend of "granular" historicism, the training of an ever more close-up lens upon our texts that in the end relegates criticism to description (32), by reenvisioning twentieth-century poetry as an affirmation of the status of the person (35). What Izenberg makes patent, astutely, is that "a tradition of poetic thinking in which the insistence upon difference (between poets, verse genres, as indeed between one person and another) is the very problem in need of solution" (34).

Toward a Definition

In an attempt to solve the problem of irresolvable difference, the theory at hand concerns itself with the cognitive faculties of the human animal, a fit subject of scientific inquiry. The largely neuroscientific basis of the book will no doubt cause some readers to bristle. Yet it cannot be denied that as members of a species, human beings bear resemblances to their fellows, resemblances that prevail regardless of the concept (morphological, biological, or phylogenetic) used to define the species.[5] The human brain has evolved during the relatively short span of human life on earth: this is a basic biological tenet. But the human cranium, at least, has remained unchanged over the last 150,000 years, a duration far longer than the historical period by which one is confined with respect to any direct, inductive study of literature. The human organism may in the future evolve differently, in which case human products may alter considerably, perhaps even radically. That they have yet to do so underscores the fact that the history of our poetry admits but minor variations on a theme, selected emphases culled from what remains, in whole, a consistent art form. It is possible to identify if not a permanent, at least a *stable* biological basis for this particular artifact that has in all likelihood been with us as long as has our literature.[6] To defer to such a basis is not to claim it as ultimate or deterministic: neither biology nor culture is an absolute source of human development, but rather a co-contributor to it. In fact, neither biology nor culture is meaningful in this context as a discrete concept because each exists as it constructs the other. The informing power of the cultural, as inclusive of the social and biographical and as an aspect of environment, is realizable only in conjunction with a biological dynamic that shapes our cognizance of the same *as it is constituted by it*. Lyric poetry, I argue, engages this mutual co-construction. To undergird an ecopoetics, one must admit a biological paradigm, not as a substitute for a weathered humanism, but within a synthetic model that renders cultural differences indispensable, if partial, and, in so doing, allows a view into the lyric as a *genre* rather than a ragtag assemblage of the special creations of singular contexts.

It is the thesis of this book that lyric poetry recapitulates the perceptual activity of an embedded, embodied human organism. As a basic cognitive function that subsumes action, perception effects the mutual co-construction of organism and environment and is, in this sense, ecological. I use the biological term "recapitulate" loosely to suggest a homologous relationship—one of common origin and structure—between percept and poem. The lyric poem is then distinguished by its understanding of the way that perceptual processes are neurologically and environmentally contextualized and constrained. As such, it both records the dynamic via which perceptual meaning emerges and occasions it: the receiver of the poem engages with it perceptually in her turn. The lyric, as its notoriety attests, is an "individual" genre in rendering the emergent processes of enunciated perceptual acts (and in some cases those of a unified set of voices functioning as one percipient). It is a species-level event in inscribing the cognitive structures and dynamics common to members of the species *sapiens* and the genus *Homo*.[7]

The genre's focus on a cognitive and necessarily isolate act distances it to some extent from social situatedness. The lyric as such suggests, at times enacts, a symbolic removal from the social, one that foregrounds the private act of perception and is implied by it. This rupture, often folded into the process of recovery from it, is the event that induces and sustains poetic utterance, what Frye meant when he said "the poem revolves around [its] occasion" ("Approaching" 32). In purporting to distance the perceiver from the familiar, the lyric instigates first or naive sight, where sight is a synecdoche of perception in general, a claim that accords with the dually sensorial nature of the genre, its aural and its visual modes (melis and opsis). Lyric is the literary form most attentive to preserving the brain's creative reaction to novelty and the purest exponent of the structures of its response. Other literary forms, and perhaps other art forms, may exhibit certain of the features of perception identified herein, but the lyric differs from them in the extent to which they are present, exist in close proximity, and can be said mutually to assume and to construct one another. This is not to say that the genre repels communal significance: as noted, it rather implicates the social as it is processed through the inner workings of an individual brain. Lyric fictionalizes social dislocation, but it is not for all that asocial. What is consistently *lyrical*, and thus ecopoetic, about the poem, however, is precisely what transcends cultural specificity: the species-level dynamic of cognitive emergence transpiring at the interface of organism and environment.

Lyric Impediments

If the difficulty in pinning down the lyric is due, in part, to the multitudinous incarnations it has enjoyed, the lack of commitment to the term is further complicated by the twentieth-century response to one of two foils that are incompatible with one another, yet continue, sometimes tacitly, as movements: Romanticism and New Criticism. Objecting to the former's aggrandizement of the subject self (what Charles Olson calls "the lyrical interference of the individual as ego" (24)) and the latter's myopic preoccupation with tidy unities of form—or both—much subsequent poetry views itself as either not lyrical or so differently lyrical from either touchstone as to preclude an understanding of the genre as such. Any definition of lyric one musters is in consequence outdated, stifling, or oppressive, if not all three at once. The "blame-it-on romanticism" tack is taken by Annabel Patterson:

> "Lyric" remains a name for an ill-assorted collection of short(er) poems; but the genre continues to be defined normatively, in ways that exclude dozens of poems that their authors once thought of as lyric. The reason for this is clear. The modernist view of lyric as an intense, imaginative form of self-expression or self-consciousness, the most private of all genres, is, of course, a belief derived from Romanticism. (151)

Patterson voices a widespread opinion in pointing out that a strict Romantic conception of the lyric is too narrow. It is this notion of the genre Cecil Day Lewis has in mind when he complains of its excessive breadth: "From the late eighteenth century the lyric impulse became diffused over an ever-widening area, till today one could almost say that there is no lyric poetry since every poem has a lyrical quality" (13). The poetry influenced by Olson's and Creeley's tenets rebelled against both Romanticism and the New Critical correction whose fearful symmetries were thought equally to be impediments to innovation, or modernization. The rebellious new lyricism that emerged harkens back, for some, to what we know as the original expressions of the genre: Genette goes so far as to ally pre- and postromantic lyricism (59). If he is right—if language poetry, for example, exemplifies contemporary lyric—the opposed pre/postmodern and modern sensibilities remain irreconcilable centers of the genre. Despite luminous insights, primarily on the parts of Jonathan Culler, Northrop Frye, and Paul de Man, inadequate theoretical work has been done on the lyric since these two centripetal modern movements, with the result that the impasse has been insufficiently weakened. The recuperation of what might be considered "old lyric," however, serves as evidence of the literature's endurance.

The ambiguous status of the genre has been further cemented by the preoccupation with narrative within structuralism and post-structuralism and the consequent marginalization, almost antiquation, of poetry *qua* poetry (by which phrase I mean to invoke a sense beyond the aestheticist's). Witness the slim corpus of writings on poetry compared with the tomes of narrative theory the twentieth century saw fit to birth. In particular, there is a conspicuous dearth of structuralist theories devoted to the lyric: the most highly formal of genres did not, for some reason, invite extensive formal analysis.[8] The need to salvage narrative from its low esteem as a content-driven form, to revamp its "prosaic" image, coupled with the subsequent adoption of the term "narrative" as a comprehensive synonym for any form of fiction-making that is more or less sequential, has resulted, at times, in the subsuming of poetry into this class. The habit, post-Foucault, of reducing the lyric (and poetry in general) to a mere collocation of fragments to be stitched together into a linear, if discontinuous, narrative sequence has served to obscure rather than to elucidate the concept by driving it further into the recesses of neglect. Despite its avid champions in the academy as a whole, lyric poetry has become a shadow genre as well as something of a whipping boy: quaint, useless, antedated, anti-theoretical, apolitical, socially irresponsible, irrelevant, and, if one is to side with Adorno, inhumane in the wake of the systematic, large-scale destruction that for him described the twentieth century ("Cultural" 34).

Contemporary objections to defining lyric make up a diverse lot. Several of the more common ones are addressed here briefly.

Objection No. 1: Lyric features are merely conventional. Peculiar to numerous theories is the idea that lyric attributes (or, for that matter, those of any literature) are mere conventions tacitly directing reading strategies. This explanation would not be sufficient for the anthropologist, and it should not satisfy the literary critic. It follows upon a misassignment of cause to effect: customs have functional bases, and the argument that they are ultimate sources of genres assumes that they are arbitrary or accidental, and thus significant only of themselves. One may, of course, grant convention cultural significance, but this move simply does not account for the vast similarity in poetic practice that subtends diverse expressions. Convention bespeaks a consistency the argument to convention pushes aside. It is my premise that the common features of this genre are rather based in physical exigency and shared biological processes, and that the aesthetic, as Friedrich Schiller realized early in the game, is a "species-level" phenomenon (67).

Objection No. 2: It is invalid to consider, much less to define, forms belatedly. I recur to the argument for species consistency as well as to my earlier point that we recognize and respond to ancient poetic artifacts as lyrics. That we do not respond to them exactly as their contemporary audiences may have is in part the point, and not a counterpoint. Each era, including our own, is constrained by its situatedness, which gives rise to foci and biases within an environment informing cognitive activity. Environmental shift is a given, yet, as noted, biological processes have survived the historical period. Certainly, we have reached a point, posterior to the advent of writing, when a body of literature and criticism large enough to supply a sufficient number of puzzle pieces has accumulated, when a span of time long enough to permit the discernment of constancy through change has elapsed.

Objection No. 3: Categories cannot contain diversity. The contention that the term "lyric" can be defined only locally, and then only imperfectly, is based as much on a misunderstanding of the nature of category formation as it is on a belief in the irreducibility of literature. To make such a negative claim (that is, again, totalizing in itself), even in the service of a relativism, is to perpetuate the fallacy that Aristotelean set theory, in placing impermeable borders around categories in which each member is equally a member, describes the way we think. The work of Eleanor Rosch and George Lakoff on prototype theory suggests that the human mind rather organizes categories around a perceived central member referred to as a "prototype." Other constituents radiate out from the best representative of the category and are lesser members perhaps, but members nonetheless. In Rosch's term, categories presume "gradience," or degrees of membership (Rosch, "Prototype" 81–3; "Principles" 35–7; Lakoff, *Women* 39–44).

Rosch's work assumes, first of all, that categories are defined functionally. If category membership were accorded based upon the possession of characteristics (as is often presumed) rather than the function its members perform, categories would cease to be serviceable, and the structure of language as we know it would partially collapse. A chair is a chair because it is something manufactured with the end of facilitating sitting. It need not have any of the characteristics commonly associated with the piece of furniture, including four legs, a vertical backrest, the quality of softness, or a horizontal surface on which to place the buttocks—to wit, the beanbag chair. A functional view of categories accommodates diverse membership and thus the expansiveness, and the expandability, of the category. The principle of its coherence—its definition—does not preclude the admittance of new representative types. A prime example of this fluidity may be found in the categories formed by the denotations and connotations of language. Most words denote several things, some more readily than others; these latter meanings are prototypical. The senses of a word may be incongruous, metaphors of one another, antagonyms even (a careful study of etymology usually reveals the nature of their interrelationships), but each meaning has the same purpose, that of defining the word. An understanding of the category "lyric" must likewise be based on what it is that lyrics do.

Objection No. 4: Definition is prescriptive and hence a bar to innovation. One finds the term "normative" used more or less interchangeably with "prescriptive" in the course of mounting this objection. The claim that theories of the lyric in some way preclude or dilute originality carries with it the assumption that, poems, like all art, innovate, an assumption with which I agree wholeheartedly, as it accords with my thesis that lyric utters original perception, an utterance regarded, at times, as spontaneous.[9] First of all, it is common sense that a genre concept cannot be prescriptive; if it were, we would have inferred the prescription long ago. There exists no template for lyric as there does for the more rigid *forms* the genre subsumes, the sonnet for instance. My full response to this common misconception will become clear as the present theory is articulated; for now, I defer to the argument for functionality as a unifying principle accommodating novelty within categories. More importantly, if a genre is defined by the way that it permits meaning to emerge, as the lyric is here, its definition assumes that original response is not only possible but also rife, and the objection is thereby countered.

The misattribution of prescriptive stability to genre theory gives rise to the corollary that definition closes down interpretative possibility and with it both potential and actual meaning: the bar to poetic innovation is also the bar to innovative response. What happens here is that a theory of genre cohesiveness is misinterpreted to be theory of local meaning, one that prescribes meaning to the individual case. The idea that new approaches to literature must enrich the reading process by, as Perloff and many others contend, increasing the ways of reading a poem is a dubious assertion in the first place, one often meant to encourage the voicing of previously neglected perspectives. This particular quibble arises to some extent from the concern that historically marginalized examples will be excluded, that definition is ineluctably a tool of political oppression. I agree with Jonathan Culler's position, reiterated in *Theory of the Lyric*, that "poetics should take precedence over hermeneutics" (viii). It is valid, indeed essential, to come to understand how literature works. (How odd that it should seem obligatory to make such a claim for an academic pursuit.) Adding a new interpretation to a fold need not be the aim of all criticism.

Objection No. 5. Blended forms destabilize categories. It is impossible to corral lyrics into a clearly demarcated sector, so the argument goes, because there will always be ambiguous examples; the genre is therefore indefinable. An awareness of category bleed has led to the establishment by Eduard von Hartmann, for example, of composite forms such as the epical-lyrical and the dramatic-lyrical (697–738). Such overlap creates in effect a continuity Goethe acknowledges in positioning the major genres on a circle that encloses the hypothetical space between them (378). That clear lines do not divide genres and that genres may in some vague sense form a continuum is granted. It is no doubt a mistake to perceive lyric to be fully discrete from narrative or drama. Literary types may be interlarded or even interfused with others, as they are in Coleridge's and Wordsworth's poetic narratives of *Lyrical Ballads*. The results of such crossbreeding may manifest formally as, for instance, the prose poem, a hybrid that makes the most of an unsuitable physique. It is the supposition of this book that lyrical episodes and archipelagos inhabit texts that might possess a different, more striking generic identity. Yet it is ludicrous to forsake understanding, to relinquish sovereignty on the basis of border disputes. A conventional lyric is simply more likely to register as a lyric, to fit the bill as a central or prototypical member of the category, in the way that a wingback is more chair-like than the chaise on which I sit as I write. Hybrid forms may assume multiple identities: a novel that is primarily a narrative is also of the category "lyric" when it is acting as one; at those moments it is lyric-like.

My immediate goal is not to label individual poems in any respect, including by degree of lyricality, or to arbitrate, much less vet, their membership, but rather to establish how it is that lyric poems constitute a cohesive body deserving of the title "category." The affiliations this project sets out to justify assume that the individual poem is integrated within an arc of cognitive experience emergent from a condition of embeddedness. A poem may enact a slice of that experience (as do most literary periods and poetic movements, whose corrections often serve to reemphasize a phase of perceptual emergence that has fallen into neglect). Much poetry inhabits a limited section of the arc: the most intensely lyrical will leave footprints through the full range each lyric instance implies. These are the prototypical associates of the genre. Poets like John Ashbery indulge in the spectrum promiscuously over the course of a career, producing a corpus that ranges the category. The designation "lyric," like that of lupus or attention deficit hyperactivity disorder, is a diagnosis of degree. It is bestowed in the presence of a sufficient number of "symptoms" to identify the poem as performing a basic cognitive, that is, perceptual function. As individual poems may participate in different phases of a perceptual act, the adjectival and nominal forms of the category name merge into one another. I therefore use the noun "lyric" as an adjective with the standard "lyrical" because what is lyric might remain descriptive, or it may achieve the systemic coherence of the nominal. To emphasize the presence of degrees of inclusiveness, I often omit the article "the."

Objection No. 6: Defining genre demystifies poetry. There is another, more widespread and subtle motivation that needs to be teased out of the general reluctance to limn the contours of this genre and that is what I interpret to be the rejection of any approach that seemingly threatens to demystify literature.

It is almost as if the concept of lyric were a charm that, if explained, would lose its seductive power. We thus guard our most intimate objects and keep our mythologies close to the vest. Lurking behind this misconception is the instinct to self-preservation, the notion that we would be forced out of business as interpreters and analysts of verse if we were to attempt to fathom the genre's consistencies. Yet, understanding a genre comprehensively is not the same thing as understanding a poem comprehensively, as exhausting it. The present theory addresses the way meaning emerges rather than assigning it.

Still, one must avoid the pitfalls and potholes of genre theory. There is no dearth of them, as critic after critic reminds. The kingpin of anti-normative arguments may be the one mounted by the early-twentieth-century scholar Benedetto Croce, who attempts to pull a rug out from under an entire enterprise with the assertion that in defining a genre concept we must rely on a "scientific" method to approach an utterance that is created and apprehended intuitively (38). It is not possible, in his mind, to "deduce the expression from the concept" (36). Admittedly, lyric is a medium that resists description in part because it is experiential in nature. One does not read or write primarily by applying a received idea of lyric, but by engaging one's own brain and mind as they function typically. If lyric is indeed an original utterance, it must be graspable in some way prior to the advent of explicit critical concepts. That said, Croce's first assumption—that poetry is strictly an intuitive undertaking—is already a suspect and limiting surmise, one not unrelated to the equally reductive claim that lyric is an expressive medium, a cousin, as it were, of the scream. In addition, because lyric experience does not proceed from the imposition of a conscious "concept" *per se*, it does not mean that the poem is a posteriori inconceivable. It is possible to conceptualize intuitive knowledge in discerning the means by which it arises, and this means is my present subject. If this were not the case, the scope and the methods of inquiry into cognition would be severely curtailed, impacting efforts within the fields investigating it. In an age that has witnessed the arrival of highly conceptual mechanisms for understanding the experience of, for instance, emotion, by definition an intuitive means of knowing, the incommensurability of these two types of knowledge becomes an untenable objection. Intuitive responses can be understood rationally in the absence of a deductive process, assuming Croce intends the narrow meaning of "deduce." Indeed, much literary interpretation and analysis proceeds inductively, at least initially. The deductive derivation of a particular instance from an ideal is a mathematical method that, as Alfred North Whitehead argues persuasively, has minimal utility within a reality marked by continuity, because it presumes the existence of fully bounded constituent entities, which an ecological orientation and an ecological understanding of poems rejects (8). The stark division between intuitive and conceptual knowledge has been erased by contemporary cognitive science, which sees the two as imbricated, and the latter as built upon the foundations of the former.

Croce sees the dichotomy he sets up as a deadlock, but it is one based in an untenable distinction. His logic is akin to that which bristles at the idea of a theory of chaos, assuming it would reduce chaos to a predictable order. Yet, "chaos theory" is not reductive because it describes the emergence of unpredictable behavior revealed, retrospectively, to be orderly. (The argument perplexing the application of scientific concepts to a "nonconceptual" genre presupposes a fully predictive, linear science, the applicability of which has been increasingly delimited throughout the twentieth century, including within cognition.) Although I begin with a set of neurological concepts, they are physical principles that are engaged unconsciously within intuitive perceptual and poetic experience. They are not superimposed upon poetic events, but rather undergird them, giving rise to original expression that cannot be deduced. The fact that poetry is among the more complex and astonishing achievements of the human mind simply makes its adequate definition elusive—it doesn't preclude it.

It is true, however, that deductive approaches to the genres as a whole have slowed an understanding of the lyric. It was William Rogers who first pointed out that the development of lyric theory has been impeded by the perceived need to schematize it in relation to its classical sisters, epic and drama, in order to subserve a preexisting metaphysical unity (11–12). He dubs this approach the "logical space" argument, one that assigns each genre a fixed point within a schema that in turn allows for the insertion of generic blends (33–4). The ill fit of overarching theory with particular works of art is due in part to the attempt to deduce genre boundaries from an ideal order bequeathed by the Western metaphysical tradition. Running through neoclassicism and Hegelian idealism, this time-honored approach continued unabated in modern thought until it was replaced by postmodernist resignation to the sheer impossibility of definition.

The Lyrical-Perceptual Continuum

Literary studies is at core an empirical discipline in that it confronts its objects of inquiry sensorially, objects that are most often held to be primary, though stray from them we may. While I am not advocating an empirical approach to literature in the strict sense involving testing (such an approach would likely amount to a quantitative demonstration of the obvious[10]), the present theory is an inductively devised definition of lyric informed by cognitive science, not one deduced from whichever sisterhood of genres seems exhaustive at a given historical moment or from any other concept. I contend rather that the "generic" quality of lyric consists, observably, in the poem's structural and functional replication of the perceptual activity of an embedded and embodied mind and brain engaged in making meaning in the confrontation with novelty. As will be revealed, the lyric is a perceptual act derived from a perceptual act.

As the lyric coherently reflects as well as effects the dynamics of perception, its integrity derives from a complex of associated features that mutually construct—and thus presuppose—one another. The recognition of this coherence is then what allows an understanding of the genre to move beyond the descriptive and into the realm of the theoretical. The lyric further gels as a category when it is seen to express the cognitive continuum extending from the embeddedness of the perceiving organism within the environment it implies and constructs to the organism's emergent consciousness of its separateness from that whole. There is a tension, if not an outright contradiction, inherent in decentering a human product (poetry) formed of a human product (a word-based language), as much ecopoetry aspires to do. Yet, as an embedded perceptual event, lyric poetry as a whole entails both anthropocentric self-awareness and the biocentric utterances common but not exclusive to ecopoetry that countervail self-awareness. In launching the publication *Ecopoetics*, Jonathan Skinner identifies such a gamut in observing that "a lot of nature is getting into poems these days—in ways that … subvert the endless debates about 'language' vs. lyric, margin vs. mainstream, performed vs. written, innovative vs. academic, or, now, digitized vs. printed approaches to poetry" ("Introduction" 6). Understanding that egocentric poetry is a logical extension of ecocentric poetry accounts for the subversive, dichotomy-collapsing nature of at least some of the work to which he refers. It permits a syncretic theory that contextualizes discrepant features, a transhistorical claim in the strict sense: one that encompasses the recorded history that includes the transcription of a body of lyrics. As an inclusive account of the genre, this project is meant to comprehend the types of poems Perloff and Patterson see as having drained through the sieve of Romantic lyricism, including the hymn, the psalm, and the prayer, as well as much postmodern poetry.[11]

In his book *The Discovery of the Mind*, Bruno Snell crafts a delicate and intriguing argument that the inception of lyric poetry in Hellenic society coincided with an aborning awareness of the mind's autonomy, of a personal agency apart from, and sublunary to, the supernatural will of the gods. Snell attempts to tease out the historical moment when, in contradistinction to the epic character, who believed himself to be a vehicle of divine will, the lyric poet (here Sappho) grew cognizant of her intrinsic motivations and in turn her self. Sufferance in love, the memory of the waxing and waning of affection, of being in a state that one had visited before and therefore might pass through again, and the awareness that the heart is fickle are the mental contents, he argues, that gave rise to the earliest glimmer of self-continuity in the face of external changes inflicted by the gods. The mind is first "discovered," if you will, within the lyric poem (43–70). Snell's pinpointing of its emergence within the writing of a seminal Western lyricist is no accident: the lyric poem conceived broadly (or prototypically) moves through layers of awareness, becoming, at times, fully self-aware as it realizes the terminus of the perceptual process. Individual lyrics may not achieve self-consciousness, but across the genre, self-concepts cohabit with their determining even as they are resisted. However, as I shall argue, the lyric stops short of stabilizing identity and rendering it transcendent.

Of the Lyric Mind

This is perhaps an appropriate place to gather the features common to individual lyrics in order to amass a body of traits one would have to account for in developing a theory of the genre. It is meant to be a survey of minimal responsibility. While the list includes well-known criteria, certain items have received far less critical attention than have others. Some features are observed to be unique to the lyric, others are attributable to poetry at large, and still others are associated with different types of literature.

1. Lyric assumes an embodied performance. A consciousness of bodily experience is reflected in its presentational situation: the poem's primary mode of delivery is oral, and it is conceived, regardless of its presentation, as an utterance. The original lyricist sings and plays an instrument percussively; the Romantic lyricist conceives himself to be a resonant body in the form of an instrument. Moreover, the salient rhythms of the form recall, as they engage, bodily rhythms, those of the breath and of the beating heart. The engagement of the breath is manifest most prominently and most literally in the singing of lyrics demanding its modulation and control. Within written lyrics, the breath presents figuratively. To enter

into a lyric state as receiver involves an immediate physical attunement of body to the pace of the poem. The genre is also allied with gesture; for instance, the Pindaric Ode is verifiably rooted in dance.

2. Within lyric utterance, a musical quality is present, either literally or derivatively, in the form of prominent, patterned sound. The degree to which said quality manifests may vary considerably.
3. Lyric is a linguistic form, an obvious fact but one that should not be overlooked. Within lyric poetry, the medium of language exists in concert and in tension with the medium of music, both when the latter is a present accompaniment and when it is reproduced linguistically. In each case, lyric exploits rather than limits language's semantic breadth.
4. The genre affords an economical and efficient means of the production of meaning. Its compendious quality is enabled by an intensity often conceived of as density, depth, or polysemy. The resulting obscurity or semantic resistance sets up the expectation of a hermeneutic and an analytic "decoding" process. Engaging in this process demands of the reader a high level of attention and, most often, rereading.
5. The lyric is a private medium. From this characteristic arises the frustration of impenetrable subjectivity and with it the notion of the reader as eavesdropper (Mill 13). When a poem does not articulate an I, or otherwise suggest a subjectivity, a sense of its concealment is often given by its difficulty or obscurity.
6. The lyric addressee is frequently inanimate, unhearing, and/or unresponsive. Apostrophe is positioned as a central figure within the genre.
7. As lyric is a private or interior medium, an especial "poetic" logic of meaning-making often prevails over, and at time frustrates, the logic of reference or representation the language of the poem, as language, also employs.
8. This internal dynamic is activated by the regular deployment of disjunction, the introduction of a signifying break or pause. The various forms of lyric discontinuity are often adduced as the "conventions" that distinguish it from other linguistic forms.
9. As a consequence of disjuncture at all levels of scale, the lyric manifests a structural propensity to nest, to embed units within units, a technique giving rise to further disjunction and creating a hierarchical structure.
10. The lyric repeats itself. Its repetitions exist in relatively close proximity and across levels of scale.

11. Interplay within and across levels of scale enabled by the proximity that, among other things, calls attention to repetition is a product of the fact that, as Poe mandates, the lyric is a relatively brief form.
12. Despite recycling common themes and motifs, the lyric maintains an investment in fresh expression that is set against consistencies of form. As will be made clear at several junctures in this argument, freshness in the lyric resonates as perceptual freshness, as first or naive sight, or the "estrangement" described by the early-twentieth-century Russian Formalists.
13. Thinking about the lyric and mythologizing it betray an awareness of a sense of space the poem cultivates, one reflected in the terms "verse" (the metaphorical "turning" at the end of a row when plowing a field) and "stanza" (the Italian word for "room"), as well as notions such as field poetics.
14. The lyric is to some degree an emotional expression, and its emotional content plays an integral function in the cognitive aspects of the poem.

The assumption that a mind may be discerned within, or inferred from, a literary text is pervasive, inherent, for example, in stream of consciousness technique and psychologically based criticism. Often, the activity of the mind registered by literature is treated as an exclusively mental event. However, perception, as the basis of cognition, is also a physical process subsuming the bodily movement with which it is intimately and inextricably entwined. As the poem likewise exists as a phenomenal presence, a material incarnation, and an action, it is inadequate and indeed unproductive to regard it only as the stuff of experience. Lyric records and gives rise to mental experience in the manner of other literatures, but it uniquely reproduces the physical activity of the neural substrate and thus the basic dynamics of cognitive functioning. It differs from other literary forms in that, rather than simply representing the mind, it recreates, formally, the most basic meaning-making apparatuses of the brain and its environment in order to recapitulate, and to prompt for the reader, the dynamic emergence of meaning. Further, lyric language is intensely active, generating meaning in the manner of perception, whose alpha, omega, and coconspirator is action. The lyric impulse is the impulse to draw upon the primary and creative negotiations of perception and action (as well as, as will become clear, the emotion that fuels them) deeply rooted in our animal brains, and to disclose those negotiations—the means of meaning-making—in its product. In both cognition and poems, concept formation and self-awareness are built upon the neuronal dynamics of these basic functions.

Ecopoetics has, in fact, gathered each lyric ontology under its umbrella. A poetics intent on reconstructing ecological processes stresses the materiality of language in positing instances of the medium to be analogous to the physical world. Indeed, language enjoys a kinship to natural processes in that it coheres, flows, and yields to its own conversion: words denote other words and in a sense give way to them. Reprioritizing the physicality of language, and by extension the natural world, also facilitates the eco agenda to temper poetry's egoistic proclivities and to reground the organism. Arguments in this vein include that of Scott Knickerbocker, who attributes to certain eco-oriented poetry a "'sensuous poeisis,' the process of rematerializing language specifically as a response to non-human nature" (2) that allows it to mediate a connection to the earth (3). Poetry's existence as mental content barely needs defending, as any focus on poetic content prioritizes it. Within an early ecopoetics, Leonard Scigaj turns to the phenomenological framework of Merleau-Ponty to recover for poetic language the referential function phenomenal experience entails (21). He attributes to ecopoetry what he terms *référance*, the power to refer to nature beyond the poem and to achieve, thereby, what he calls "an atonement or at-one-ment" with it (38) precluding "the degradation of ecosystems" (5). Last, as noted ecopoetry and traditional nature poetry are widely ascribed a meta-activating (i.e., an *activist*) function, but I shall argue that poetic activity is first something more immediate and perception-based, a quality of language accentuated, typically, by lyric.

Regarded ecologically, reference in fact becomes complex, embroiling the physical and phenomenal levels of perception as well as action toward what is perceived. As will become clear, the lyric genre's threefold manifestation enables a constructivist dynamic that in turn complicates the long-standing, much troubled idea of mimesis. In *The Logic of Literature*, Käte Hamburger divests lyric writing of its task of imitation, granting it a status as "real" she at once denies to narrative writing. (Her insights are a foil to Wellek and Warren's earlier designation of the lyric "I" as "fictive" (Hamburger 273).) Since the lyric does not concern itself with objective reality, she reasons, it does not engage the notion of fictionality (271). Neither is genre determined by its form, she argues, but within the "statement-system of language" (242): "The lyrical genre becomes constituted through the so to speak 'announced' intention of the statement-subject to posit itself as a lyric I ..." (241), that is, as enunciated by the text. In an understanding of subject/object interplay that is quasi-constructivist if unidirectionally so, she argues that an "object-nexus" is created by the subject announcing itself as such, an entity with which it enjoys a "mutually interlocking" relationship of contiguity. Lyric language therefore does not reference the objective world, but forms its own internal "sense-nexus," or system of meaning-making, revolving solely around the "subject pole." What words denote, then, is an idea of an object belonging to an articulated subject (261). The objects themselves "disappear beneath the words, which become independent" (259). Hamburger's argument is interesting for its removal of the burden of imitating objective reality from the shoulders of the lyric project and for its identification of a proto-constructivist dynamic at the heart of the genre that accomplishes the same. In allowing for the object-nexus to be *inspired* by the object and constructed by the subject, she hints at, but does not develop, the means by which a subject-nexus might also be inspired by a subject and constructed by an object, and thus at the complementary dynamics characterizing perception.

While praising Hamburger's thesis for its repudiation of fictionality, Jonathan Culler expresses his discomfort with the fact that regarding the poem as real evokes the other term of the dyad, thus perpetuating the idea of fictionality (*Theory* 108–9). He is right: the dichotomy is a cage in which genre perspectives have been trapped for far too long. It is for the best that Plato and Aristotle chose not to wedge the lyric into their mimesis-based systems,[12] for it is impossible to disembroil the idea of objective representation from the idea of imitation, which copies the action, verbal or otherwise, that is represented. Within a cognitive medium, one does not reenact a behavior or an utterance (itself a behavior), and thereby imitate it, but rather reconstructs said object in a new medium in order to enable interaction with it. A cognitive rendition of an object affords grasping the object, literally within perception and metaphorically by means of the concepts to which perception gives rise. Perceptual processes may be said to "copy" objects only in the most skeletal way. Lyric language likewise muddles representation (including the representation of other language acts). It can reproduce neither objects, as Hamburger recognizes, nor subjects because, as will become apparent, the process of lyric emergence at length constructs each. The replication of a cognitive method in a linguistic medium is the means by which lyric originates, the modus of its originality. One might conceive of the genre as imitative of a dynamic (an object more rarefied than a discourse), but as that dynamic is constructivist, it cannot itself effect imitation in the classical, representative sense. If the poem is imitative of anything, it is imitative of the situation of embeddedness and its negotiation by perception and action that makes objective access an artificial construct, but I rather think it more useful to cast off the mimetic concept once and for all and to regard poems as *constructive of* subjects and objects via fundamental, cognitive processes.

Coleridge had much earlier secured such a provenance for the lyric, undermining any mimetic role it had been assigned in construing the "secondary" imagination productive of poetry as an "echo" of a "primary" perceptual imagination ("Biographia" 257). Recognizing that the constructivist nature of lyric derives from perception permits the tracing, in turn of the origins of perception to the ultimate source of nature as a whole, and in turn an understanding of a perceptual act as an environment in relation to the poem in the way that nature is the environment of the perceptual act. A poem then becomes an environment in relation to the perception-like activity prompted for its receiver, thus creating a nesting of cognitive actions Gregory Bateson calls "minds." Understanding lyric activity as the echo of a perceptual dynamic, and its reception as the reconstruction of that dynamic, yields a less neat, but eminently more feasible explanation of the genre than any distortion of the innately representational concept of imitation. It recognizes that the poem, in constructing meaning within a system in which it is embedded, is as Culler observes an event in and of itself (35), one that nevertheless enables interaction with the world beyond it. Mimesis is a misappropriated and inappropriate basis for the lyric's genre identity.

The New Cognitive

The view of the poet as imitator and the derivative idea that poetry represents the world is as much the baggage of philosophy as it is a formative insight of literary critics. The complementary approaches of empiricism and rationalism share a model of the mind as a reflective mechanism representing a discrete and cognizable world as it is, a task it either completes or flubs through misrepresentation. The view that perception is a creative, mediating activity is now commonplace; yet, the assumptions of empiricism are still espoused within the twentieth-century movement of cognitivism, which perpetuates the long-standing philosophical tradition in construing the brain as a disembodied processor of symbols, a Turing machine running on wetware as it were. The notion of the brain as a rational entity capable of objective representation, a position developed by Alan Turing and Kenneth Craik,[13] assumes substance dualism, the separateness of the agent and object of representation necessary for accurate representation. (Cognitivism further posits the interchangeability of the physical platform on which "mental" events transpire.) Yet, in an embedded system, Blake's "eye altering" that "alters all" in perceiving is itself altered, physically, and not simply in a metaphorical sense, evincing not only a bidirectionality of influence but also the mutual co-construction of subject and object. As a cache of research from the last decades attests,[14] and as most neuroscientists now hold, the mind does not function primarily as a computer or otherwise realize a one-to-one correspondence with reality. The last decades of neuroscientific inquiry have reclaimed the term "cognition," offering an alternative view of the faculty, one that allows the formulation of preliminary answers to the question of how the poetic process is kindled by or in some way indebted to it. It is now possible to explain the manner in which a particular kind of perceptual acuity is the genius of the poet, an observation so pervasive as to be shared by classicism, where it is valued negatively by Plato and positively by Aristotle, Romanticism, and Charles Olson's anti-Romantic projective verse. To do so, I draw upon the following assumptions of the correction to cognitivism.

The brain has evolved through time. My argument relies on a theory of cognitive functioning that assumes that many of the characteristics of the brain have adaptive value and that the structures of cognition were selected in accordance with Darwinian principles as they are augmented by the neo-Darwinian synthesis.[15]

It is a short, logical step from the assumption that a lyric poem operates according to the principles of an evolved cognitive system to the assertion that it is itself a complex adaptive system, one that is both residual and living. Each lyric poem registers the aligning of an organism to environmental flux and assumes the introduction of difference (what Northrop Frye calls a "block" or departure from the "ordinary" ("Approaching" 32)) that prompts adaptation.[16] As noted, poems often imagine difference in terms of environmental shift, the sudden confrontation with novelty. Gregory Bateson made the first step toward tracing the formal consistencies between "mind" and "nature" when he conceived a homologous relationship between these two systems. In deriving from nature, the brain, and by extension the mind, is also an evolving, that is, learning system, one whose adaptation to its environment is fine-tuned (Bateson). The poem, in deriving from the mind, is a similar type of system.

The organism is embedded in an environment and the two construct one another through reciprocal processes. The simple belief in a holism is often facile: it may be asserted in the absence of rigorous inquiry and remain a vague ideal. The implications of organismic embeddedness, the reciprocity and the mutual co-construction of organism and environment, have only recently been granted their full significance within the hard sciences, for instance in the neuroscientific model that replaced cognitivism. Our as-yet unexhausted Cartesian inheritance continues to sustain us, and its heuristic value is indisputable. However, its deeply ingrained suppositions have hindered both scientific investigation and humanistic study. An understanding of lyric poetry must therefore account for the techniques by which the mind and, in turn, the poem acknowledge and effect the organism's continuity with, or embeddedness in, an environment.[17] The term "embeddedness" assumes the following:

1. The decision to consider an organism separate from its environment subjects that organism to an artificial act of extrication. Its points of attachment to the world are never fully severed, even when they remain perceptually unavailable or otherwise remote. Though cohesive and bordered, an organism cannot be completely separated from its informing context. It is at all times attached to it and part of it: an environment includes the organism that is defined in relation to it.
2. The perceived environment that is often considered separate from the organism also constitutes the organism, which assimilates and shapes it, both ontologically and epistemologically. (At a certain point, these concepts are collapsed into one.)
3. The trajectories informing the emergence of embedded entities are bidirectional. The individual is constituted by its environment and vice versa in a continuous process of mutual co-construction. In a luminous critique of the recalcitrant assumption of separateness that finds its most popular expression in the nature/nurture dichotomy (the developmental version of the organism/environment dichotomy), Susan Oyama artfully dismantles the assumption that these entities are discrete. Pointing out that even the term of popular resort "interaction" assumes discrete units that interact, she lays bare the logical shortcomings of this entrenched view, among them, the problem of infinite regress. If the gene is the cause of the organism, what, then, causes the gene? (As Emily Dickinson phrases it, "Germ's germ be where?")[18] Oyama argues that the gene must have a causal origin beyond the organism itself, within the environment (12, 14, 17). Biology and environment are parameters shaping one another, informing one another in a sense that is quite literal. Organismic actions, including perceptual actions, are constructed of both present environment and present neurobiology, which is itself formed by the individual's history, its experience with the world, that is in turn formed in a manner that is biologically possible. The subordinate position taken here is that lyric

utterances, as derivative natural acts, are formed of both organism and environment, which, as the co-constructed complements of one another, cannot exist independently. The lyric subject and object create one another. (This assumption provides, in addition, a basis for understanding the active construction of meaning on the part of the reader.)

4. Perception occurs at this formative point of contact and is a means of the mutual co-construction of organism and environment. Perception also creates the appearance of absolute distinction, the discernment of contrast. Points of detachment tend to be perceptually available while points of attachment do not. Poetic obscurity then becomes, perhaps counterintuitively, symptomatic of organismic embeddedness, of the obfuscation of physical continuity.
5. Due to discrepancies of scale, the impact of the environment upon the individual is in most cases far more significant than the impact of the individual upon the environment, especially the environment at large. A linguistic environment likewise affects a poem, which has a lesser effect upon the language (but an effect nonetheless).
6. The best explanation to date of the dynamic of co-construction is that provided by dynamic systems theory, which is here assumed to describe the constructive activity between mind and environment within perception as well as that between the cognitive faculties of perception, action, and emotion.

Conceptualizing the negotiations of mind and world in a manner that fully objectifies neither is a difficult task for those of us nursed on Western substantive certainty. The late neuroscientist and Buddhist scholar Francisco Varela adopts the term "middle way" to characterize the nexus of negotiation that I argue characterizes lyric output. (The lyric theorist William Rogers offers the designation "middle term" to describe the lyrical tropes effecting "reciprocity" between mind and world, but his is not a constructivist ontology (180–1, 251, 269).) The notion of "betweenness" is itself problematic, because it may be taken to signify separate entities flanking that which bridges them. This is not to say that lyric may not establish subject and object poles (it is, after all, so often defined in accordance with those terms), but it does so only in the copresence of a continuity from which they emerge. Lyric remembers embeddedness, a notion that disturbs traditional understandings of representation. The lyric "I" is composed of its object as the object is composed of it. If their connectedness is conceded, it must also be granted that the cognitive act transforms each: the object is assimilated, transformed in the act of assimilation that alters the perceiver. In resisting the extrication of an environment from he who utters it, in embodying the coextension of the two, lyric enacts this co-construction. The hermeneutic is creative: lyric expression is for this reason recalcitrant, irreducible. This is the beauty and the bane of interpretation, perceptual and otherwise.

Given that the extrication of the organism from the environment is an event that follows from the precondition of continuity, the assigning of causality by critical approaches and philosophies to detached, alternative sources results in abstractions that are artificial and thus unsuitable—or at best partial—bases for understanding the poem. To regard a text as purely cultural, to abstract this construct the environment subsumes, ignores the fact that culture, as an aspect of environment, is created by the individual biological organisms it simultaneously creates. It is a mistake, therefore, to conceive of any work as simply a product of its culture, or, conversely, to regard culture as a bounded influence on artifacts. Genette presciently makes room for the influences of both nature and culture in our categorical schemes in calling for an inclusive understanding of genre: "For at whatever level of generality one places oneself, the phenomenon of genre inextricably merges the phenomena—among others—of nature and of culture" (69). The cognitive merger of these "phenomena" in the lyric allows for both the admittance of contingency into the poem and the maintenance of a stability as consistent as the existence of the species. As organism and environment are mutually wrought, cultural, historical, and biographical influences are folded into the poem, and are legitimately extricated, *given an awareness of how they are first implicated.*

An embedded organism is situated and thus particular. Another implication of the lyric's acknowledgment of embeddedness is that poetic utterance is engendered within a singular situation, from a particular vantage point, at a particular moment. (This is also a ground-level assumption of culture-based criticism.) It is by virtue of its unique embedded condition that a situated organism experiences its circumstances sensorially (Gibbs 69). Even when a poem makes abstract statements, it does so via the perceptual dynamic that negotiates its specific circumstances. This project then assumes for poems a common dynamic, but a particular stance. (This common dynamic, it should be noted, need not be realized by a universal technique. Creation, by its nature, precedes convention.) This is not to say that lyrics are inspired by "real" perceptions, although I see no reason why they could not be. The manner in which mental acts, whether real or hypothetical, inspire lyrics is addressed in Chapter 3.

Cognition is embodied. Another assumption of anti-cognitivist approaches is that cognition is embodied, in the sense that it is necessarily a physical (i.e., neuronal) activity and in the sense that it is distributed throughout the body. The poem's embodiedness is reflected in both its foregrounding of the materiality of language and in the complicity of the autonomic processes evoked and engaged within its experience—such as breathing and the beating of the heart, parameters constraining neurological functions.

Perception and action are intertwined processes primary to other types of cognition. I use Francisco Varela's term "enactionism" in the strict sense he delineates, noting first that "perception consists in perceptually guided action" (173). Action is of the same processes as perception. It is anterior and posterior to perception at the same time it is of it, constructing perception as it is constructed by it. (The latter directionality is usually taken for granted.) The prioritizing of action with respect to perception and their integration are corrections to the sequencing assumed by cognitivism, which, in the empirical tradition, sees the organism as a passive receiver of stimuli from the outside world to which it reacts.

Varela's second enactionist tenet is that "cognitive structures emerge from the recurrent sensorimotor patterns that enable action to be perceptually guided" (173). Perception (with the action it enfolds) is primary evolutionarily: "Human minds evolved with neural resources that are primarily devoted to perceptual and motoric processing, and whose cognitive activity consists largely of on-line interaction with the environment" (Gibbs 12). As such, it constitutes the neurological basis for the so-called higher forms of cognition implicating it. Concepts, including self-concepts, are grounded in the coevolution of action and perception. As cognitive artifacts, poems may concentrate themselves around the perception/action nexus, the perception/conception nexus, or the conception/self-conception nexus, or they may enact all three of these levels of cognition. They may also orient themselves toward the pre-perceptual.

Cognition emerges through systemic neurodynamic hierarchies. The systemic activity lyric instantiates and stimulates proceeds hierarchically. This is not to summon one of the multitude of schematics that rank the genres on the basis of their humanistic value, but rather to stipulate that a hierarchy of scale enables meaning-making activity within the poem. The poem is hierarchical in the way that perception is hierarchical, that is, progressively more integrative, engaging a more expansive "level" of the system as it proceeds. As in any hierarchy, the germane activity of the lower levels is preserved as it is integrated into higher-level schemas, which in turn constrain lower-level functioning. This dynamic to which the genre is prone and the disjunction upon which it depends are the subject of Chapter 3.

Unconscious structures are potentially conscious. If an argument is to be made that the physical, neuronal structures of the brain are in some sense present in a product of the mind, the objection that unconscious structures must by definition remain unavailable to consciousness must be quelled, for the premise that they are realized in the literary work assumes their availability. Vastly complex neurological processes with their multitudinous components remain unconscious, it is often reasoned, because awareness of, or access to, them would clutter the mind to such an extent as to preclude mental functioning. This is a cogent rationale and probably a correct one, and I do not wish to refute it, only to point out that to deploy it as an objection to the possibility that poetry foregrounds unconscious dynamics is to misunderstand the location of conscious awareness within the creative process. The structures of the poem analogous to those discernible in the brain become available as the creative act transpires, and not because the poet is consciously aware of his own brain's dynamics as he creates. The content of the Freudian dynamic unconscious is similarly believed to be unavailable to its correlate, the conscious; yet according to Freud, the mind's productions encode it and may be decoded to expose it.[19] The claim that brain dynamics manifest mentally is granted scientific defense by the work of neuroscientist Gerald Edelman, who assumes that the physical substrate must share the structural qualities of consciousness, including coherence and unity[20] (*Universe* 146–52). It is provided a logical rationale by philosopher John Searle, who maintains that the structures of the unconscious must be potentially conscious because the notion of an unconscious exists only on a conscious level (152). This linking of unconscious and conscious activity (if not content) in kind is an implicit insight of Romantic, especially Coleridgean, poetics, which, as has been noted, sees the poem as the ur-product of an imagination rooted in, and analogous to, perception. In the words of Maureen McLane, "To define poetry via the human faculty of the imagination was not only to give it, as Coleridge desired, a philosophical foundation: such a definition also gave poetry an anthropological foundation. Poetry is defined, in fact, as the discourse of the species" (32). I set out to unmask the ways in which this sapient, human address is fundamentally of the species' engagement with the environments embedding it.

A Biosemiosis

The rooting of linguistic activity in perceptual activity is finally a biosemiotic gambit, a conceiving of biological systems as sign systems. Following Jakob von

Uexküll and Charles Sanders Peirce, Thomas A. Sebeok asserts that the sign system of perceptual-motor events is foundational to the sign system of verbal events and further bases the very advent of language in Uexküll's concept of the *Funktionkreis.* This functional circle of perception and action Sebeok regards as a "pivotal model" for organismic functioning (*Sign* 54–5). To ensure survival, mental models of the world, including the simplest of animal perceptions and actions, must signify reality not objectively, but appropriately (*Sign* 57). As sensory systems allow the comprehension of environments, a comprehension that is, as Sebeok writes, "surely life's cardinal propensity" ("Roots" 228), "any … communication system must be a natural extension of its sensorium" ("Roots" 231). Verbal signs are modeled on nonverbal signs.

> Solely in the genus *Homo* have verbal signs emerged. To put it in another way, only hominids possess two mutually sustaining repertoires of signs, the zoosemiotic nonverbal, plus, superimposed, the anthroposemiotic verbal. The latter is the modeling system … which, in truth, is phylogenetically as well as ontogenetically secondary to the nonverbal. (*Sign* 55)

Signally, Sebeok does not judge the "anthroposemiotic verbal" system of signs to have originally functioned to communicate: he rather sees communication as an "exaptation"[21] of language, a use that developed belatedly, subsequent to the adaptation that was the development of an implicitly noncommunicative linguistic system. In his view, language evolved rather to enrich cognitive models of reality:

> Accordingly, language—consisting of a set of features that promotes fitness—
> had best be thought of as having been built by selection for the cognitive function of modeling, and … not at all for the message-swapping function of communication. The latter was routinely carried on by nonverbal means, as in all animals, and as it continues to be in the context of most human interactions today. (*Sign* 56)[22]

In positing an original, verbal language modeled on and reinforcing perception, Sebeok creates a primary role for language that foreruns the now ubiquitous task it performs of facilitating the praxis of human interaction, opening a space that may indeed be where the lyric sits.

It is, of course, impossible to know whether such an aboriginal language existed and, if it did, how it might have sounded. However, in granting a *signifying* function to biological processes, biosemiotics suggests the possibility of a structural consistency between cognitive and verbal signification. My goal is to point out the similarities between perception-action and the inherently ecological literary form that has come down to us from prehistory as the lyric. The philosophical-poetic speculations of Herder, Rousseau, Vico, and Bovet that language is aboriginally poetic might find an ounce of redemption here. The instinct to make lyric the very earliest of genres, to locate it at the point of the emergence of language, is perhaps not so far off base, not because its advent necessarily precedes that of the other genres, but because it remains an enactment of the creation of a relationship to the universe, one that is of necessity original. As Shelley professes,

> In the infancy of society every author is necessarily a poet, because language itself is poetry; and to be a poet is to apprehend the true and the beautiful, in a word, the good which exists in the relation, subsisting, first between existence and perception, and secondly between perception and expression. (312)

A Glance Ahead

As the cognitive faculties discussed herein are complexly interconnected, and as they enable the negotiation of a relationship of organism and environment that is already one of continuity, any linear presentation of a theory indebted to them is bound to be misleading to some extent. Given the ongoing, mutually co-constructive nature of perception, I found it necessary at times to introduce only briefly concepts I develop later on, and so I must beg the reader's patience with this inherent difficulty in the argument's design. Given the need to sequence, the book proceeds as follows. Chapter 1 surveys myths of poetic origin and salient theories of lyric, interpreting them to encode the perceptual nature of poetic utterance. Chapter 2 commences to discuss the perceptual process itself, positing that the obscurity common to lyric recognizes the state of potential meaning initiatory to embedded perception, the invocation of which imparts a sense of originality or first sight. Chapter 3 continues to uncover perceptual mechanisms, treating lyric disjunction and the hierarchies to which this propensity of the genre gives rise as reflective of the hierarchical disjunction enabling potential to be decided perceptually. Chapter 4 addresses the formative role of action in perception and in the lyric as well as that of the emotion associated with the genre.

Notes

1 To cite an early example, in the 1994 book *Ecological Literary Criticism* Karl Kroeber argues that an ecological perspective on literature needs to avail itself of a

scientific understanding of the physical world if it is to move beyond the hermetic concerns of the literary critic (20–1). All such theoretical models, of course, postdate the presence within poems of the processes theorized.

2 Genette contends that Plato construes the term *diegesis* to refer to narrative. However, choral hymns to Dionysus must have possessed a lyrical quality. The interpretation of the dithyramb as nonlyrical may be disputed, for the form, barely extant, is barely exposed to our gaze.

3 See, for instance, Ernest Bovet's misattribution of a discussion of lyric to Aristotle in *Lyrisme, Épopée, Drame: Une Loi de Histoire Littéraire Expliquée par L'Évolution Générale*, as well as Irene Behrens's refutation of his claim in *Die Lehre von der Einteilung der Dichtkunst, vornehmlich vom 16. bis 19. Jahrhundert: Studien zur Gerschichte der poetischen Gattungen.*

4 This tendency is perhaps best exemplified in the assignment of a mythical priority to the lyric within the theories of Vico, Rousseau, Herder, and Bovet. See Johann Gottfried Herder's "Essay on the Origin of Language," Jean-Jacque Rousseau's "Essay on the Origin of Languages Which Treats of Melody and Musical Imitation," and Giambattista Vico's *La Scienza Nuova.*

5 The argument for the structural and functional consistency of the human brain is in fact buttressed rather than undermined by the presence of difference as the neurological aberrations conferred by pathology often provide a window into the typical, nonpathological brain.

6 The unfounded rejection of biology as a literary tool arises in part as a response to the horrific consequences of the misappropriation of the mechanism of natural selection by Social Darwinism. That said, one does not forbid the use of fire because it might burn one.

7 The perceptual dynamic limned herein is common to many animals as well; however, while perception (and by extension lyric poetry) may be said to be "animal" in this and perhaps other senses, animals do not produce utterances similar enough to poetry for their output to fall under the egis that is this theory.

8 The plethora of classical, neoclassical, and Romantic schematizations of genre are structural in their attempt to systematize, but they do not address the internal workings of the lyric.

9 The spontaneous quality of lyric utterance is stressed, for instance, in the "myth" of Caedmon's origination of English verse and in Allen Ginsberg's mystical poetics, the creative assumptions of which are touched upon in Chapter 4.

10 I am indebted to Donald C. Freeman for this expression.

11 This gesture toward historical inclusiveness is in no way meant to suggest the presence of an historical continuum analogous to a biological process. The historical emergence of the form does not necessarily recapitulate cognitive emergence.

12 In noting the misattribution of a theory of lyric to Plato and to Aristotle both, Genette roots the genre's problematics in the mimetic view of art that governed classical investigation. Aristotle's definition of art in general as an imitation of human actions (*Poetics* 1447a, 1448a) is, he argues, the reason the lyric is neglected by classical critics: an understanding of art outside the rubric "mimesis" was beyond the purview of classical thought. The slot Plato left open for the lyric, dithyramb, or *pure* narrative was, per Genette, hypothetical: "If the dithyramb is a phantom genre, pure narrative is a fictitious mode, or at least a purely 'theoretical' one" (22). By the time Aristotle was writing, the form of the dithyramb was antiquated. He discards Plato's nebulous third category, which for him has no constituents, in an abandonment by an empiricist of what is not empirically verifiable (22, 23).

13 See, especially, Alan Turing's "Computing Machinery and Intelligence" and Kenneth Craik's *The Nature of Explanation*.

14 Important predecessors to the turn away from cognitivism include John Dewey, Maurice Merleau-Ponty, Gregory Bateson, Susan Oyama, and J. J. Gibson.

15 Though not directly relevant to the present enterprise, the theory of neutral evolution is hereby acknowledged. It holds that most mutations at the molecular level arise as the result of genetic drift and are not beneficial to the organism. (Thus, they are not selected.) In other words, most such mutations survive if they are not deselected.

16 It might seem to follow, then, that the practice of lyric poetry could have direct survival value, possibly as the honing of individual response to the anomalous. I have, however, no interest in making this sort of an evolutionary psychological argument, which is tangential, at best, to the present line of inquiry.

17 The deep investment in the separation of the subject and object on the part of empiricism and rationalism alike may explain why the lyric was a subordinate form throughout the Enlightenment.

18 This line is taken from Poem 998, "Best Things dwell out of Sight."

19 See *The Interpretation of Dreams*.

20 "Coherence" refers to the state of consciousness at a given moment, the impression that it is singular and precludes other states. "Unity" refers to the integration of a conscious state, the sense that it cannot be decomposed into constituent entities.

21 This term was coined by Stephen Jay Gould and Elisabeth S. Vrba in the article "Exaptation—a Missing Term in the Science of Form."

22 Karl Popper makes the same assertion in his "Three Worlds" model set forth in his lecture "Three Worlds: The Tanner Lecture on Human Values."

1

Occasional Cries: Prelude to Lyric

Appearance clings to being, and pain alone can tear them from each other.
—Simone Weil

If every poetics does not understand lyric utterance to echo the vital activity of perception, the terms of poetry as they are negotiated within seminal thinking on the subject nevertheless indicate the genre's perceptual bent. Within the plot twists of myth and in knots tied and tightened by philosophy, one can interpret the poet to be a perceiver— if at times a forced perceiver—*extraordinaire*. A foray into archetypal stories explaining the origin and role of the lyric poet lays bare the basis for this common insight and provides a platform from which to understand poetry as a perceptual act. I begin, then, with the intuition, pervasive within poetic lore, that the poet, to be a poet, must be removed from his native circumstance and *subjected* to original experience.

The trope of the singer's ouster from society arises from diverse cultural and historical matrices, yet its motivation varies, at least on the surface. Within the Western tradition, Plato's expulsion of the poet from the Republic submits as grounds for banishment the unfit status of a deriving mind, one sodden with truth-fogging impurities. Unlike mere enthusiasts of poetry, who are to be "loved" and "saluted" if condescendingly, the poet is a subversive, a *provocateur* whose seductive ways must be steadfastly opposed ("Republic" X.606e–607a). As the polemic establishing artisanal and artistic inferiority by virtue of their second- and third-degree remove from the truth is mounted, a certain urgency arises whenever poetry is its subject. Book X's trajectory at length exposes Platonic anxiety before the form to be a reaction to the vulnerability of ideal knowledge to emotion. In Socratic thought, the remembrance of the glimpse at truth (*anamnesis*) that is a precondition of human birth ("Phaedrus" 249e–250a) is a rare and tenuous event that follows upon mastery over emotion as much as it does the renunciation of semblance. In fact, the former achievement follows logically from the latter, and Plato's argument pivots at the site of their linkage. Imitative practice causes identification with the imitated, which arouses in the spectator the emotions portrayed.[1] The ability to discriminate that brings one nearer the recognition of the perfect is thereby compromised ("Republic" 603b): "The imitative poet implants an evil constitution, for he indulges the irrational nature which has no discernment of greater or less"[2] (605b). Left to his devices, such a poet panders to the ignorant, perpetuating their delusions. As Plato's tack evolves, it becomes clear that it is affective possession that poses the more virulent threat to his utopia. He who grieves, he tells Glaucon, best moderates his grief and maintains, at all costs, equanimity fit for public display. Immoderate emotional response, if indulged at all, must be confined to private quarters where it may be quarantined. The dialectic method, the end of which is to steer acolytes toward *anamnesis*, tacitly concedes the dependence of doctrine on *decorum*. The hope of restoring ideal forms to consciousness is then socially preserved because the conditions fostering its realization are socially facilitated. *Logos* is a civic virtue.

That platonic practice hinges on the maintenance of what is, in sum and substance, a value system is to be expected. Its metaphysics subsumes its ethics: truth, beauty, and goodness merge in the divine and stand in for one another in their earthly manifestations. As is true of any value system, its preservation rests to some extent on consensus, here the consensus to resist the erosive influence of art.[3] Plato's wish to maintain the social order is underscored by his resort to the forcible expatriation of the nonconsenting poet. His fiat to exile decrees, as such fiats did, the removal of an unruly element, one with the perceived capacity to infect that which is self-contained: "Few persons ever reflect, as I should imagine, that the contagion *must* pass from others to themselves"[4] (X.606b) (emphasis added), he writes of the empathic connection art begets. His choice of a metaphor of disease to characterize the effects of art makes it impossible to regard the poet as quaint or spectacular, the author of a mere pastime or *divertissement*.

In Book III of the "Republic", Plato takes pains to distinguish two diegetic, or narrative, modes. The first and more problematic of the two employs a purely imitative technique in which the poet speaks as if he were another, that is, he mimics him. In the alternative mode, the poet dispenses with imitation to speak on his own behalf. Drama is the most menacing of genres because it is wholly imitative; as its imitative vehicle is character, it runs the greatest risk of exemplifying—and thus inducing—disruptive behavior (III.394c). Would-be citizens must beware "lest from the imitation they imbibe the reality"[5] (III.395c). As epic blends mimesis with direct narrative, that is, the recital of the poet himself, it is qualified on this basis to be less pernicious (III.394-b-c, 397d). Plato's attitude toward the lyric, which would seem to avoid the trap of imitation altogether, is less clearly formulated. His brief mention in Book X of the dithyramb, a barely extant form comprised of Dionysian hymns and heroic narratives epitomizing the direct report of the poet, is by way of rounding out the categories established in Book III. He will dispense of it as well, but not before salvaging encomium, sung praise for the just, and according it the full privileges of literary citizenship (X.607a). This subgenre of songs extolling the virtues of gods and heroes is deemed worthy because it is thought to inculcate the goodness it relates. The unidentified remaining examples of direct address, poetic forms such as Pindar's odes or Sappho's love poetry that today strike us as quintessentially lyrical, though the least imitative of the three types, are at last glance no less threatening. While Plato does not account for lyric in his taxonomy of mimesis (a fact significant in itself), it is hard to imagine that he would approve of its emotional power. It is safe to say that the genre is more or less intact upon its banishment in spite of the fact that it is not delineated by Plato as such, and that he considers it to be, with epic, the instrument of "the honeyed Muse," purveyor of pleasure and pain, menace to law and reason (X.607a).

Despite outranking drama on his scale of admissibility, it is also the epic, and Homer's rendering of it in particular, that is Plato's target. Eric Havelock sheds light on an attack that seems at best heavy-handed and at worst misconceived to modern sensibilities, to which an aesthetic medium is hardly to be judged by the same criteria as carpentry (25–7). The philosopher's repulse, he argues, has no such aesthetic basis, but is rather directed at a prevailing educational system (12–13, 23–4). Epic was the primary means by which social mores, customs, and ethics were imparted to Hellenic youth. Replete with detailed descriptions of behavior to be emulated or avoided, it functioned as what he calls a "tribal encyclopedia"[6] (66): instructional passages interpolated into the narrative modeled desirable behavior of one sort or another (chapter 3). As a form that was transmitted orally well into Plato's time, an era that was at best semiliterate, epic poetry was constructed for mnemonic efficacy in order to ensure that its lessons would be recalled (43–5, 96). The mnemonic devices employed techniques that included rhythmic lyre strumming and dancing, as well as the verbal devices of parallelism, echo, and refrain the Greeks called *mousike*, combined to enrapture audiences. One was inhabited by what was sung; one embodied, empathized with, *possessed* the characters (45, 145–60). As a result, "the whole memory of a people was poeticised" (134). As information was drunk in, true knowledge, attainable only by a mind undulled by this reason-drowning liqueur, was, in Plato's view, rendered impossible. Poetic knowing precludes the indifference and the distance the dialectic method demands.

Though derived from Socratic thinking, the famous dictum is emblematic in placing the poet in a comfort zone acoustically well beyond social perimeters. Like Milton's Satan, the outcast is deemed to be viral, dependent on the parasitic ravaging of others to manifest his own vitality, imperiling the aspirant to intellectual purity, the *philosophe*, as Lucifer might doom his righteous if hapless hosts seeking to purify the heart. Satan's evildoing is likewise derivative: wickedness is mediated, that is, realized through another medium, the earthly creature in whom it is reproduced. Like the poet, Satan "implants an evil constitution," choosing "fit vessel, fittest imp of fraud, in whom/To enter, and his dark suggestions hide" (*PL* 9.89–90). Self-propagating at the expense of others, each figure is cast down and out from the ideality he threatens. Irresistible, he must in consequence be exorcised. And although he at times sings admissible songs, it is finally the lyricist who internalizes the predicament of exile and exile's consequences for perception.

The Always Already Rejected, Infected Poet

The banishment of the poet is not a remedy peculiar to Platonism, or even the West. For lyric to arise, "individual" and "society" must be disentangled as terms, however provisionally. Exile, as concept, is seminal for lyric: its poetic significance is deeply seeded in a response to the danger of Orphic absorption, of Orphic sway. In articulating a prevailing attitude toward the poet-lyricist among conservationists of the status quo—one that will inspire the reactive forms of *apologia* and defense—Plato assumes that a dedication to the poetic entails turning on the expectations of social circumstance. Logically, the purging of a dangerous element must be preceded by the decision on the part of that element to embrace nonconformity. Yet, within poetic lore, this "decision" is often portrayed to be the outcome of the exile itself.[7] An understanding of the way lyric's paradoxical beginning and complex temporality are inscribed within lyrical utterance may be cultivated, fruitfully, within the adumbrations of myth.

In his book *Sound and Sentiment: Birds, Weeping, Poetics, and Song in Kaluli Expression*, anthropologist and jazz musician Steven Feld decodes the bird-inspired poetics of the Kaluli islanders of Papua New Guinea. To account for the genesis of an inherently lyrical poetry, the Kaluli tell the story of a fateful fishing expedition undertaken by a young boy and his older sister. On this particular outing, the girl nets several crayfish, her brother none. Complaining of his hunger, the boy begs his sister for each of her fish, but she allocates them instead to other family members: the children's mother, their father, their older brother, and so on. Though the boy's pleas grow more plaintive, his sister persists in her refusal to share her bounty. At length, he catches a single shrimp and places its shell on his nose, which shades to the distinct, reddish-purple hue of the beak of a fruit dove the Kaluli call *muni*. His hands sprout feathers, at length mutate into wings, and when his metamorphosis into a bird is complete, he takes to the air. Faced with the consequence of her selfishness, his sister grows inconsolable. Tearfully, she begs her brother to return, offering him all of her fish; yet, he does not heed her pleas. He rather intones, in his new bird voice, a sorrowful, half-sung oration:

> Your crayfish
> you didn't give it to me
> I have no *ade*
> I'm hungry. (Feld 20–1)

Feld's ethnographic study of Kaluli poetics uncovers the symbolic order structuring the myth. The tone of the *muni* bird's cry is said to verge on weeping: its melodic contours descend in mournful cadence. As such, it is the source of the Kaluli's sole original song form, the *gisalo*, a ritualistic genre in attendance at funerals and séances (36–7). Employing an elaborate semantic system derived from the tones of rain forest birds, *gisalo* signifies the pain born of the denial of nourishment and of the loss of communal sustenance such a denial entails. The relationship of an older sister to her younger brother in Kaluli culture is one of primary caregiver and protector once the boy is no longer an infant, that is, once he speaks. A brother and sister so related call one another *ade* (*ah-day*), a term of endearment that both mediates and betokens their mutual fondness (24–7). It is conventional in songs of the dead to express sadness for the loss of an *ade* only after mother, father, sister, and brother have been lamented; that this sequence is inviolable attests to the Kaluli's ultimate regard for the *ade* relationship (158). In the story of "The Boy Who Became a *Muni* Bird," the sister's refusal to share her food, and especially her expressed intention to serve other family members when confronted with her brother's hunger, negates the caretaking and the sharing that construct an *ade* relationship and in turn its primacy (27).

For the Kaluli, as for many cultures, food is both symbol and currency of social connection. Sharing a meal signifies intimacy: once bread has been broken, the partakers may refer to one another by the name of the food they have consumed (27). "Hunger and loss are thus at the center of a basic Kaluli symbolic equation; they stand for isolation and abandonment" (28). To begrudge an *ade* food is perhaps the ultimate transgression of custom, and the young girl's actions thus undo the most basic of bonds. The boy's complaint that he has no *ade* then levies a symbolic charge. His betrayal is sufficiently egregious to compel his permanent withdrawal from native circumstance and the crossing over into a fundamentally different realm. To the Kaluli, birds signify the spirits of the dead (30). The transformation into a *muni* thus consummates an irrevocable exile, one inextricably bound up with the birth of a new expressive order, that of song.

In an essay building upon Feld's analysis, the poet Nathaniel Mackey elucidates the Kaluli myth's insight into the link between the loss of the communal and the recovery of the musical, contending that the boy's plight is tantamount to an orphaning: "Song is both a complaint and a consolation dialectically tied to that ordeal, where in the back of 'orphan' one hears echoes of 'orphic,' a music which turns on abandonment, absence, loss" (88). His gesture to the Orpheus myth is pregnant, for it too imagines the supremely moving quality of poetic song to be inspired by unnatural severance, by the open wounds of overwhelming grief. Each myth suggests that the innate musicality of words is liberated within the lament for lost community. Lyric is conceived in what Wallace Stevens calls "the cry of its occasion" ("Evening" XII.1), or so it would seem.

Holding Orpheus and his fate in abeyance for the moment, I turn to the Greek story of Philomela, a portrayal of the origin of poetic expression bearing a sustained similarity to the Kaluli myth. Raped by her brother-in-law King Tereus while under his protection, the maiden Philomela is further violated in order that the knowledge of his crime, the "knowing" that is his crime, might remain concealed (Ovid VI.401–562). Her mutilation at his hands is a muting: her tongue severed, she is rendered speechless, ignorable as the Kaluli boy is perfunctorily ignored. The injustice inflicted on Philomela is both familial and civil: Tereus, as king, personifies the state. Her subjection to a political will—one thereby empowered—follows upon the betrayal of a *parent* in both the French and political senses of the word. Like the Kaluli boy who is abandoned by his caretaker and closest relative, Philomela should have been, by all rights, afforded the protection of her kin[g]. Her double connection to Tereus is neither an insignificant fact nor one attributable solely to a blurry line between extended family and political unit that is more sharply drawn in the here and now. It bespeaks a necessary *genetic* resemblance between transgressor and transgressed, a resemblance of type that subtends civic connection. The poet figure is tainted by one most near, in blood or in law, by a sibling or sibling-figure who is entrusted with her care and who also represents the social order. (The English words "kin," "king," and "kind" are in fact cognate, deriving from the Indo-European *gene.*) The Kaluli girl nourishes everyone but her *ade*; Tereus maintains his marriage at Philomela's expense. Younger brothers and sisters-in-law are degraded and deemed impure, unworthy in relation to the ideal forms they necessarily reflect as lesser types, or *reproductions* in the way that a child is an imperfect type of his parent. Those prompted, indeed doomed, to sing are betrayed by a protector, a nurturer, one to whom one's existence is bound and through whose existence one's identity is constructed. The boy is made *ade*, made *like* his sister by virtue of her preexistence and her care. Philomela's social identity is that of sister to the wife of the monarch who wields the power of life and death over her. As each violator is also a parental figure, a maternal surrogate and a patriarch, respectively, the abdication (indeed, abuse) of parental responsibility effectuates what are in essence orphanings. The origin of lyric, it would seem, presumes the sullying of the pure (a maiden or a child) by one most alike typologically in what is essentially a self-assertive exercise aimed at preserving the status quo—*for others*. This is precisely the plight of the poet of the Republic, who is besmirched and deemed outcast rather than reformed. In what strikes one as a terribly unfair twist, the violated, now bearing a derivative relationship to his or her former self, the self whose potential to mature into a functional citizen has been thwarted, becomes a source of danger to the state, a term cognate with "status." The poet is treacherous because she is deemed treacherous, impure because he has been defiled.

As the myth proceeds, Philomela is able to aestheticize her trauma through the resort to a practical skill associated with frivolous embellishment, fine detail, and occupation for idle female hands, as, justifiably or not, has been poetry. She weaves or embroiders, in different versions of the story, a message to her sister Procne (571–86). Her stitchery is the refusal of her silence, and it foreruns, even as it stands in for, poetic speech, having in common with poetry a tactility, a two-dimensional, warp-and-weft texture, and the fashioning of discrete units into a meaningful whole.[8] By virtue of the missive's representation of intense emotion, one might even say trauma, Procne is, so to speak, infected. Its receipt precipitates a grisly retaliation—the killing of Tereus's son and the serving of Itys to him at dinner (587–674). Her plot to take revenge, that mighty Hellenic fixation, reclaims agency for the victim as infection renders the passive active, the destination source. The fatal cascade of events that ensue may be said to validate the Platonic fear that the momentum of affective contamination is unstoppable.

Most taboos violated—adultery, rape, incest, mutilation, cannibalism, and the murder of a son at the hands of his mother—Procne's vengeance rends the "natural" laws of human congress.[9] The drive toward ruin is self-propelled and ineluctable.

Idealism breeds the fear of such an outcome, for the motion it is vulnerable to is unidirectional: it is not possible to grow more ideal. Corruption tends to beget further, more egregious corruption by means of a positive feedback cycle at odds with the negative, self-correcting system that is the dialectic process. The Socratic method strives to maintain equilibrium, to prod the errant and to rein in that which goes astray. Reason inoculates to the extent that it forestalls such aberrant motion, whose thrust is at odds with the self-determined movement that defines the reasonable, reasoning soul:

> All soul is immortal, for that which is ever in motion is immortal. But that which while imparting motion is itself moved by something else can cease to be in motion, and therefore can cease to live; it is only that which moves itself that never intermits its motion, inasmuch as it cannot abandon its own nature; moreover this self-mover is the source and first principle of motion for all other things that are moved. Now a first principle cannot come into being, for while anything that comes to be must come to be from a first principle, the latter itself cannot come to be from anything whatsoever; if it did, it would cease any longer to be a first principle. ("Phaedrus" 245c–d)

The unremitting, self-propelled motion of the soul is hence the basis of its immortality. As prime mover, its unbegotten and thus eternal existence is compromised the moment it becomes subject to another force. Melic poetry is dangerous because it disturbs the self-motivated continuance that is, paradoxically, the soul's ontological repose. Analogous to a virus, it redirects the course of the already-in-motion and alters its organic development by manipulating its DNA, however subtly.

Within the parent–child relationship, the infecting offspring becomes a usurper who must in consequence be disowned. As children are parented, they are by virtue of their existence threats to the idea of an ultimate source, the unparented soul-ideal-God, reminders that one is oneself mortal and flawed. The twist within these poetics is that the disavowal is preemptive, Cronus devouring his children. The multiple levels on which the idea of a paternal source may be interpreted extend its significance beyond the family drama to the opera of the polity, to fathers heavenly and founding. This, then, is the source of Plato's disease. It stems from the vulnerability of the reasoning, philosophical self that is implied by the contamination of *those most like one*, one's genetic and political brethren. It is no mere contradiction, then, that Homer's verse was beloved of Plato: the philosopher's admission that it is physically possessing ("Republic" X.605d) evinces his susceptibility to the bard. That Plato, as Shelley proclaims, "was essentially a poet—the truth and splendour of his imagery, and the melody of his language, are the most intense that it is possible to conceive" (314)—is a historically tested judgment and not merely the upshot of Shelley's desire to preempt reason with the imagination as the faculty by means of which his own idealized version of universal harmony might be perceived.

In systematic thinking within and beyond the Western tradition, poetry is dangerous because it wields the power of emotional dominance over the reason and the will. As has long been realized intuitively, emotion is motion's prod and precedent: those subjected to affect are said to be *moved*. As a destroyer of the ideal, poetry is an agent of death itself. In Kaluli society, poetic praxis meets with no overt censure: it is neither devalued nor ostracized. In fact, its mastery is often sought as a means to woo a wife (Feld 38). Yet the poetic wellspring is safely secreted in the afterlife and accessed only under the protection ritual affords: poetic talk emanates from the symbolic complex of dead kin-bird-poet channeled by a spirit medium during a séance ceremony. The Kaluli posit a parallel invisible world beyond the physical one (66) that is populated by birds inhabiting the fringes of the village—the accessible beyond—who are believed to embody the spirit correlatives of the dead (61). The intent of *gisalo* is to evoke sadness or nostalgia, and to inspire grief and anger that is then vented in the ritual singeing of a ceremonial dancer's back in an act of retribution for pain inflicted (215). (The dancer, who sets the pace of the song, assumes, through costuming and the quality of his movement, the form of a bird (180–1).) By banning the poet-maker himself from the earthly and thus the civic realm and recalling him safely, the Kaluli have institutionalized a means of accessing poetry and insuring its containment. The respeciation of the poet as bird is both self-protective and retributive, a distancing of danger and an act of revenge against the infector.

The metamorphosis that creates the poet signifies doubly for her as well. In the séance ceremony in which *gisalo* is performed, the words attending the melody that replicates the *muni's* cry tend to take the form of a mournful call for "help, attention, and recognition" (144), re-creating the boy's seminal plea. Philomela's weaving likewise exhorts (as does Orpheus's famous song sung in Hades) in an attempt to rectify offense and to forestall the transformation to poet. As Feld explains, "What appears in myth as the scenario of mediation, 'becoming a bird,' reappears in expression as a pervasive metaphor for form and performance" (220). The metaphor in fact permeates a tradition in which birds flock to poetry: the Seafarer's mournful cuckoo, Poe's cryptic raven, the Boy of Winander's screaming owls, Keats's achingly poignant nightingale, and Stevens's blackbird in its thirteen aspects are, like Philomela, the "lover of song," figures of poetic performance. The bestowal of bird form is comparatively egalitarian within the Kaluli ethos (all souls come to inhabit bird bodies; every death is a poetic fountainhead) whereas, in the West, the suffering poet is singled out, elevated at the same time she is degraded. In both views, the mysterious agency that in the end transforms Philomela to a nightingale and the boy to a *muni* is also a force of mercy, a balm affording the means to express and to assuage pain through aborning lyric utterance. Philomela Nightingale and the immortal *muni* are condemned *and* freed to mourn "in full-throated ease."[10]

One finds in the myth of Orpheus the central Western account of poetic song, the extant versions of which constitute a nucleus of sentiment toward the poet and his craft, which, while it resists unified interpretation, reflects, even as it inflects, this core story of poetic genesis. More complex and detailed than those of the preceding narratives, "Orpheus" both negotiates and moves beyond the terrain they cover. In Ovid's rendering in his *Metamorphoses*, the injury that befalls the poet is seemingly motivated by fate as the sputtering of Hymen's nuptial torch portends the disastrous outcome of his wedding day. Bereaved of his bride, Eurydice, on the morning they are to be wed, Orpheus is deprived of his immediate, as well as the source of his future family, and her taking is catastrophic in terms of its effect upon his social embeddedness. As the goddesses who determine lifespan, it is within the power of the Fates to sustain Eurydice by forbearing to decide hers. They thus also function as would-be protectors. Further, they are in a sense Orpheus's kin, for he is in many versions of the myth semidivine.[11] In Virgil's earlier telling of the story in his *Georgics*, Aristaeus, who indirectly causes Eurydice's death by his predatory pursuit of her, is Orpheus's fellow poet figure, arguably his alter ego, symbolically his close kin[12] (IV.453–527). His indecorous aggression toward a bride on her wedding day is a breach of propriety as sinister as the smiting of Eurydice by a lowly serpent in the grass. The narrative here loosely follows that of the other myths in combining the roles of relative and protector to create an unlikely agent of betrayal.

As mentioned, Orpheus's story further accords with Philomela's and the Kaluli boy's in that the first significant expression of the bereft is a cry for help, an attempt to gain reparation and implicitly an accusation. Philomela's weaving, the younger brother's half-human song, resound as Orpheus's plea in Hades for the return of Eurydice. What is perhaps most salient about each utterance is its sheer rhetorical force: lyric persuades in an attempt to rectify.[13] To revivify his bride, Orpheus braves Hades, descends into death's landscape, and, in one of the most cogent renderings of the power of artistic reception in the West, provides a momentary reprieve from hell's cyclic punishments: "*inque tuo sedisti, Sisyphe, saxo*," Ovid writes. "And you, Sisyphus, sat idle on your rock" (*Metamorphoses* X.44). Eternity pauses. The shades weep, the king and queen consent, but in no case can the breach be mended. The chain of events, as evidenced by Orpheus's eventual turn, is fated—irrevocable loss is a precondition of poetry and its continuance. The bard's deft diplomacy, however effective in the moment, is finally a vain attempt to undo what is undoable. The failure to restore a preexistent social order in each of the myths serves as proof of the irrevocability of acts situated on an irreversible arrow of time. A plot involving recourse or revenge stipulates a linear cause and effect structure, dooming poeticizing to fail in its attempts to reunify society and singer. The Kaluli boy's indictment announces a *fait accompli*, one that ensures that lament will be perpetuated.

Unlike the other poet figures, Orpheus is seemingly born a poet. His consummate poeticizing precipitates his removal from society, an event that seems only to redouble his power. There is no need to oust or banish him, for he takes this task upon himself, as if aware that he has no alternative. In Virgil's rendition of the tale, he embarks upon a self-imposed exile to the deserted Strymon shore (*deserti ad Strymonis undam*) (IV.508). Although he departs to Rhodope and Haemus in Ovid's later version, his wandering is more aimless, his exile primarily esoteric, "a withdrawal ... from the empirical realm and a desire or need to live predominantly in [an] inner world"[14] (Knapp 2), as is evidenced by his rejection of all forms of intercourse with women and thus the social unit originally violated. In poetry, the effects of exile are necessarily esoteric, whether or not the fiction of an exoteric exile is maintained, and it is this withdrawal into the self within a new environs, into the act of singing the self that mourns its separateness, which compels and sustains lyric expression. Born of isolation and the confrontation with novelty, poetry figures the solitary activity of perception, an activity dangerous to all because all, perceiving via the same means, risk infection by song.

The ancient practice of exile was a draconian political tool, the plight of the exiled a dire one. Removal beyond municipal walls was in many instances a guarantee of death by exposure or at the hands of one's enemies. Though the same severity and intense dread do not necessarily attend the modern event, it remains a profound experience, both actually and symbolically, one Edward

Said has described as an "unhealable rift whose essential sadness can never be surmounted" (173). Orpheus and his exiled brethren stand, in their essence, as figures of unrelieved mourning, which finds an outlet in song. Music, writes Mackey, is "wounded kinship's last resort" (88). It is the means of deliverance of those engrossed in their wounds, expression deformed in the cries of pain. The intrinsic musicality of poetry is released in the rending of the individual from the society that preexists and forms him, and from which he is, if not expelled, compelled to go forth. Lamentation is lyric's first mood. "No poem without accident, no poem that does not open itself like a wound" (Derrida *Che cos'è* 289). In myth, trauma inspires song: the stories accord it a needful primacy, but do not permit its resolution or transcendence. Singing, though palliative, is not finally restorative, as wound remains to fester. Since the song-response pain prompts is inextinguishable, it is banished to the perimeter, the treetops, the mouths of the transmogrified, the symbolically and literally dead.

Yet, in the wake of treachery, lament becomes at once consolation. The evacuation of pain, the "expression" of it (a word we use readily but understand imperfectly) is always already itself a source of pleasure, not merely the pleasure of release, of suffering bound for the destination of its absence, but that given by the physicality of vocalizing. Infants, including deaf infants not privy to even the affective qualities of voice, babble, an activity prior to vocal mimicry that is reinforced because it is orally gratifying.[15] There is pleasure in the touch of speech and its expressive antecedents, in sounds caressing throat in the process of their expulsion. The body electric is sung and, in singing, it is electrified, an instrument played, as in Pindar's exemplary use of the ode in which body literally vibrates as it dances, is danced. It is at the site of pleasure attending in spite of pain that consolation emerges and shades over to celebration, and it is for this reason that lyric can encompass the odic extreme of a Whitman as well as the consolatory merits of the Greek *paregoria* and the Spanish *consuelo*, the opposite pole of the elegy, *planctus*, complaint. Celebration attempts to repair what lurks at the back of it. It marks triumph in and through continuance, because death, including social death, exists. This emotional complex, or ambivalence if you will, finds an apt, if not a full, expression in the too-sentimental term "bittersweet," a mood that lingers in lyric as the emotional residue of the rift, as undertow. It is this paradoxical affective stance that sees death in beauty, the eternal in the ephemeral, and suffering in desire, which prompts Plato to utter the injunction, "pleasure and pain will be enthroned in your city" ("Republic" X.607A), as one of his most rhetorically potent warnings against the power of *poiesis*.

This paradox of the coextensive lyric currents of lament and celebration distills in the centrifugal Greek word *pharmakos*, a term commonly applied to poetry. *Pharmakos* means at once a poison (a cause for suffering and thus a source of lament) and a remedy (a source of relief and thus a cause for celebration). In classical poetry, *pharmakon* often denotes a kind of "drug that can both alleviate and cause the pain of love" (Segal 11). Derrida famously exploits a nexus of reference in "Plato's Pharmacy," a deconstruction of the "Phaedrus" in which he seeks to reclaim writing from its abject status within Socratic thought (and thereby to overturn the foundation of Western philosophy) by interrogating the facets of the word that permeate the dialogue in fact or in spirit. In probing the structural necessity of the concept's semantic range (71), he indirectly lays bare the set of assumptions that undergird the Platonic marginalization of the poet, exposing the dynamic relationship of the poet to society that is common to the myths.

According to Derrida, Socrates first uses the word *pharmakon* in the dialogue to refer to the concealed speech Phaedrus has brought with him on their walk, a document the urban denizen Socrates accuses the younger man of using to lure him out of the sweltering city. Derrida interprets the ploy: "Operating through seduction, the *pharmakon* makes one stray from one's general, natural, habitual paths and laws" (70). The sense intended here is that of "poison, drug or allurement." The word next surfaces when Socrates retells the myth of Thoth to demonstrate that mythos and writing inspire *hypomnesis*, "merely repeating without knowing," and not *anamnesis*, the living memory revelatory of the knowledge that is the natural destination of the soul. As *hypomnesis* can only remind one of what has already been remembered, it is merely a semblance of *anamnesis* (135). In the myth, Thoth invents writing and presents it to the god of gods, Thamus, calling it a *pharmakon*, a cure for defective memories (96–7). Thamus, however, refuses to sanction Thoth's invention, declaring it to be a danger to memory in ultimately weakening it, a likeness that can produce only delusory knowledge (105). In Derrida's argot, the *pharmakon* "substitutes breathless sign for the living voice" (92). Unlike the father of *logos*, the embodiment of reason in speech, the progenitor of writing is displaced by the text he creates. Writing is therefore "denounced as a desire for orphanhood and patricidal subversion" (77), the place of displaced reference that, as Mackey points out, is the place of the begetting of poetry: the orphan finds himself severed from the unity of which he was a member, the presence to which he innately refers (Mackey 89). The son (writing) who replaces the father (speech) then embodies the Derridean notions of substitution and trace that characterize the poet as a stand-in for his spawning culture, the trace of which remains in his utterance.

What Thoth does in inventing writing is to induce *différance*, meaning that is both different and deferred. Although his inventions include the world's many languages, he rarely originates language, rather developing it (*Dissemination* 88). "[Thoth] can become the god of the creative word only by metonymic substitution, by historical displacement, and sometimes by violent subversion" (89). In fact, he frequently involves himself in conspiracies to usurp kingships (89). Writing, then, as the irrepressible means of dissemination and *dilution* of meaning, agent of *différance* and death, is subversive and thus is targeted as a *pharmakos* in the third meaning of the term: "scapegoat." Derrida's unraveling of the "Phaedrus" culminates with the story of the ritual in which a deformed citizen, considered impure, is led out of the city to a brutal death by flogging in order to rid it of pestilence and plague. Homogeneity is restored to the polity through the removal of difference (130–3), which defers the scapegoat's referencing of society, a second purport and consequence of exile.

Writing here stands in for poetry. Within Socratic doctrine, the two are linked transitively. In the "Republic", Plato affiliates poetry and painting (X.602); in the "Phaedrus", Socrates equates painting and writing (275d).) I do not mean to except the lyric's oral forms, but rather to point to the alliance between poetry and writing as marginalized, absented media threatening to the stability of the logically derived state.[16] Each is balm at the same time it is venom, sacrificed because irresistible. And while my argument with respect to the lyric is not deconstructive (it will claim an ecological dynamic for linguistic indeterminacy), Derrida's perspective is useful in understanding the relationship of singing individual to audient society. It is precisely the *différance*, as he conceives it, embodied by the poet figure that poses an existential threat to the state. It would be no revelation to claim that in poetry the play of *différance* is extreme, within both the dynamic of its origination and the textuality of the poem. Presence and absence are negotiated physically in the myths positing a metamorphosis by means of which the poet is moved out of his group (and out of his former self), thus deferring his representation of the society he has left behind: the utterance of *another species* enables an extreme play of *différance* in each sense. The ouster of the different expressive order of poetry relieves the exilers, if only temporarily, of the confrontation with the truth that the poet represents them, sings themselves, undergoes what they can or will not, and perceives what they fear to perceive. As the citizenry remains within earshot of the absented poet, the exile must be reenacted. Clearly, difference here is also fundamentally emotional. Emotion itself is a moving out (an "e-moting") of stasis by virtue of its ability to penetrate: it threatens to induce ontological difference, altering being not in the play of concept/nonconcept, not as concept, but by altering mood in the Heideggerian sense. For both poet and audience "affected," intense emotional states become temporary exiles: "No poem that is not also just as wounding" (Derrida, *Che cos'è* 289). Lyric emotion is intimately entangled in the referential web of the word *pharmakos*: it contains the oppositional meanings of curative and inducer of pain, as well as that of the scapegoat in whom they are merged.

To partake of lyric then presumes an immeasurable trust in the lyricist, the trust one must accord any purveyor of pharmaceuticals. It exacts an assumption of risk. The chance that the infiltrating agent will co-opt one's self-determination, that one will fall victim to the Pied Piper, is ever-present, particularly so when poetry is performed. The primary vehicle transporting *poiesis* into the inner sanctum of being is that other *pharmakos*, the fourth meaning of the word: *mousike*. Charles Segal notes that in portrayals of Orpheus in classical art, his listeners appear to be enraptured (15). The compelling, incantatory power of song, the animal magnetism with which it holds its hearers spellbound, all find distillation in the death of Orpheus. The myth demonstrates that when lyric piques desire but defers its quelling, it becomes dangerous. The intensity of Orpheus's grief (he mourns the loss of Eurydice with a fervor; he loves her as one loves possibility) prompts the seemingly nugatory yet fatal act of spurning the overtures of the Thracian women. Having fallen under the poet's spell, the frenzied Maenads retaliate for their unrequited lust. The first spear they hurl is aimed at the poet's mouth with the end of silencing him. But the weapon, enchanted by his song, falls prematurely to the ground. Orpheus's voice is drowned out only once the women's cries overwhelm his melodies and break their spell, at which point the poet and his entourage are violently rent at the hands of these "mothers." Their first victims are poet-surrogate birds (Ovid XI.37–41). Like the burning of the Kaluli dancer, Orpheus's murder is not only an act of retribution, it is a subdual, a cry of "enough" that reclaims self-guidance for the profoundly affected—or infected, as it were.

The sensibility of the Orpheus myth is in some respects more modern than that of its counterparts treated here, especially its portrayal of the poet's exile as self-imposed. Yet, it rehashes the basic plotline of poetic genesis, sharing with the stories of Philomela and the Kaluli boy the superseding of human contact by the crossing of communicative barriers imposed by speciation. Although Orpheus does not become a bird, there is something regressive in an evolutionary sense about the quality his expression assumes, something primordial, as with it he is able to summon beasts and trees and inspire stones hurled in his direction to abandon flight mid-course. Even the inanimate are *moved* from their trajectories, establishing once more for poetry a core emotional efficacy born of loss and beholden to sound as much as it is to the referential function of language. Lyric entails a turning back, a beginning at the beginning, a rooting of utterance in the primal efficacy of quasi-linguistic expression, in the gesture, dance, and percussive instrumentation posited to have been the genre's original, coextensive media, media it continues to evoke.

Drawing on Victor Zuckerkandl's idea[17] that music forms a "critique of our concept of reality" (88), Mackey notes that there is an order of experience it might express or indicate, but not denote: "Music bears witness to what's left out of that concept of reality, or, if not exactly what, to the fact that something *is* left out" (88). What is missing from our ossified concepts is that body of nascent experience the exile perceives and sings, having transcended the ordinary through his compelled submersion into the foreign.[18] Like the song of the canopy birds of Papua New Guinea, the exile's *poem* serves both to express his bewilderment before the strange and to orient himself within it. For the Kaluli, birds "are both the spirits of the dead and the major source of the everyday sounds they listen to as indicators of time, location and distance in their physical environment" (88). The music of lyric is, like birdsong, self-contained, yet strongly evocative of what lies beyond it, even to the uninitiated. It is capable of estranging all the while it remains vaguely and suggestively familiar, imparting the sense that it encodes a meaningful, semantic order that one has not yet mastered, but still might. In revealing enough to entice, yet withholding enough to intrigue, the music of lyric seduces. In song, formal coherence exists as potential meaning, as promise. As music resists semantic reduction, it becomes a sign that new meaning must be sought and a guide to usher one along toward it.

Feld repeatedly emphasizes that Kaluli poetry reaches an artistic pinnacle in maintaining a tension between the opposing motions of obfuscation and clarification (139). Like Janus, the abstract patterning given by the lyric's rich sonic aspects gestures in two directions: toward coherence and away from it. Following Wallace Stevens, Jonathan Culler describes the lyric's bent toward opacity as a "resistance of patterns and forms whose semantic relevance is not immediately obvious"[19] (*Structuralist* 179). Opaque expression, a further feature by which lyric begins to differentiate itself from other literary forms, may be provisionally ascribed to the goad of experience lived outside the perimeter of stable signification. Obscurity, the preconceptual, describes the Orphic; it characterizes a poetry that reaches back into the vague, animal sources of clarity. This, then, is the final significance of Philomela's weaving: her message telling of diremption inhabits what is also decorative pattern, the abstractly harmonious. Her *j'accuse*, like the recrimination voiced by the Kaluli boy, alleges a particular crime at the same time its nonreferential elements make tangible the promise of coherence in another realm. It represents her song even as it foresees it. The musical, because it points toward new order, is a palpable sign that an old order has been abandoned, that social upheaval has come to pass. This precise complex of betrayal, accusation, lament, consolation, and obscure message as guide to freedom in the flight to new meaning, coheres in the singing of spirituals by African American slaves to relay plans of escape. The topoi of parental rejection and severed or indefinite reference common to the myths are reiterated in the predicament of the escaped slave, who also no longer refers unequivocally to a paternalistic owner. Orientation becomes an exigency in the no-man's-land between municipal walls where language's referential range is compromised. In its indication of new relation, of relative location, the poem is also the precursor of a map, and as such demands intense attention to one's surrounds.

That lyric is in some sense an inaugural genre and that it reinvigorates language are ideas that have been aired again and again. Within the fiction of the removal of the poet from the familial and the familiar, there is, logically, an imperfect correspondence between the native language he has at his disposal and the novel environment he encounters so that his language must be renovated, tortured if necessary, to begin to account for the experience exile motivates. The full extent of language's plasticity, its versatility, must be called into service. There is a sense in which poetry is quintessentially mediate, not only because it is a linguistic medium expressing thought and feeling but also because the poetic, the lyrical, mediates old language and new environment, old embodiment and new environment, new embodiment and old society, new environment and new embodiment, old and new embodiment. The mismatch between the words of the clan and the categorical needs of experience beyond it is a given. The lyricist by default speaks the language of his tribe, is born into the social institution of language, but must revise linguistic conventions in the face of the scenario he must brave. It is precisely because conceptual categories must be altered, denotative ranges shifted, and connotative fields enlarged, to name a few of the consequences of lyric use, that lyric language grows opaque and is reified. The materiality of the word in poetry is a consequence of the multiple pathways it must mediate, of its location at a busy crossroads. If language cannot refer unequivocally, as was philosophy's dream, it especially cannot in light of the use to which lyric puts it. The reason *les mots de la tribu* must be given *un plus pur sens*, as Mallarmé urged, is not to make poetry novel, but because lyric poetry, by default, contends with the novel, contends with it perceptually, and its musical propensities both reflect and facilitate this contention. The manner in which the effects of exile the myths narrate congeal to entail perception now begins to reveal itself. Poetry is birthed in an *ousting* from the familiar that coincides with utterance, itself an *outing*, a movement into new environs compelled by the emotion-laden momentum of expulsion: it is precisely motion compelled by emotion that occasions—even forces—perception, a fundamental activity mediating organism and environment that is here made fresh by new embodiment and new milieu. In implying that the poet perceives afresh, performing an activity that is necessarily individual, the myths provide the backstory as well as the story of the creation of the perceiving-singing individual in the scientific sense, that is, as a member of a species. Poetry, I contend, proceeds in the manner in which the species perceives.

The irreconcilable breach between Platonic forms and the poem is based lastly in the necessity that the latter engage in its namesake "making" (*poiesis*). Poetry is constitutive rather than revelatory of knowledge in coming to terms with and taming its new milieu. Platonism acts as a foil to such creativity since all of its central virtues—truth, beauty, and goodness—are preexistent. Their stabilization acts as a social preservative and, in so doing, fixes a basis for the determination of privilege in the form of access to said virtues. Societies cannot contend with moment-to-moment newness en masse: it is up to the individual thinker to receive, to integrate, and to reconstitute, work that has often been ascribed to genius.[20] What the poet "makes" and how he makes it is by its nature threatening to an existing order. Lyric endangers an established regime by virtue of its ability to infiltrate the solidity of its concepts and weaken them through unauthorized, individual creation: poetry is particularly threatening because it enjoys widespread influence accorded by the fact that it replicates the dynamics of cognition and is thus of—and for—us all.

As I have noted, when the Platonic recourse of exile is examined within the myths, one arrives at a causal conundrum in which the poetic obtains as both provocation to exile and its high consequence. Civil order depends upon the rooting out of the disorderly creative principle, which is paradoxically born by virtue of its extirpation. There is a complex etiology at play in the birth of song that speaks to the irresolvable priority of individual and group. Within the exigencies of Platonic philosophy, the marginality of the poetic enterprise has as its basis the perceived radical gap between the philosophical and the poetic. Havelock's observation that Plato rejects a preanalytic epistemology, one in which knower and known become fused in the act of knowing, is a key piece of the puzzle, one that will be visited in Chapter 2. By removing the source of a type of knowledge inflected to penetrate the knower and placing it in a remote beyond, Socratic thought makes analysis, the method of its own justification, possible. One is thereby enabled to perform the logical manipulations that forestall the dissolution of the rational self, which is salvaged as the site of knowledge. The ironic outcome of Plato's curative is that analysis is thwarted, unavoidably, *in spite of* the analytic act of removing the individual from a social context. Mythic time is linear and cyclical, both generically and within each of the narratives treated here.[21] Each myth posits two points of poetic origination, one unprecedented in fact or quality and a second signifying the continuity of the first. Orpheus's song in Hades precedes the supernatural dimension his minstrelsy takes on; Philomela's weaving is reiterated through self-regenerating song (she is *the* and not a particular nightingale); the Kaluli boy's farewell lament is resurrected within the set structures of séance. As each story unfolds and the social breach is to some degree mitigated through singing, the reenaction of the breach is guaranteed. The poetic is always already with and of one: as will become apparent, it is the way one negotiates the world by and as an individual organism, one embedded in, and constituted of, the source of its knowledge.

The Universal Particular Subject

It would follow, then, that many theorists of the lyric wrestle with the inextricability of an individual from society, the paradox of a bounded entity bound for elsewhere who communicates privately, expressing himself for himself, at the same time he speaks to and on behalf of others. In Derrida's undressing of Platonic philosophy in "Plato's Pharmacy," the complementary concepts signify one another inevitably. Society exists as trace with respect to the individual that refers to it and vice versa: the tracks of an absent individual linger in society's midst. Other treatments of the lyric's social significance concern themselves with the means by which this individual utterance conveys social freight, regarding the genre to be the matrix in which such conveyance, mediated or not, occurs. In so doing, they acknowledge the tension between these terms, an essential tension within perception.

Foremost among these is Hegel's idealist rendition of the logical space argument. His dialectic positions the lyric as the subjective literary genre, antithesis to the objective genre, epic. (Drama is the synthetic term.) As a "subject," lyric is the paradigmatic means of both mediating and unifying the universal.[22] In setting out his influential formulation of the relationship of the individual to what is larger than himself, Hegel contends that the collective emerges with and through the realization of the individual self, which in turn effects the universal (*Right* 160–1). It is only through human consciousness that the spiritual "inner depth of the world" he posits as absolute may be realized (*Phenomenology* 81).

Hegel all but conflates the universal and the social, as each of the manifestations of the latter marks a phase of the former: not only is society composed of individuals, but it also moves toward its own realization with and through individual self-realization. Conversely, the social pervades, courses through, the individual, whose consciousness develops because he thinks on behalf of, *is* the absolute thinking. The individual is effectuated through its sublation (*Aufhebung*), Hegel's term for the contradictory motions of preserving and overcoming, within the synthesis of the whole that raises it to a higher level (*Phenomenology* 62). It is not possible, ultimately, to distinguish between individual thought processes and the "fulfillment of the whole" (*Sciences* 174).

In speaking the universal, the poet organizes what is "essential." She must therefore cull the absolute for what is to be preserved, a distillation she effectuates by means of the intuitive and imaginative faculties, which are themselves suffused with feeling (*Aesthetics* 1114). The poetic self is then "vessel" of select objective experience that it unifies within the medium of a particular mood, or occasion with which it identifies itself (*Aesthetics* 1133). Given the "variegated" and splintered content of the poetic mind, such unification in turn serves to demarcate the self, which above all must be *independent* (the bird flown) within an enclosed inner world[23] (*Aesthetics* 1115). Lyric unity is an inward unity, enabled by mood (*Aesthetics* 1114) and realized by integrating objective material as one's own (*Aesthetics* 1118). As Jonathan Culler emphasizes, Hegel's understanding of subjectivity diverges from the Romantic stance with which it is often linked, the idea that poetry is the authentic self-expression of the empirical poet, as much as it does the contemporary view of the subjective as "personal, affectively colored experience" (Culler *Theory* 100). For Hegel, lyric is attributable to a subject that is a *unifying function*, not one that is individuated (*Theory* 95, 105).

Any theory that posits the subject's unifying mediation of the object within a process realizing each bears, at minimum, a tangential relationship to perception, which achieves the same end. Though the comparison is perhaps rough-hewn, the faculty of perception is in a basic sense a selector, an organizer, and an integrator of diverse input by an individual in the biological sense, input hypothetically available to all, if uniquely at hand for an individual in a given instance. To borrow Stevens's line, "The squirming facts exceed the squamous mind" ("Connoisseur" III.5) and must, therefore, be gleaned if one is to perceive. The amalgamation of what is selected is necessary to the coherence of the percept and its conversion into an action. One must, of course, shed Hegel's idealism and his teleology to carry the comparison further. What is universal about perception is not the truth it filters, distills, and thereby expresses, but the dynamic by which it does so. Perception realizes an individual, expressing its circumstances through its assimilation of select elements of an ecological whole, which assimilation in turn adjusts the organism's integration into an environment (incorporated into which are socially determined affordances). It thereby reinvents the whole, maintaining it as a whole (rather than realizing it as a predetermined fact). As will become clear in subsequent chapters, an artifact structured in the manner of perception permits another individual to enter a perceptual frame and to enact a homologous process of emergence: this is the basis for poetry's universality.

Theodor Adorno repositions Hegel's dialectic within a materialist worldview and would seem in so doing to move closer to delineating a dynamic born of the individual's physical perception of the world. He carries forward Hegel's insight that aesthetic particularity is the means by which art may partake of the universal, emphasizing the co-emergence within lyric poetry of the individual subject and the society it mediates (38). However, Adorno argues that lyric *objectifies* subjective experience, thus making it available to another subject, while neglecting, indeed rejecting its opposing function: rendering the object subjective. His theory is not wrong, but it is partial in characterizing the ontological status of the poem as a subjectivity made object, a speaking of the universal that reifies (and thereby clarifies) the relationship of the individual to society. In his view, the lyric genre cannot finally evade said reification because it is linguistic, and language is a social medium (42):

> For language is itself something double. Through its configurations it assimilates itself completely into subjective impulses; one would almost think it had produced them. But at the same time language remains the medium of concepts, remains that which establishes an inescapable relationship to the universal and to society. (43)

As language is already of society, poetry is most social not when it concerns itself thematically with the social situatedness of the "I," but when it does not, for the very possibility of objectifying the subject—of alienating it—is socially sanctioned (42). Lyric poetry, he goes so far as to opine, arises *only* in societies that harbor a concept of the individual, as the poet's disengagement, his individuation, and "even the solitariness of lyrical language itself is prescribed by an individualistic and ultimately atomistic society" (38).

Adorno's alienated lyric subject is finally a modern subject aspiring to humanize itself by transcending what has become an astringent reality. Lyric performs a utopian duty, he suggests, not by organizing and making comprehensible what preexists and enfolds it, as it does for Hegel, but by torquing language—the material, social medium in which individual experience is mediated—in an attempt to reintegrate the individual into the society from which it is estranged. This classification of lyric with modernity, the argument that as the expression of a liberated subject it describes the poetry of a finite historical phase with occasional anomalous precursors[24] (40), bears refuting. In spite of poststructuralist conceptions of the text as sui generis, however qualified those conceptions might be, individuals compose individually; a poem emerges as a voice issuing from a single mind and body. (Collaboration in any form is but the additive sum of the output of single contributions, no matter how the collaboration is mediated.) A notion of individuality as a political value or an inescapable cage need not obtain for a mind to express itself, or for a form of expression that is rooted in sensory perception and thought—which are by definition solitary—to exist within a given society. There is a certain arrogance in proclaiming retrospectively that premodern humans did not recognize their thoughts as their own, did not express them with distinctive voices. While a stable concept of a self may not have informed premodern poeticizing, it need not have: a bourgeois notion of a hypertrophied, politically sanctioned individual doomed to suffer alienation does not undergird all lyric utterance. Ultimately, self-awareness is unnecessary to lyric experience, as the survival of the genre and my subsequent argument attest. The appropriation of lyric by a modern sensibility and within a modern ethos erects an obstacle. As many critics of genre theory concede, the definition Adorno adopts excludes a host of earlier and subsequent poems: lyric examples run through societies sanctioning individuality to different degrees. While cultural mores may indeed give rise to lyric types that in turn survive their initial reception, this narrow construal of lyric limits the genre, derailing it at its terminus. The subject that experiences itself apart from its environment (rather than as a part of its environment), and dwells on that condition, is one positioned at the culmination of the perceptual process.

Interestingly, for Adorno, lyrics do strive to effect a reentry into nature, what might be called an extrasocial reembedding[25] that mends the rift alienating the subject (41) and alleviates the affective response born of the subjection to exile. However, he regards this natural state he calls "pure subjectivity" to be "illusory," its apparent presence a testament to its absence, to the singer's ironic love of distressing estrangement. In fact, the lyric's "harmoniousness is actually *nothing but* the mutual accord of this suffering and this love" (41) (emphasis added). This core emotional conflict is, again, an indigenous and irresolvable lyric response. However, what Adorno deems "illusory" is rather simply elusive: a healing recognition of the embeddedness grounding perception that threatens subjectivity, poetic and otherwise.

Ultimately, the dialectics of both Hegel and Adorno disengage the individual lyricist from society so that he might assume the position of universalizer and in the end deem that break impossible. For Hegel, the individual is sublated into the universal; for Adorno, the social absorbs the breach in conceiving of such a possibility in the first place. We have come upon the same paradox that gives rise to the inevitability that the scapegoat must again be excommunicated. As the myths also suggest, such an extrication cannot occur by means of a simple loosening of the warp and weft of the social fabric into its constituent threads. One might argue that for Hegel, the lyric event of channeling and remolding the universal gives rise to an exile into individuality, into the solitary task that is unification. From Adorno's perspective, the retreat into the poem attempts to repair a break that has become endemic. The two prioritize causation differently: for Hegel, poetry prompts, *is*, an exiling it also redresses, while for Adorno, alienation conditions poetry. In each case, it is the continuity of society and its constituents that allows the distinguishing of the individual to be framed in the manner it is. Within a dialectic process, the copresence of rupture and unity is resolvable temporally, and thus temporarily, if only apparently, as it is in embedding biological systems. The fallacy of viewing banishment as a *fait accompli* is explainable without resort to a philosophical construct given an understanding of the dynamics arising from and effecting the embeddedness of the individual as organism. The central tension of irresolvable priority extant within the lyric genre, I argue, is a paradox of cognition, of the private activity of perception that distinguishes the cognizer while maintaining his physical connection to an environment. The chief stumbling block to generic cohesion, the division of musicality and subjectivity into quasi-centralized, but irreconcilable genre criteria, may be averted with this recognition. The distinction Adorno doesn't draw is that between a concept-laden language, which is convention-dependent and socially informed, and the forms, features, and dynamics of lyric that imply a cognizing, embedded individual in the biological sense: the lyric genre also re-embeds (in Adorno's word "transcends") subjective utterance, de-objectifying the subject it objectifies.

One might regard pain itself to signify both continuity and abruption and thereby account for its basic status. From the individual's perspective, it is impossible to endure the perfidy of exile without pain and memory's maintenance thereof. Pain is an indicator, a preserver of lost connection, not only in referencing it, but because its experience defines the boundaries of the individual, engrossing and thereby delimiting it, swelling it to the perimeter of the whole world, or a fit vessel thereof. From the point of view of the society constituted of individuals, a shift occurs whenever it is deprived of a member. The societal value that excludes, for better or for worse, an element through which it is realized commits an ultimate version of betrayal, a decisive breaking of faith. The divestiture is effectively an amputation, the effects of which will reverberate within the body politic. One might argue that "dismemberment" is so radically implausible that the fiction of respeciation is necessary to render it conceivable. Regardless, society continues to feel the presence of what behaves as if it were a phantom limb. The pain of the loss of the individual member, particularly the expression of said sorrow, reverberates within the higher unity as the effects of song are felt and reabsorbed into society. As the exile's song is never free of its spawning social context, despite the fiction of physical removal, as society resonates within the song, the song resonates within the acoustic range of society. It is therefore always *recallable*, as the Kaluli know—this is the purpose of their séance ceremony. Because the lyric resounds through society, *is* the song of its own mourning, it must be ousted, insuring that the cycle continues, that wound is unalleviated in perpetuity. The song ousted is the song of the individual *and* the song of society, and the need for exile goes on.

The trope of exile is finally primary for lyric because the action of compelled removal, which permeates the genre in literal and derivative forms, is evidence that a concept of singularity exists, a concept of solitariness exists, in societies that are not in the least bourgeois or fragmented. The act of exiling implicitly recognizes an individual being. What the device does for premodern societies is to imagine a state of affairs in which an isolated individual is forced to develop self-reliance by virtue of the necessity of making a new personal plan. The idea of exile presumes a psychic distance from a native group that permits fresh perspective, originality, and the attention to perception as the perception of oneself (as one's own perception and possibly also as the perception of one's "self"). It allows the lyric poet to exist beyond its society, whether or not that society is "individualized and atomistic." Physical delivery into an alien environment is reformulated as an esoteric state by the nature of modern subjectivity. With time, the trope of exile softens; it is recast as the predicament becomes less dire, and a concept of the individual arises. As the metaphor of social death recedes into the background, the emotional pitch of the cry of the poetic occasion modulates, but the idea that the poet and her poetry exist apart never fully subsides. As stated, Northrop Frye generalizes the impulse to lyric expression as a "block," by which he means an interruption of ordinary experience compelling the production of the poem ("Approaching" 32). The situation instigating composition is carried over into the poetry, resulting in the sense that something routine has been left behind, and that an ineffably present absence continues to haunt the poem.

Poetic Exiles

Before the modern descendants of the exile are visited, it may be useful to consider a poetic enactment of a literal removal from society, one with a curious historical basis. Anglo-Saxon lyrics tend to survive in fragmented form, often appearing to be scenarios with missing pieces or arcane tales whose full understanding eludes us by virtue of our distance from them. It is possible, however, that their obscurity might not be resolvable by the recovery of inferred "whole texts" or the recreation of a fuller cultural context, but is instead a sign of their prototypical lyricality.[26] Within the Old English poem "The Seafarer," which is as far as is known intact, the speaker undertakes what is widely interpreted to be a voluntary exile, a self-imposed banishment onto an inhospitable winter sea courting all of the perils of a forced exile. Its end is divine communion to be accomplished through the rejection of earthly comforts. The Seafarer arguably exists beyond social support: he is *winemaegum bidroren* (deprived of kin), without *medodrince* (mead, or nurturance), and *earmcearig* (wretchedly sorrowful) as a result. The mead hall, whose absence hovers over the poem, has been read as the metaphorical embodiment of the social order that constructed it (Irving 161), the place where benefits are meted out by a secular lord and alliances cemented through the authority ceremony invests and displays. That the Seafarer considers himself to be estranged from this institution and all it represents is implicit in lines 36–8:

monað mōdes lust maēla gehwylce
ferð to fēran, þaet ic feor heonan
El peodigra eard gesece. (36–8)

And constantly the heartfelt wishes urge
the Spirit to venture, that I should go forth
To see the lands of strangers far away. (Hamer 35–7)

As evidenced by a substantial body of Anglo-Saxon pilgrimage literature, the plight of the stranger came to symbolize the transient condition of the earthbound once Christianity influenced secular poetry and prose. When read as self-inflicted, the exile suffered in the poem may be deemed a means of transcending what is mutable and earthly by its rejection in this realm. While the Christian trope of the stranger on earth (which also structures "The Wanderer") has been traced to the doctrines of St. Paul and St. Augustine, its ultimate source is perhaps found in the nomadic and finally righteous Abel, whose lot contrasts with that of his erring brother, Cain, a builder of cities bound to land and to wealth (Bradley 329–30). This notion of pilgrimage is curiously distinct from the later form it will assume: rather than sojourning to a site endowed with communal meaning, a place of congregation, such as a Canterbury or a Lourdes, the speaker of "The Seafarer" intentionally travels away from social contact.

The poem's elegiac tone and its alternating expressions of loss and consolation arise, then, from the speaker's isolation. Elegy is a central Anglo-Saxon lyric type, and Rosemary Woolf has argued that this poem may be further classed with "The Wanderer" in the subgenre *planctus*, a form of medieval complaint that responds to intense loss of any kind, thereby broadening the elegy's affiliation with death. "The Seafarer's" well-documented theme of mutability, exemplified by its *ubi sunt* motif (a device that will reemerge in the Middle Ages), follows from the perception that loss is inflicted by the passage of earthly time. However such lines are drawn, what is pertinent here is that most forms of loss imply social deprivation: death renders it, the loss of youth regards the separation from society as impending, the loss of position dislocates one socially, and the loss of love construes society on a small scale.

Regardless of what the Seafarer lacks, he is most often thought to fare alone of his own volition. The famous debate between Stanley Greenfield and John Pope concerning the number of speakers in the poem came to center on the best interpretation of the word *sylf* (35b) once Pope retracted his two-speaker theory in favor of Greenfield's single-speaker hypothesis. Pope refused Greenfield's translation of *sylf* as "of my own accord," arguing for the meaning "alone" to support his newly adopted theory of a solitary Seafarer. Greenfield's contention that *sylf* suggests "independent action" (as he points out, *ana* is the common Old English word meaning "alone" or "unaccompanied") buttresses the Christian interpretation of the poem as a pilgrimage ("Sylf" 235). This particular meaning has the effect, he argues, of underscoring the necessity that the individual perceive or recognize for himself the transitory state of the earthbound and the unknowability of divine judgment. "This is a voyage he must *by his own cognition* take to save his soul, to attain the heavenly joys (whether we take the voyage to be literal, symbolic or allegorical)" (235) (emphasis added). He points to the presence of words of perception and conception that tend to be found in tandem with *sylf* (237–9), for instance, *gehohtas*, "thought" (which Hammer translates as "desires"), in the passage spanning lines 33b–35:

For þon cynssað nū
heortan geþohtas *þaet ic hēan strēamas,*
sealtyþa gelāc *sylf cunnige.* (33b–35)

And yet the heart's desires
Incite me now that I myself should go
On towering seas, among the salt waves' play. (Hamer 32b–34)

The situational ambiguity here proves fruitful. If the speaker is a sailor who has drawn the night watch, as has been widely posited, there would be other souls aboard ship who would presumably be asleep. He would in either case stand alone at the watch, and the poem is imbued with all of the symbolic significance such a post confers. Even if he engages in a dialogue, as Pope initially suggested, the solitude that is the poem's subject matter is not diminished. What is significant is that the comforts of society, those advantages living in its midst afford for survival, are attenuated and at a remove, and an alternative environment, one which is by default natural, is claimed. Absent the distraction of conversation, deprived of an audience, the mind's isolation is foregrounded, signifying and exacerbating the seminal rift. This prototypical lyric then reaches toward a full expression of the exiled mind's activity within the new environment it enters: it manifests the mind's solitary performance, that which it must do "of its own accord" in its isolate state.

Not incidentally, the lament for the loss of communal sustenance in "The Seafarer" is voiced in part by birds. The mournful tenor of the cuckoo bespeaks the distress of alienation in a kind of presaging lament for summer's imminent close. The songs of the other birds populating the poem—the swan, the gannet, the curlew, and the sea mew—take on another function, that of substitute sources of conviviality, entertainment, laughter, and mead-drinking, as the Seafarer finds solace in his fellows in exile, singers whose songs echo his own expression of lament and whose flight comes to figure the turns of his mind. The frequently referenced lines 58–64a feature the word *anfloga* (literally, "lone flyer"), which has been translated as "thought" or "soul":

For þon nūu mīn hyge hweorfeð ofer hreþerlocan,
mīn mōdsefa mid mereflōde
ofer hwæles eþel hweorfeð wīde,
eorþhan scēatas, cymeð eft to me
gīfre ond graēdig, gielleð anfloga,
hweteð on wælweg hreþer unwearnum
ofer homa gelagu. (58–64a)

Even now my heart
Journeys beyond its confines, and my thoughts
Over the sea, across the whale's domain,
Travel afar the regions of the earth,
And then come back to me with greed and longing. (Hammer 57b–61)

The mind of the Seafarer takes wing, ranges expansively over the terrain of the sea, and comes at length to desire it. Expatiation, a voyage undertaken by the mind in its unfettered navigation of an unfamiliar and perilous new world, is the bird's prerogative. The singer is, so to speak, at sea, where he must function independently (*sylf*) because he is alone (*sylf*).

Modern lyrics are not always explicit in their portrayal of communal loss and its cognitive consequences, but if such loss is not the ostensible subject of the poem, it often permeates it on some level. Portrayed, enacted, figured, or assumed, this seminal rift gives rise to the intermural otherness to which the poem is indebted. It is within the lyrical borderland of the exile that poetry finds a cross-cultural generative trope. Examples abound. Poetic dislocation has been figured as societal, lapsarian, romantic, and developmental. And although the poetry tends to break down categorically, it is common for specific utterances to straddle classes. The brief taxonomy that follows is meant to be neither prescriptive nor exhaustive.

Physical Exile. Of the Old English vernacular elegiac poems, the bulk of the period's surviving lyrics, fully half—"The Seafarer," "The Wanderer," "The Wife's Lament," and "Wulf and Eadwacer"—render physical exile explicitly. "The Wife's Lament" and "Wulf and Eadwacer" couple this reality with the form of disunion that will come to dominate many later lyrics: that in which lovers find themselves separated. Literal exile is also the subject of many Old Irish poems. Further, the lyrical moments in ancient epic poetry tend to be prompted by the protracted absence from home that is a condition of war if they are not inspired by other forms of loss. Many Early American poets, among them Anne Bradstreet, were themselves, if not exiles, de facto expatriates. The American colonial experience tended to foster an exilic temperament that infiltrates poetry, a stance beyond society, realized through the combination of self-reliance as value and the needful confrontation with the wilderness. Emerson (as lyrical a prose writer as they come) prized his solitude in nature. Dickinson's soul shut the door on society at large.

Religious or Lapsarian Exile. The fall from Grace, the Judeo-Christian version of the sentence to disunity, unravels the seamless integration of the human and the divine. The lyricism of Milton's epic *Paradise Lost* is the product of twin exiles, the first from heaven and the second from Eden. As intimated earlier, Satan is a prototypical lyric type: cast out of the angelic order as Lucifer, he rebounds within a milieu of his own. An interlude inhabited by lyrical possibility follows his fall and silent, stunned survey of Chaos (*PL* I.84–124). On occasion, divine exile is experienced in concert with the renunciation of society, as through cloistering or virginity, eschewals of the human intended in this context to facilitate communion with a god. The impossibility of the fulfillment of divine union during life's earthly term functions as a natural, insurmountable barrier, mysticisms notwithstanding. Arnold's "Dover Beach" fits within this category because it entertains the prospect of permanent divine desertion. The very notion of faith assumes that the possibility of redemption and reunion will at times be doubted, and thus much religious lyric poetry is in some degree a diluted form of the crisis of faith poem. Poems of praise and celebration (hymns, odes, encomia) anticipate the possibility of divine rejection in their attempt to forestall it. It is no stretch to inscribe abandonment by a deity beneath the rubric of the social, given the Judeo-Christian conception of an anthropomorphic God rendered so by creating man in his image, as a diminished type of himself. Poets from Caedmon to Herbert, Donne, Hopkins, and Eliot have produced exemplary poems of this sort, to name but a few of the writers who have been drawn to conventionally religious themes.

The Courtly Prototype: Exile and Romantic Love. The exile, perforce bereaved, is perhaps most commonly figured as one bereft of romantic love. Courtly love poetry distills society into a unit of three, a reduction that posits a lover and a beloved who are *pro forma* and institutionally separated. The adulterous nature of the would-be alliances pined for in Provencal lyrics proves crucial. The knight errant, a figure peripheral to court life at the same time he is sporadically a part of it, is further situated outside of legitimate society by virtue of the married status of the object of his affection. His recurring rejection attests to his marginal standing.[27] The conventions of this subgenre allow for the perpetuation of courtship and desire into an inconclusive state of affairs, creating an immovable bar to the society of the beloved. Unrequited feelings, the prohibitions of families, and the whims of mistresses are ostensible reasons for the separation implied by the very necessity of wooing. (Wooing is pre-social: it seeks a communion yet to be enjoyed.) The *carpe diem* poem of seduction is lyrical because the day is never seized. Sappho's poems, which have enjoyed a long, influential reach forward, are among the earliest incarnations of the lyric of unfulfilled love. Dante Rossetti places the Blessed Damozel in heaven while her lover mourns her on earth. In "A Valediction Forbidding Mourning," John Donne ordains his marital love on the occasion of the couple's impending separation, a romantic gesture intended to mitigate their prospective "breach." Wallace Stevens's *inamorata* is the earth itself.

Romanticism and Exile from the Natural State of Childhood. The lake country Romantics left London to rusticate as strangers among peasants. This literal exodus from society is undertaken by the young Wordsworth with the simple, exaggerated anticipation of a child on an outing:

> O welcome messenger, O welcome friend!
> A captive greets thee, coming from a house
> Of bondage, from yon city's walls set free,
> A prison where he hath been long immured.
> Now I am free, enfranchised and at large. (*Prelude* 1805 I.5–9)

In a layered twist on the theme, the poet foregoes community to commune with nature in an attempt to repair the breach of natural companionship that is incurred with age; such is the impetus for Wordsworth's project. The originary moment within his poetry, in particular, the source of his wistful lament, occurs at the point of exile from childhood, a period he explicitly characterizes as a natural society. Nature herself effects the disjunction as subjects grow into an awareness of their separateness. Exile of this sort thus subsumes what one might term "developmental exile." The Boy of Winander's mimicry of owl calls evokes a response from said birds that evolves into a scene of gay camaraderie in a naturalized Orphic performance not to be reprised in adulthood (*Prelude* 1805 5.364–79). Moore and Bishop's animal poems often portray a familiar creature of nature from whom the speaker is nevertheless estranged. In another version of this motif, Sylvia Plath's lyrics "Nick and the Candlestick," "By Candlelight," and "Event" plumb the underexplored terrain of childbirth and breastfeeding, activities in which the natural and the social blend seamlessly. The society so construed by these innate practices is fated to be disjoined.

Exile in Mortality. Death is the ultimate domain of the exile, and the dead or dying figure may function as subject or object within a poem. Keats's self-elegiac lyrics are sometimes doubly exilic, positing both accomplished and imminent exile as his speakers isolate themselves to face premature death. Chidiock Tichborne's "On the Eve of His Execution" and Raleigh's "The Lie" each confront death as a consequence of a social betrayal. Given their necessary entailment of the threat of death, war poems comprise a noteworthy subdivision of this type.

Exile of the Invaded and Colonized. Colonizing phases have often proven to be fertile intervals for lyric because the culture of the colonized is infiltrated by that of the colonizers and thereby made strange. In extreme instances, civilizations are razed by invaders, their inhabitants literally exiled. For instance, the fall of invaded civilizations is poignantly mourned and memorialized in the Arabic tradition of the "lament for lost cities."

Exile as Alienation. "We have become accustomed to thinking of the modern period itself as spiritually orphaned and alienated, the age of anxiety and estrangement" (Said 173). As was perhaps first fully explored in French *symboliste* poetry, the fragmentation and depersonalization of modern culture becomes, as Adorno understood, an alienating force, one that is widely internalized. In a sense, the poetry of alienation is among the most unadulterated of lyric types because it has shed its scaffolding of physical circumstance to imagine exile as an existential constant. Yeats's poem "The Second Coming" goes so far as to mythicize the cultural disintegration that led to modernist alienation.[28]

Exile as Globalization. In its traditional poetic forms, exile preserves the hypothetical of returning to a native social unit. It assumes boundaries between within and without, here and there, the spatial schematic on which the very idea of self-expression, the outward projection of that which is internal, depends. When these geographic distinctions are confused—when the territory of exile is both omnipresent and nonexistent—the lyric subject often dissolves under pressure. It becomes fragmented, flustered, multiple. The stresses to the self registered within postmodern-era writing are those experienced by a subject trapped in a cultural milieu in which foreignness has been recast as the incomprehensibility of a complex, interconnected world. It becomes difficult to assert a self against the shifting ground of a culture whose technology and whose aspirations drive it to be all-inclusive, a world bent on erasing borders. The greatly tempered emotional pitch of much postmodernist poetry indicates that exile is both constant and irremediable. One becomes inured to its effects, being always, so to speak, beyond the wall.[29] At an extreme, the mournful tenor and jubilant tones of poetry flatline into apathy. While the subject alienated from a culture to which he is indigenous—the modern subject—often exaggerates his subjectivity reactively, the postmodern subject who has known only homelessness lacks stability against which to define himself.

However it is conceived or explained, the rift between the individual and its gestating society produces a being adrift. The outcast, by definition, subsists in a state of intercultural suspense, where he must carve a niche beyond civic walls. His status will expire only at the moment of definitive repatriation or assimilation, an ideal that, in lyric poetry, must go unrealized: the exile of the poet in its many forms leads to, even as it stands in for, the isolate condition of the biological individual thinking in its most basic sense, by perceiving and acting. Though it may begin and end in a social context as it incorporates social significance and is received socially, this activity resists reassimilation: in a fundamental sense, we perceive alone. *Cognizing a new environment is itself an ousting.* The implications of basic organismic functioning for subjectivity are exaggerated in certain historical periods and minimized in others—the postmodern dissolution of the subject is a protracted emphasis and not a novelty—but such functioning is always solitary.

Dickinson, Heidegger, and the Negotiation of Subjectivity and Being

There is, then, a further unsettling consequence of exile that the lyric genre absorbs. The rare, cognate term "exility" denotes the condition of being small, insubstantial, thin, fine, or tenuous. And indeed, the subjectivity of the poet as it is dramatized within the myths treated here may be seen as exilic in this sense, as within them, the lyricist's human capacities are diminished, rendered birdlike, generic, slight. If subjectivity is defined in the usual ways, as the unity and continuity of experience that gives rise to the awareness of a self defined against a non-self (a category including, but not limited to, other selves), a stronger case for subjective presence may be made with respect to those genres that aspire to full-fledged characterization and the representation of so-called bourgeois consciousness, namely, novels, plays, and narrative and dramatic poems. By this standard, even the height of Romantic expression must be seen to construct a flimsier kind of subjectivity than, say, a contemporaneous Jane Austen novel, which painstakingly renders the social context from which selves emerge rather than contending with its absence. This assertion would seem to contradict flatly the notion that subjective expression anchors the genre. In fact, the Hegelian argument for the essential subjectivity of the lyric opens itself to the objection that channeling the universal compromises a unique, delimited subject. The logical consequence of the claim that lyric articulates society best as it individuates is that the tenability of a subject as subject, its cohesiveness, must loosen to accommodate the universal and to voice it. In speaking the universal, even as it is selected and unified, the individual sacrifices his self, at least to a degree. As Frye remarks, the simple equation of the lyric with the subjective is facile ("Approaching" 31), an insight implicit in the fictive placing of the lyric subject outside the boundaries that define it, where it is bound to be abstracted into a state of relative exility. If one looks closely at lyric poems, one finds that the subjectivity they assert is almost always simultaneously undermined, even with respect to the most self-conscious of speakers. In recognition of this fact, an already tenuous presentation of subjectivity has become increasingly rarefied, as reflected in the devolution of the understanding of subjective presence from that of poet, to that of speaker, to that of voice speaking, to voice figured, to voice shattered. The most glaring manifestation of this heightened troubling of subject status in the lyric has been the gradual disappearance of the first-person pronoun. As W. R. Johnson puts it, perhaps too dramatically, "The lyric I grew first ashamed and bewildered, then terrified, by the idea of saying I" (15). Experimental American poetry of the late twentieth century found itself mired in a self-described crisis arising from the vanishing of the first-person pronoun from the landscape, one I shall argue constitutes a pendulum swing to the limits of the genre.

The downfall of the grammatical subject is by now well documented. Its demise has been attributed to the grand theories of Marx and Darwin and their subordination of individual agency to system dynamics. The eschewal of the first-person pronoun within poetry, ascribed routinely to the rejection by Mallarmé and the French symbolists of the "unity between the work and the empirical person" creating it (Friedrich 172), enables T. S. Eliot's doctrine of impersonality to understand affect originating within the poet's personal experience to be "transmuted" into a "new compound" that is the poem ("Tradition" 41). Rejecting authorial intentionality, New Criticism fictionalized the poet into a speaker, a construct that has since been taken to task for its rigidity and mimetic assumptions, in order to regard the poem as an objective artifact. In his 1950 manifesto, "Projective Verse," Charles Olson responds to Romanticism's goal of realizing the poet as an ontological presence in the poem by celebrating the end of what he called "subjectism" (24). Its antithesis is "objectism":

> The getting rid of the "subject" and his soul, that peculiar presumption by which western man has interposed himself between what he is as a creature of nature … and those other creations of nature which we may, with no derogation, call objects. (24)

Freed of the burden of subjectivity, the poet, as a "creature of nature" with "instructions"—a mandate as it were—does what she does "naturally," as a bird, perhaps, or the entity Emily Dickinson, a poet as attentive to the origins of poetry as any, configures as "being."

Notorious for her reclusive habits, Dickinson was most attuned to social dislocation and its attendant effects, and her personal and poetic dispositions were, by nature or by design, exilic. Deploying a version of the trope that conceives of social loss as death, she several times stages the withdrawal from society in an altogether original way, allowing a space interstitial to life and afterlife to percolate into sensory presence. Exemplary of this class of poems is number 340, "I felt a Funeral, in my Brain," presenting the ironic situation in which the mourners at a funeral function as an efficient cause of pain for her oxymoronic invention, the dead speaker. While a fixation with animate death runs through her corpus, it is here portrayed uniquely as a profoundly painful experience for the deceased. The poem opens with the registration of the footsteps of the mourners in attendance at her funeral.

> I felt a Funeral, in my Brain,
> And Mourners to and fro
> Kept treading—treading—till it seemed
> That Sense was breaking through— (1–4)

The bereaved comprise an immediate social network, a retinue for whom the consequences of a death reverberate. They here embody a social presence that intrudes rhythmically, repercussing within the brain of the deceased until "Sense"—or the appearance of sense—penetrates the mind. As "sense" may refer to either sensation or the meaning the poem qualifies as emergent, the word imparts an ambiguity that is both eloquent and apt: its two facets are linked causally, for sensation yields to meaning as sensory input is cognized. But this culmination is eventually thwarted: the insistent, pounding footfalls of the mourners, which would seem to inflict a cosmic headache, at length render the mind of the speaker insensate, which condition would seem to preclude the coalescence of meaning:

And when they all were seated,
A Service, like a Drum—
Kept beating—beating—till I thought
My Mind was going numb— (5–8)

One senses the beating, explicitly felt and implicitly heard, pulsate within the body of the departed as the ritual rhythms of the Service are registered. The pain of death inflicted posthumously by a society of familiars whose "Boots of Lead" intrude upon the soul reduces being to an aural ontology that waxes to become the full measure of consciousness:

And then I heard them lift a Box
And creak across my Soul
With those same Boots of Lead, again,
Then Space—began to toll,

And all the Heavens were a Bell,
And Being, but an Ear,
And I, and Silence, some strange Race
Wrecked, solitary, here— (9–16)

As the impact of the merciless tramping becomes more immediate and more intimate (as it "creak[s] across [a] Soul"), a gesture of lyric recuperation is forced with the tolling not of the voice of the poet, but of "Space" as instrument, of Heaven as bell. Although Dickinson's paratactic repetitions tend to disorder the linear progress of the poem as much as they cobble together a sequence, the passage from pain to the sensory ontology of the poet is duly rendered. "Being" is here embodied, yet purified to the organ of audition that cannot but *perceive* a musical, foreign realm. Death's aftermath is, for starters, Dickinson's version of a regressive shift into a purely perceptual form of existence where "Being" as ear implies its counterpart, the vocal apparatus, while "I"—the socially constructed identity with which silence forms a "strange Race"—is shipwrecked, disabled, at a remove from "Being" primed to vocalize. In qualifying sense as apparent, as seeming, the poem portrays the back end of the passage from actual sense perception (occluded by death) to imagined sense perception—the source of the poem. It plays on the idea of "audition" as a poetic sense modality *and* a rite of initiation that, if performed successfully, leads to the enactment of a more fully realized imaginative product. In so doing, the piece ritualizes lyric incipience.

As hearing supersedes the poem's initial sensory modality of feeling, which here evokes both pain and emotion, and Being swells to become an organ of hearing, relative location becomes indistinguishable because its discernment depends upon the duality and relative position of the *ears*, plural. The sense of space rendered is therefore inscrutably vague, the boundless, ubiquitous beyond of what is perhaps a resonant Christian heaven and what is certainly the unknown. As a "strange Race," the "I" and "silence" represent the tribe that has been shipwrecked from the point of view of Being, the destroyed ship of State, a racialized subjectivity that is unavoidably present, yet *silenced* and purged from the being that can perceive the unearthly tones of heaven's music. One might say that Dickinson tests the conditions necessary to the lyric's utopian transcendence of society and, in so doing, arrives at an impasse. Relief from emotional pain is typically sought through its expression—and Dickinson's death poems accomplish that end—but in Poem 340, the regression to being has gone so far as to flirt with, and finally to enact, the silence that is the consequence of utter disengagement from the social, what defies articulation because it is alogical (*alogos*)—beyond logic and thus without words.

> And then a Plank in Reason, broke,
> And I dropped down, and down—
> And hit a World, at every plunge,
> And Finished knowing—then— (17–20)

In the final stanza, the extended dropping of the "I," presumably within the medium of air (within an "air"), lends the further sense that it is out of its element, beyond support. Given the recovery of the sensory imagination, reason's floor, reason as foundation, collapses and with it, the "I," which falls through worlds, the conceptual structures rationality governs. Reason's "stories," its systemic wholes or narratives in the broad sense and its carefully ordered levels, are crashed through one by one. In the poem's last line, Dickinson breaks her habit of capitalizing nouns, instead capitalizing "Finished," adding stasis to the verb's expression of finality while inscribing the participle "knowing" in the lower case, a gesture that enervates rational knowledge and points to a new form of experience that will follow. Though metrically complete, the poem ends prematurely in silence, flirting with, testing the brink of irrevocability that is the final deictic "then—." It risks the silencing of the social identity from which the poet is disassociated and finds that such silence entails the suppression of the poetic. As Adorno writes, lyric "language should also not be absolutized as the voice of Being as opposed to the lyric subject" (43). The subject is articulated in language, which speaks as the subject's own voice, and thus cannot be surrendered fully to Being (44). If social context is evaded, the poem cannot continue, so Dickinson would seem to warn us.

Sharon Cameron has claimed that the submersion or repression of pain at the heart of Dickinson's poem "lacks an etiology"[30] (97). In a fundamental sense, the etiology is the funeral itself, is the send-off from a socially determined life that prompts the entry into "Being's" imaginative potential. Though the poem wrenches a division between being and the first-person pronoun, each entity presents within the poem, maintaining a fundamental lyric tension at several levels: between externally generated, social rhythms and their internal impact; between the conceptual acuity that informs the poem and the aborning sensation it describes; and between the conceptual certainty conferred by fluid syntax and the conceptual parsing effected by paratactic constructions and interruptive punctuation. Most profoundly, the poem generates a tension between silence and the defiance of silence: it drives a motion in the direction of dissolution, or exility, and a simultaneous countermotion toward self-expression. The coincidence of a "totalled" "I" and an articulate "Being" whose voicing evinces a will to survive points to a complex lyric presence, one subject to the entropic action of disintegration into its new environment at the same time it is ensconced as a grammatical subject. One can read this poem as a narrative of the precondition for the entry into lyric, over which a lyric itself is layered—the poem is simultaneously a prelude to poetry, the emergence of which would seem to follow it, and poetry itself. The irony of the piece is that it manages to realize the lyric entrée into naive perception before executing its silent glide "downward to darkness on extended wing" (Stevens "Sunday" VIII.15). Dickinson's death poems go to the paradoxical core of lyric experience and unabashedly probe it.

The poem's dissolution or "dropping" of the "I" into silence then enacts exility, having charted its causes and its implications. The promise of lyric is that the loosening of social identity will precipitate a journey to recovery that begins in the ideal of pure perception. The "then" of Poem 340 gestures toward an "after"life based in sensory experience, recovering something like an embryological state in its transition to an acute focus on hearing, the primary sense, the development of which begins in utero. An aural being revisits this state by "sounding" for meaning in order to rebuild the wreckage of the "I" within a new, as-yet unspeakable milieu. The poem charts the process of leaving the concrete world for the imagined sensory realm of composition. As Dickinson writes elsewhere, "After great pain, a formal feeling comes—"[31] (1).

The social dimensions of language are far too complex to treat within the confines of this project, which is concerned rather with the enactment of being as it might be understood biologically. Suffice it for now to say that what is social inheres to a great extent in the referential bent of language, which may be minimized, but not overcome. All language is social and, in this sense, received; lyric language is also existential. Perhaps not surprisingly, Heidegger's poetic philosophy of being, though distinctly modern, can help to account for the lyric's basis in existence as well as its core emotional complex. The situatedness at a remove he ascribes to being in his opus *Being and Time* is reflected in the vague adverbial and deictic quality of the term *Dasein*—"being there," where thrown. For Heidegger, being is always in and of the "world"; conversely, the world is part and parcel of being (11, 14). Yet, *Dasein* is rendered alien to the world when thrust into a condition in which the "there" is also "theirs," as a result of which it is subjected to the tyranny of others (represented metonymically by Dickinson as "Boots of Lead"). Anxiety (*Angst*) rooted in the relinquishment of being to the values of others is then the fundamental human mood (178–83). Accepting anxiety as a given enables one to make of one's life a project, to imbue it with meaning existentially (279–82); the emotion in this way both constitutes existence and reveals it. In calling forth authenticity, the pursuit of a life project liberates oneself from the "they," but without ever fully subduing anxiety, the source of which is bidirectional: *Dasein* fears as "they" trespass onto itself, and it frets before death, at the prospect of ultimate separation from the "they." We have here a version of the trope of exile, which recognizes that the poet negotiates anxiety (sorrow in a less fraught ethos) originating from each source. To make one's life as authentic and self-realizing a project as possible, one is placed alone in a life or death situation, whether one is at sea or "dying" of desire, and is thereby liberated from the tyrannical "they" at the same time he confronts the apprehension to which said freedom gives rise, and concomitantly, his mortality. The anxiety-inducing rupture of the self from society simultaneously recovers being within a new set of anxiety-inducing circumstances (afterlife, foreign place, self-authored project).

It is then *Dasein*'s reaction to the imposition of the "they" (the Kaluli sister's refusal to nourish) that prompts his ejection into difference and death. Although anxiety clearly pervades certain lyrics ("The Seafarer," for example), the emotional response to thrownness is prototypically cast as one of boundless sorrow: as John Clare writes, "I am the self-consumer of my woes" (3). The original threat of "their" presence—a presence that is finally undivestible in lyric because it resides in language—is all but offset when the self-liberating project closes in on success, and celebratory response irrupts to moderate lament. Consolation shades over into celebration as the "I" musters the fortitude to rejoice at its freedom from the "they," when it delights at the prospect of reconciliation with them (as in encomia), or, in a variation, when it realizes that they are already of him (as does Whitman's "I"). Lyric poetry navigates this ever-double and ever-doubling emotional nexus. In effect, Heidegger disentangles the genre's etiological knot: the poet is the poet in society because he experiences the encroachment of the "they," which forces him from society, where he is the poet because confronted with the forecast of his death.

However ambivalently Heidegger may have regarded the implications of his work for literary criticism, he characterizes his theory of being as a theory of poetic being in establishing song as the means of situating *Dasein* within the world, as the vehicle of its project. In his essay "What are Poets For?" he explicates the unpublished poem Rainer Maria Rilke called "Improvised Verses," formulating a poetic stance in the process. He interprets Rilke's concept of "the Open" as that which is "ventured," or risked by being, "the great whole of all that is unbounded" (106) to which *Dasein* exposes himself in entering into it. The Open is a "draft," a gathering into itself to which all who dare being are subsumed (106). In consequence of entering into this wholeness, Being becomes whole, a condition conferred by the whole of "the Open" that swells to accommodate it (136). The Open offers shelter, and yet, in exposing itself to it, *Dasein* also courts danger, leaving itself in Heidegger's parlance "unshielded" from the risk of objectifying itself as well as things through a kind of self-assertion that arrives, ineluctably, at mere objectification (115). Both the yielding to the wholeness of the Open and its fragmenting by objectification are the natural doings of human beings. But there is a refuge in which one is protected from the tendency to objectify, that of language not limited by its signifying function:

> Language is the precinct (*templum*), that is, the house of Being. The nature of language does not exhaust itself in signifying, nor is it merely something that has the character of a sign or cipher … all beings, each in its own way, are *qua* beings in the precinct of language. (132)

Being consists in being in relation to what is not yet signified, and thus not yet mediated, a relationship that obtains within poetic language, is afforded by it, because poetry permits internal representation (132). The evasion of object status is achieved through the entry into an inner space of creation. Poetic image making is a type of making in which the unfamiliar is recognized: "Poetic images are … not mere fancies and illusions but imaginings that are visible inclusions of the alien in the sight of the familiar" ("Dwells" 226). Inhabiting the "precinct" of poetic language thereby creates for us a haven from the presence of anxiety-inducing objects by allowing us to integrate them imaginatively into our histories. This anxiety-relieving integration of the unfamiliar into what is known, which Heidegger brands poetic, *is* the activity of perception, particularly when what is perceived is new.

The assumption of one's place in the whole, then, entails the relinquishment of the objectified, objectifying social self accomplished by singing, the uttering of the whole of which one is a part ("Poets" 140). In speaking the whole, song marks the limits of reason and its basis in objectification: it is not productive of that which can be commodified, including one's own self (137–8). The admission into and the admitting of the Open involve an abandonment of the assertive, willful subject Dickinson wrecks through the metamorphosis into an exilic presence that can sing the whole, thereby healing it (138). To convert the parting against the Open, to recall its unwholesomeness into a sound whole, the poets "sing a healing whole in the midst of the unholy" (140). "Their song over the land hallows. Their singing hails the integrity of the globe of Being" (141). Throughout "What are Poets For?" Heidegger gathers and correlates a set of terms that translate to the English cognates "whole," "hale," "heal," "health," and "holiness": the German "*heil*," "*heilen*," "*heilig*" in turn derivative of the Indo-European *kailo*. Singing manifests as *sound* in all relevant senses of the word: as aurality, as birdsong, as music, as a probing of the whole, and as a health. The healing work of poetry works to mend the initial breach created by the objectifying, the scapegoating of the poet in turning toward and importing a new wholeness that makes him whole. Orpheus, Heidegger tells us, as singer of being, "lives in-finitely in the open" (139). Indeed.

Being is the state of existing, and in existing, animals perceive, emote, and act. By restoring being, poetry becomes the language of perception. As I shall argue, it "deconceals," to borrow Heidegger's term, the essence of being as emotion, action, and perception situated within the whole it confronts and utters, thereby risking objectification. In "… Poetically Man Dwells …," Heidegger explains that by dwelling poetically man is "able to be commensurate with his nature" (221), a nature I maintain is fundamentally cognitive and necessarily physical. Exile in its various forms serves as the means by which social connection is attenuated to force attention to the formal, linguistic, cognitively based means by which meaning is made by a being that, in so making, sings. As a device, it isolates and foregrounds an individual so that "thinking" may proceed undistracted and by necessity. Lyric is a survival mode, the voice of the individual in the wild, the cognitively untamed, recurring to being in synthesis with a new environment in which it is embedded.

The respeciation featured in the myths also serves to foreground the poet as an individual in a biological rather than a philosophical or sociopolitical sense. The devolution to a bird marks one as a generic member of a species, a being separate but representative: *the* Nightingale, *the Muni*. A bird "being" a bird in a general sense resists objectification as a particular bird. Thus, the indeterminate priority of song and its recursive ousting points also to a resistance to individuation: the individual is always of the species, in a biological sense unbanishable and therefore suited to filter the universal. Perception, as a fundamental activity of being, both avails the singer in circumstances apart and functions as a site of conformity and connection because members of a species perceive by means of the same mechanism. The poet becomes a mediator of her new environment by deconcealing the "universal" processes of perception, the content of which is necessarily singular, particular, concrete. Lyric techniques offer a scaffolding on which perceptual activity is built, one affording connection between individuals by means of a dynamic common to them and unique to the genre. As perception transpires to a great extent within one, to be engaged perceptually as and by another, as and how another has been engaged—the process lyric occasions—is to be in a sense infected.

As a conceit of estrangement from the ordinary, exile in addition becomes an allegory for the shift to a usage of language that competes with its social usage, minimizing entailments that are, as Adorno reminds us, never fully divestible. This way of understanding poetry acknowledges what he points to as the doubleness of language, the medium in and through which being in the world, the environment as inclusive of the singer's actions within it, emerges. The position that poetic language, as the language of existence, speaks something other than the social suggests a malleability, an adaptability that poets exploit. The common sentiment that it is the role of the poet to refresh the native tongue is given canonical voice by Hegel, who urges that it is incumbent upon lyric to remodel "the prosaic consciousness's ordinary mode of expression into a poetic one"[32] (*Aesthetics* 977). Exile is moreover the removal into an extreme mode of language usage, a pulling away from reference in order to approach pure aurality, if provisionally, to begin as the bird.

In Summary

What is accounted for within these stories of lyric incipience may be said to qualify as basic characteristics of the genre, characteristics the remainder of the book will map onto perception together with the other core features of the genre:

1. *Emotional Paradox.* Lyric emerges from and airs a fundamental emotional range encompassing lament and blame at one extreme and celebration and praise at the other. Praise, itself a form of celebration, seeks to reachieve a unity as much as it responds to freedom from the social pressures that objectify. Lamenting and blaming function to console the bereaved in his solitary existence before the unknown.[33] The ambivalence this emotional complex assumes is also the upshot of the condition of physical embeddedness, an alternate form of union from which perception evolves the cognition of separateness. Different cultural moments tolerate different degrees of affective intensity in their poetry, but poetry does not eschew emotion, which may be subtilized, but not erased. (A complete lack of feeling would suggest insentience.) Hegel tells us that poetry is a liberation *in* and not *from* feeling (*Aesthetics* 1112) (emphasis added).
2. *The Absenting of the Lyric Audience.* A rhetorical consequence of the separation imposed by exile is the absenting of audience from the dramatic situation of the poem or, at the very least, the minimizing of its importance. John Stuart Mill's pithy account of lyric as "an utterance that is overheard" implies that an audience is unintended within, or incidental to, its performance scenario. Frye defines genre in terms of the "radical of [its] presentation" (*Anatomy* 246–7), which for lyric is "the concealment of the poet's audience from the poet" (249), a precondition of eavesdropping. While it is true that the primary method of dissemination of early lyric poetry was oral, and that it was sung to an audience, to argue that the bard's listeners were the intended recipients of his words (the hearers rather than the overhearers of the poem) is to confuse the poem's external presentation with its rhetorical situation. Poems addressed to a "you," though they may seem to reduce audience to one intended listener, tend to read as soliloquies, utterances that apostrophize an addressee, rather than messages. Mill's insight accords with the placing by many theorists of the figures of apostrophe and its complementary term, prosopopoeia, at the center of the genre.[34] From the French *symboliste* movement onward, the lyric set out to rid itself of even a symbolic auditor, and its Stellas, Lauras, and Amaranthas grew patently superfluous. As the concept of a speaker yielded to the notion

of a phenomenalized voice, the listener was consequently abstracted, reduced to an "ear." The lyric's shyness before its public lends it a heightened, even an overdeveloped sense of privacy, an idea bound etymologically to "privation," specifically the privation of society.

3. *Compromised Referentiality.* In its embrace of novelty, lyric dishevels reference, skewing toward the condition of music, which expresses the inaugural quality of the poetic, as well as poetry's core emotional valence. As organized sound, lyric musicality points toward new meaning; it promises that sound will yield sense within a foreign milieu.
4. *The Exile of the Subject and Its Transition to Being.* The Kaluli boy is symbolically starved, Philomela is symbolically muted, Orpheus summarily beheaded. The disintegration of the "I" and its recuperation as being is a further consequence of its uprooting; these events occur in tandem with the independence of the lyric singer (Hegel, *Aesthetics* 1118). As being emerges, it risks self-objectification, which results in a tension between the recession of the subject and what appears to be its excessive foregrounding, a tension endemic to perception.

If the lyric were to stabilize a subject, to realize it fully, it would exhaust itself in so doing. Once being has negotiated an obscure new environment, perceived and conceptualized it, it has reified itself. At the end of this spectrum, the lyric "I" is no longer troubled by its existence, no longer strives to speak. This is the point at which poetry must be renovated and the circumstances that cause the "I" to flounder recast, the point at which the pendulum swings back to the instant the poet must once more face ejection. Lyric thus also shatters or assumes the shattering of the "I" that was Olson's goal, reimmersing it in nature, in biological, species-level behavior prompting perception and initiating first sight.

How the exiled figure, the castaway, or victim of existential angst assimilates to his new environment becomes the stuff of the lyric poem. In making his experience coherent for himself, in making himself coherent, he makes the same coherent for his readers, renovating his language in the process: this is the achievement of major poets. The lyric poem is a postcard sent home.

Notes

1 Eric Havelock goes so far as to argue that Plato *equates* imitation and emotional engagement: by the latter half of Book X, mimesis comes to refer to the emotionally

driven act of identification, not only what gives rise to it (26), a hypothesis that accounts for the lyric's exclusion from the Platonic system.

2 This particular translation is Benjamin Jowett's (446). Unless noted, translations are those of Paul Shorey.

3 The elevation of prevailing social values to the status of wisdom is a fundamental move Plato absorbs from Socrates, who in turn quotes Diotima as she prescribes content for poetry. "Now, by far the most important kind of wisdom, she went on, is that which governs the ordering of society, and which goes by the name of justice and moderation" ("Symposium" 209b).

4 This translation is also Jowett's (446).

5 It is perhaps worth noting that this argument for the negative influence of art is extant in contemporary popular culture with respect to visual media. Although seemingly an overreaction, it speaks to the perceived power of the artifact to influence behavior that disturbs Plato.

6 See also pages 31 and 42–4.

7 This paradox would seem to support the truism that an artistic vocation is somehow destined.

8 The first two of these features may seem to have more in common with written poetry than with poetry in its oral form, which Philomela comes to create. It can be argued, however, that oral poetry is also two-dimensional, introducing repetition within a linear delivery.

9 It bears repeating at this point that law and fact or law and truth are conflated by Plato, as is evidenced by the very establishment of the Republic as the City of the Soul. Within his system, the women would stand accused of diluting truth as well.

10 In Ovid's later rendering of the myth, Procne is turned into a nightingale and Philomela a swallow, reversing the earlier version, which is treated here.

11 In Simonides's tale, Orpheus is Apollo's son, and the muse Calliope is his mother. In other renditions, he descends from Oegrus and Clio, or Polyhymnia. In still others, Aphrodite is his mother.

12 See Segal (20–4) for this interpretation.

13 Jeffrey Walker claims that the lyric gave birth to the rhetorical mode *epideiktikon*, an oratorical style deploying the primary modes of blame and its counterpart, praise, in order to exemplify behavior to be renounced and to be emulated. Epideictic poetry both precedes and survives the broadly applicable concept of rhetoric (8–9, 16). See also Aristotle's *Rhetoric* for his codification of oratory.

14 Bettina Knapp opposes esoteric exile in this sense to exoteric exile, a physical banishment beyond a periphery.

15 This assertion is not meant to contradict, but rather to supplement the understanding of babbling as a developmental stage in which muscle tone is developed to enable speech.

16 It is possible to argue that written poetry, as derivative of oral poetry, is itself a substitute of a substitute, a further enactment of différance; for present purposes, each functions as a *pharmakos*.
17 Victor Zuckerkandl's book *Sound and Sentiment* is an inspiration for Feld's opus as well as its namesake.
18 This venturing beyond the ordinary recurs in the idea of the *avant-garde*, another metaphorical naming of a situation in which a lone figure precedes his fellows in order to survey the unknown.
19 In the "Poetics of the Lyric" chapter of *Structuralist Poetics: Structuralism, Linguistics and the Study of Literature*, Jonathan Culler makes resistance and recuperation one of four fundamental criteria for lyric. The others are deixis, theme and epiphany, and organic wholes. Obfuscation is widely held to be a central characteristic of the genre. The reference to Stevens is "Poetry must resist the intelligence almost successfully" (*OP* 197).
20 In a sense, the Romantic elevation of the poet foreshadowed by Sir Philip Sidney has a qualified merit in the present context as the creator stands apart by merit of his creation. The more egalitarian view of poet that emerges in the latter half of the twentieth century likewise finds validation here as a perceptually based means of poetic making is in theory available to all.
21 Notably, the three major approaches within myth criticism, the structural, the psychological, and the cognitive, each acknowledge the cyclic recurrence of mythic events.
22 As Feuerbach's secular challenge to Hegel first suggested, the latter's absolutism, and particularly his Christian rendition of it, is in fact incidental to the totalizing dynamic he limns. See "Toward a Critique of Hegel's Philosophy."
23 To effect such a unification of the individual through the particular, poetry must originate in an exemplary, that is, an imaginative individual (*Aesthetics* 1115).
24 Adorno adduces the often-cited Sappho as an example of an ancient modern sensibility.
25 One might argue that Hegel's idea of sublation is also something like an embedding.
26 The centrality of obscurity to lyric poetry as well as its function will be explicated in the next chapter.
27 C. S. Lewis discusses the requirement in the Provencal courts of love that the beloved be of superior class status, and thus of a society from which the lover is, strictly speaking, barred. See *The Allegory of Love* (35, 36).
28 It is perhaps worth noting that the modern era also saw the en masse expatriation of its literati.
29 Current political conditions point to exile's waning significance as a figure for geographic displacement. As Said stresses, the twentieth-century version of the exile is the refugee (177–81).

30 Sharon Cameron points to the unemotional tone of this poem to interpret it as an act of repression culminating in a symbolic lapse of consciousness (96). According to Cameron, the pain from which the speaker is disassociated is not expressible because it is repressed. Rather than begin the lyric journey toward new meaning by trusting in the vehicle of song to oust, or utter, pain and thereby to make new meaning from it, it makes that pain inaccessible, thereby silencing the poem. No pain, no utterance. I, however, find this poem, which concededly describes the cause of pain rather than directly expressing it, unsettling if not painful per se.

31 The line is from Poem 372.

32 See also, pages 976 and 1006 of *Hegel's Aesthetics: Lectures on Fine Arts*. Vol. II for elaborations of this idea.

33 One might argue that the hyperbolic tendencies of lyric, one of Jonathan Culler's fundamental traits of the genre, derive, at least in part, from the breadth of the emotional reaction exile triggers. The emotional response to diremption is one of extremes. (See *Theory of the Lyric* 258–63.)

34 Paul de Man does exactly this in "Lyrical Voice in Contemporary Theory: Riffaterre and Jauss." See, especially, pages 61–2.

2

Dwelling with the Possible: Lyric Obscurity and Embedded Perception

But the highest minds of the world have never ceased to explore the double meaning, or, shall I say, the quadruple or the centuple, or much more manifold meaning, of every sensuous fact.

—Ralph Waldo Emerson

That the lyric poem imagines a radical and unceremonious thrust into a new milieu presumes that it confronts utter novelty. On the far side, before the poet, lies a foreign scene awaiting survey. On occasion, lyrics dramatize this inchoate moment of initial contact. Two noteworthy examples, John Keats's "On First Looking into Chapman's Homer" and Wallace Stevens's "The Doctor of Geneva," establish themselves as originary to lyric experience at the level of their content in so doing. Signally, each work is preliminary to the opus it inaugurates: "Chapman" initiates Keats's poetic enterprise as only the second of his surviving lyrics, and "Geneva" occupies an early slot in Stevens's first book, *Harmonium*, a volume preliminary by design to his *Collected Poems*[1] (*Letters* 834). Each poem is further seminal for its poet as an annunciation of a lyric undertaking it simultaneously enacts. Sharing a Pacific vista as a synecdoche of the new world, the transplanted "Cortez"[2] and the figure often interpreted to be the Genevan John Calvin can muster no more than a look of "wild surmise" and a stifled sob, respectively, in response to the overwhelming novelty before them. Keats represents the wondrous view as a "wide expanse," a vast oceanic offing that resists, or at least forestalls, linguistic apprehension as it is beheld from atop a mountain.

> He stared at the Pacific—and all his men
> Looked at each other with a wild surmise—
> Silent, upon a peak in Darien. (12–14)

Emulating Keats, Stevens exploits the motif of the American frontier by placing his Old World denizen at the continent's outer limit where he appears involuntarily passive and pathetically incongruous on a Pacific beach, clad, as he is, in a stovepipe hat and shawl. Flummoxed within this secular, natural context, the Doctor is not awestruck, but he is clearly ill at ease. The environment Calvin perceives, itself verbose or "voluble," agitates him into a prophetic mode via which he has no choice but to concoct a response. In the process, his mind "spins" and "hisses," producing the sound of one of the English pronunciations of the letter "C" and replicating its circular motion (the very sounds and movements that will come to pervade Stevens's Grand Poem as indicia of nascent meaning):[3]

> oracular
> Notations of the wild, the ruinous waste,
>
> Until the steeples of his city clanked and sprang
> In an unburgherly apocalypse.[4] (11–14)

His native music, the accustomed, sacred sounds of Geneva rendered discordant and defamiliarized, the good Doctor cannot prevail over uncomfortable speculation by formulating a coherent (or for that matter an incoherent) verbal response. His ultimately feckless, ultimately obscure revelation is so great a breach of decorum that he is reduced to blowing his nose.[5] And while Cortez's wonder is perhaps less humbling than is Calvin's, it is silencing nonetheless. The rendition of verbal impotence, or pregnant pause, before novelty this class of lyrics shares is somehow initiatory to poetic praxis. One can count among its members Dickinson's Poem 340 ("I felt a Funeral, in my Brain"), which, like its fellows, effects a shift of scene, liberating death as metaphor into the real in a display of imaginative virtuosity the poem cannot finally muster the agency to articulate. The reactions of silence and inaction limned in these poems are extreme: each becomes preliminary, herald, and proem, in whole a synecdoche of itself and of poem-making at large.

It would seem that this dynamic in which the pressures expelling the voice are countervailed by those compelling it to silence is fundamental to an enterprise that must simultaneously preserve a death scene and effect a rebirth. The exilic, in the sense of attenuating, or disintegrating, subject (and Orpheus's bodily dismemberment is emblematic here) is deprived of a vocal agency that is simultaneously *recoupable.* Although each of these poems pushes the risk of lyric initiation to a logical extreme, it has nevertheless been uttered: it has engaged with new terrain and has been sounded at the same time it dramatizes a lyric-precluding silence. The plot device that precipitates lyric creation within its heuristic frame is embedded in the act of recovery that supersedes it, creating, as a consequence of origination, a complex overlay of temporalities that distinguishes the genre sharply from narrative.[6] As such, an obligatory silence is elicited prior to the commencement of vatic delivery that assumes the hearing, as well as the seeing, of new environment, here the afterlife and the Pacific swell. In Dickinson's and Stevens's poems, listening to the clanking of bells conditions their voicing.

Dwelling with the Earth: Lyric Recovery

The understanding that *poiesis* is a perceptual venture essayed in the apprehension of novelty allows Stevens to conceive of it literally, as the activity of a displaced mind, and to submit the conditions of the mind's locating. The opening of what is perhaps the most candid of his *ars poeticae*, "Of Modern Poetry," tenders its subject, "the poem of the mind," as it is engaged in a search for "sufficiency" following a change of scene. Rehearsing his custom of entering a poem *in medias res*, Stevens sets his archetypal mind poem awhirl without full recourse to predication: the opening sentence fragment, "The poem of the mind in the act of finding/What will suffice" (1–2), renders present tense action despite lacking a verb. With a conspicuous absence of fanfare, the passive voice construction that sets in motion the poem's second stanza, "Then the theatre was changed/To something else" (5–6), subjects its protagonist to a change of view and venue, to an unmotivated immersion in an alternate theatricality. The signal on which the inception of the mind-poem hinges is once again the abruptly intrusive adverb "then," the preemptive temporal marker designating an episodic shift. Following this indicator of divide, a mode of search is induced whose end is the seemingly minimal requirement of sufficiency and the complex of ideas it entails.

Notably, the future tense of the concluding verb phrase in the line "it has to find what will suffice" (10) serves to defer the attainment of "satisfaction" (26) indefinitely, extending what might be considered a mode of improvisation, indeed spontaneity, occasioned by sudden change. With this gesture, the poem opens itself to the referential breadth afforded by the adjective "else," concluding with a sampling of quotidian content. Concurrently, the anaphoric echoes of the modal verbs "has to" and "must" running through the remainder of the poem instill a certain urgency as they enumerate the parameters shaping the "poem of the mind" (28). The mandate to a mental performance on a foreign platform in a play of one's making is, per Stevens, the impetus to "modern" poetry, the precondition of its composing. Restless yet compelled, the poet-actor seeks the "satisfaction" of what Stevens pinpoints as "sudden rightnesses" of sound "wholly/Containing the mind, below which it cannot descend,/ Beyond which it has no will to rise" (22–4).

"The poem of the mind" (the poem *as* mind, the mind *as* poem) in Stevens's poetics is activated by an open-ended change of scene inflicted upon it, and thus a version of exile inheres in this piece in the form of mental dislocation upon the incurring of loss and the resultant state of being lost. What, then, is the finding of sufficiency when it comes to animadversions in the root sense of the word?[7] Stevens's choice of the metaphor of the theater, as etymologically rich as it is, is not, I believe, an attempt to relate modern poetry to the *genre* of drama. It is tempting and perhaps facile to read the trope as a modernist version of the one governing Macbeth's quasi-absurdist "Life's but a walking shadow, a poor player" speech (V.5.24) and to ascribe chronic dissatisfaction to the angst, alienation, and ennui widely thought to color historical modernism. What is significant, rather, is that the metaphor imparts a sense of immediacy, a theory of the poem's own moment, for it self-mandates being "of" its time (8–10). The mind-poem must attend to its circumstances: it may be "of," that is, engage with, dailiness in all its varieties: "skating," "dancing," "combing." The insight that it is self-enacting, ever "in the act of finding," suggests that it is a poetry belonging to and not merely about the present, one that skirts the ravine between song and silence—or being and nothingness—by remaining happily attentive to the moment of seeking. "Modern" then becomes a descriptive and not a historical or categorical term, one best construed to refer to contemporaneity, a consistently singular moment whose particularity remains undesignated because it is contingent. Stevens may have discovered something about lyric poetry through the dicta and the praxis of his own historical instance, but the idea of presence is something far more deeply interfused within the genre's character, indeed its ethos, that fends off a reductive alliance with modernism and even modernity. In *Theory of the Lyric*, Jonathan Culler points out that lyrics employ the past tense infrequently,[8] embracing instead a "performative temporality" (63), what he calls "the here-and-now of enunciation" (16) grounded in, among other things, the genre's preference for the nonprogressive present tense[9] (291–2). Lyric renders mind present to a time and a place so that it may attend to the search that is its particular project.

Stevens's motif of mental displacement and concomitant restless quest cannot in fact be uniquely modern because it runs through the lyrics of prior epochs. The realization that a mind displaced must endure the chronic dissatisfaction of homelessness—the itinerancy of the minstrel—is the point of frustration, for example, within Andrew Marvell's lyric "The Mower to the Glow-Worms," which concludes with the following lines addressed to the phosphorescent insects of its title:

> Your courteous lights in vain you waste,
> Since Juliana here is come,
> For she my mind hath so displaced
> That I shall never find my home. (13–16)

The despair expressed by Marvell's arrant mower is occasioned and cyclically exacerbated by ill-spent courtesy, by the failure of hospitality, or welcome, in the daily sense of the gracious reception of the guest, or tenant, into the home. Juliana's rejection of Damon, which plays out principally in the companion piece "Damon the Mower," effects an estrangement of mind Marvell opposes explicitly to homecoming. Lovestruck, Damon can no longer walk the well-trod, perceptible path that leads to his erstwhile abode, for he has been made homeless by disposition. The theater has shifted irrevocably: routine has been flummoxed and, if he is to find his way in the metaphorical darkness, he must chart a new course. To woo Juliana and to win her, Damon must tread a path to her front door that is lit but as yet unperceived, and he must do so by encoding his perceptual processes poetically. Courtly love, including the late form adopted by Marvell, translates the highly formalized threshold ritual of reception into the codes of sexual practice. Within the courtly dynamic, the beloved estranges the lover by refusing him admittance into her graces, sexual and otherwise, suspending him between homes (what might be said to be the situation of all who woo). Courtship and wooing, as highly charged versions of the act of finding what will suffice, imply a dissatisfaction that prompts a modality of search intended to yield a desired, that is, a satisfying result.

There is clearly something within the poetic dynamic, conspicuous in its courtly variety, about foiled access to the customary *and* the unaccustomed that these poets understand to implicate the activity of the questing, perceiving mind, one that for the present finds no succor in guide lights, maps, and scripts, in the wholesale harnessing of the past experience Stevens reduces within "Of Modern Poetry" to the token of a "souvenir." (*Souvenirs* in French, the designated, integral half of his *langue*, may refer to memories themselves as well as the keepsakes that elicit them.) For both Stevens and Marvell, the satisfaction the mind seeks stands in lieu of the refuge of a former home, the site where basic needs—rest, fellowship, nourishment, and safe harbor—are tended to within the practice of homemaking and the ethos of hospitality. Home is a concept consonant with satisfaction. Perpetually ultimate as a site of *rentrer*, or return, it is the destination of all questing, all moving out from stasis. Even in Frost's cynical definition—"Home is the place where, when you have to go there,/ They have to take you in,"[10] (117–18)—grudging admittance restores one to the bosom nevertheless. As is well-established in the literature of anthropology, the ceremony of welcome is a cornerstone of social maintenance and continuity.[11] The loss of the integrity of the home evokes a pathos second only to the pathos occasioned by death.[12] Denied the aid of the familial (a cognate of "familiar"), the subject is forced to construct his own provisional dwelling, to homestead and thereby to improvise. He must engage in a process of making-do that is the hallmark of extrasocial survival and gives rise to the lyric figures of the spurned lover, the itinerant thespian, the forsaken citizen, the dispossessed shepherd, the nomad, the pilgrim, and the pioneer, to rehearse a scant catalog of versions. In poetry, home and hearth, the *vesta*, is vestigial or *vestigium*, merely trace or memento of the past, an ontology George Steiner claims is revealed by *poetics*, construed broadly:

> It is poetics, in the full sense, which inform us of the visitor's visa in a place and in time which defines our status as transients in a house of being whose foundations, whose future history, whose rationale—if any—lie wholly outside our will and comprehension. (140)

Steiner goes on to endorse poetry's role as a remediator of homelessness, writing of the poetic that it "make[s] us, if not at home, at least alertly, answerably peregrine in the unhousedness of our human circumstance" (140). Poetry becomes an attention and an accountability to this innate condition, which for Steiner is lapsarian: from his perspective, the term *cortesia* represents the ultimate reception by and before God, as well as the possibility of its thwarting (147–8). Stevens, on the other hand, strips the metaphor to expose not only a secular but also a natural form of welcome. Deromanticizing courtly fanfare and ritual, he abstracts courtship's symbolic interchange into a venture that is exclusively mental. Marked by neutrality and little identifying information, his mind-poem is drawn almost clinically, as a nonspecific "it," the pronoun, abstract by definition, of his poetic proviso "It Must Be Abstract."[13] The *inamorata*, the mind's would-be mate, then swells to become the fullness of the environs Stevens names "my green, my fluent mundo" ("Notes": "Pleasure" X.20). The trappings of metaphor doffed, the poet is revealed to minister to his vagrancy by courting what for him is an earthly reception, a wooing of the earth itself.

The forcing of the mind into a different environment, a setting in which it must learn the topography to survive, is then the upshot of the catastrophic loss that is the lot of the exile. But homelessness is not simply a fresh metaphor for the outcast's plight: as a trope it entails its complement, provisional homemaking, a not uncommon way of understanding an enterprise that calls for the building of *stanzas*, or rooms. In the poem "I dwell in Possibility—" (Number 466), from which the title of this chapter is taken, Dickinson boasts of the poetry she tacitly inhabits in styling it "A fairer house than prose" (2). Heidegger offers up the same term, "dwelling" (*wohnen*), to describe the earth-recovering activity that is inherently poetic ("Dwells" 221). The English prefix "eco," deriving from Greek *oikos* (*οἶκος*), or "home," also acknowledges that being of the earth is a kind of dwelling within it,[14] a state that requires one to be "answerable" and "alert," to perceive attentively. The mind shelters itself from its fallen estate, survives within a new locale by fitting itself to its environment, easing its desperation in what is revealed to be a cognitive quest for sufficiency. The lyric, as will become apparent, enacts this quest.

Presence, Pain, and Prophecy: Lyric Embeddedness

The need for loss to be recuperated by an indwelling kind of perception is penetrated by Emerson in his late study "Experience," which begins by declaring that entrapment in the blind interstice of pain is an endemic, yet surmountable condition.

> Where do we find ourselves? In a series of which we do not know the extremes, and believe that it has none. We wake and find ourselves on a stair; there are stairs below us, which we seem to have ascended; there are stairs above us, many a one, which go upward and out of sight. (471)

As he commences the essay whose sentences will transport him upward and out of the two-years' grief that followed upon the loss of his young son, Emerson characterizes what he regards as postnatal displacement: we are, he suggests, natively mesmerized. "All things swim and glitter," he writes with inimitable, aphoristic aplomb (471). A phantasmagoria flits, indistinct, before our half-opened eyes. The curious assertion that follows, "Our life is not so much threatened as our perception" (471), resonates with a direct sagacity that obtrudes upon the flow of lyrical tropes. The latter resume immediately: "Ghostlike we glide through nature, and should not know our place again" (471). Insubstantial, though we live, like Damon, we barely perceive—and thus do not fully inhabit—our surroundings.

Emerson evolves his version of social dislocation in an apt context. The loss of a child disrupts the integrity of the home, depriving its inmates of a kind of sustenance: it inflicts the loss of continuance legacy affords, of a clear view out over the receding steps in his spatial metaphor of time, and replaces it with treasured *souvenirs*. Lost in the grief that results when the expectations of and for one's effect—or issue—are foiled, and one's tools for predicting are shown to be unproductively dull, we believe that in our anguish we are most alive: "There are moods in which we court suffering, in the hope that here, at least, we shall find reality, sharp peaks and edges of truth" (472). Yet, the ruse of life-giving tribulation is at last revealed to be illusory. Unremedied, pain does not lift us from our quotidian course but rather dooms us to a condition of "almost all custom and gross sense" (462), a phrase Emerson uses to mean something like habituation, in which we bend before the flux that outmatches us and wear blinders during all the phases of our ascent (472). Curtailed vision follows from the initial curtaining effect of pain: it is also the plight of those, the plurality, excessively vested in habit taken as anodyne, in a mode of being Dickinson enlarges to custom, or social ritual, through the figure of synchronous marching. But this condition, a hair's breadth from the insensate (and thus drawn to the sensational), points to the existence of a finer tone in which habit is infeasible, a realm in which pain is ameliorated by being alert—or present—to what might be perceived.

Emerson, whose prose is quintessentially lyrical (perhaps more so than even his poetry), recognizes both the initiatory and transitive role of pain within vision as well as its ultimate inadequacy to the same. Pain, and especially the ur-pain of social death, elongates the past, which lingers as its source, preventing forward movement toward its relief. In conflict with transcendentalist doctrine, it confines one within the borders of the wounded self. Ideally, pain serves as impetus, the spur to its own elimination, a signal to rectify imbalance or "dis-ease." For Emerson, its transcendence is achieved through anchorage in the vitality of the here and now: "The only ballast I know, is a respect to the present hour" (479), he writes, describing what today one might call the tactic of "living in the moment." The dislocation prompted by the experience of grief must give way to relocating, to re-rooting oneself in "the strong present tense" if one is to transcend affliction's shallow streambed. It is by opening ourselves to the harmonious, ideal depths of nature that we find the relief of reconciliation with it, concomitant with the discovery that our sense that we are strangers is mere fancy.

> But every insight from this realm of thought is felt as initial, and promises a sequel. I do not make it; I arrive there, and behold what was there already. I make! O no! I clap my hands in infantine joy and amazement, before the first opening to me of this august magnificence, old with the love and homage of innumerable ages, young with the life of life, the sunbright Mecca of the desert. And what a future it opens! I feel a new heart beating with the love of the new beauty. I am ready to die out of nature and be born again in this new yet unapproachable America. (485)

Glad forgetfulness is achieved in lyrical outburst, in the attention to sensation before a "new world." Emerson's robust writing style overflows with the language of the senses: "felt," "behold," "clap," "sunbright," "feel a heart beating." Yet the sensory experience it depicts, like that of Cortez and Calvin, is not immediately processed. Emerson's response consists in "infantine" amazement, the befuddled state of initial awareness that follows from waking fully to one's surroundings, the state analogous to the moments after birth in which nascent sensation corresponds to the assumption of one's inextricable place in the whole of the new environment upon the transit in and through pain. As what is infantine is literally "without words," his progression explicates the stunned silences of Calvin and Cortez's men as symptomatic of the relinquishment, willing or not, to new environs. Emerson invokes a project that is fundamentally of *poiesis* with his turn of phrase "I make," a declaration he immediately recalls and revises to the more instinctual, more *infantine* "Oh no! I clap." His abrupt fall into silence is in a far-reaching sense the logical outcome of the self-dissolving acquiescence to a level of being below the reason the lyric demands. It recognizes that yielding to the source of sensation is an essential stage in the pursuit of what will be revealed to be the emergence of "sufficient" response.

Emerson's palliative "death" out of and rebirth into nature eventually converges with the notion of the poet as conduit, a mouthpiece or prophet who, in dispensing with known formulae, squelches the self-assertion upon which identity depends. This needful self-relinquishment on the part of the vatic figure is often neglected within lyric theory. To speak of overarching tendency, to recoup broad potential, one must sacrifice individual perspective. One must suspend volition, as Schopenhauer picks up in his famous definition of the "lyrical state" as one in which "pure knowing comes to us, so to speak, in order to deliver us from willing and its stress," a kind of knowledge he describes as a "pure perception of the environment"[15] (250). The experience of the fullness of the present moment permits the transcendence of limited acuity and view that is necessary if one is to live successfully, divinely, if one is, as the poet, to divine the natural symbols that correspond to the spiritual within Emerson's semiotics ("Nature" 1836 20). Death and rebirth in fulfillment of nature's terms is paradoxically a self-enhancing spiritual proposition, one the poet must accept if he is to interpret nature ("Poet" 448). But pain is perhaps not so easily mitigated in the absence of such a fixed system of belief, and not all lyric journeys are able to culminate by emulating Emerson's celebratory response to the prospect of submission. For many, pain is not allayed, but stays to subtend the poem as lament lingers to accompany new perception. As will become apparent, "pure" perception at length retriggers pain, accounting for the overlay of present and past time within lyric. Perception also enables praise, which often breaks through to modulate complaint, as it does in elegies and courtly lyrics, poems in which the lost society (the departed, the lady) is also the new environs the speaker regards. What's more, the relinquishment of self-awareness that attention to sensation demands may upset a balance, tipping irremediably toward the utter abandonment of the self, as it does by the end of "I felt a Funeral—In my Brain." A transcendentalist belief system can tolerate the reunion of the first-person singular with the whole, can celebrate it as a religious ideal and manage pain by surrendering to the nature it is incumbent upon the poet to speak. Less given to rejoicing than Emerson, Dickinson's curtailing of poetic action within the fiction of its beginning by arresting the poem, lopping it off after the indeterminate, terminal "then—," confronts the logical consequence of dying to abate pain. As noted, in ending the piece as she does, she acknowledges that "being" present to the bells of heaven risks perpetual silence.

Stevens contends with the tension between pain and presence by allowing their exponents to dialogue within his poem "St. John and the Back-Ache," a dramatic piece somewhat neglected as an *ars poetica*. In this late, appropriately obscure work from *The Auroras of Autumn*, he observes his custom of commencement, in this case of a tutorial, in mid-course, a practice tantamount to the forcing of origin in the sudden imposition of a contextual shift that leaves one devoid of the ballast of reference. The character encountered first in this pseudo-drama is pain, archly personified as a Back-Ache. In a significant doubling and reversal of the directionality of the figure, the Back-Ache is also a synecdoche and symbol of post-lapsarian suffering, of the consciousness of separateness to which all pain alludes (Bloom *Climate* 204). Like the figure of the orphan, it refers to its absent cause—the fall. Within a highly self-conscious dialogic format that itself instantiates duality, the Back-Ache articulates what it conceives to be the fundamental conundrum of a necessarily self-involved mind, one capable of knowing its complement—the world as presence—only as against its own limits.

"The terriblest force in the world" (2), the self-aware mind is champion and challenger both, left to defend itself against its own stubbornly dualistic bent.

The saint of revelation, John the Divine, replies to this observation by affiliating world and presence and opposing them to mind and force, setting forth the dichotomy at the poem's heart. As the Back-Ache engages exclusively on an intellectual plane, it can only wonder at what St. John calls *Kinder-Scenen*, Stevens's developmental version of presence. Positioned implicitly as a spiritual mentor, the saint responds by announcing the capacity of presence to fill the being, slaking pain as Emersonian antidote, and reeling out a suite of images that might be called a lyric proper.[16] The poem at this point appears to abandon its dialectic of initiation, and evolves, significantly, to become a soliloquy enacting presence, the mind in its signature "act of finding" sufficiency. As rhapsodic as Emerson's revelation in the West, the monologue adopts the bravado tone and ritualistic pacing characteristic of vatic delivery, realizing Calvin's failed response and providing a sense of satiety as it propels the poem toward its climax.

Within St. John's convoluted utterance, presence is positioned as the "possible nest," or birth-crib, whose name puns visually on the French *n'est* (30)—"is not." It is the origin of possibility and the possibility of origin, paradoxically, "the little ignorance that is everything" (29). Strictly speaking, presence is not sustainable or *presentable* with the precision conferred by predication: it cannot bear the falsification of descriptive "re"-presentation, and can be approached only by means of counter-spin, by the negative predication on which St. John relies. It is "neither angels, no, / nor brilliant blows thereof" (24–5), not messengers, not the tidings they trumpet, but rather their figuring, and their negative figuring at that. It is not possible, in other words, to affirm presence. In an analysis of the dynamic of apocalypse, J. Hillis Miller exposes the vatic mode as one of deferral, as a pretense to revelation that does not ultimately reveal (189, 191), precisely the dynamic enacted by the unquenchable troping of the prophet of apocalypse, who presumably has access to all tendency. Troping is the apocalyptic mode of delivery: as layer is deposited upon opaque metaphorical layer, the apparent stability of the single trope and the process of inference by which metaphors are read is undercut, shrouding the poem in an ultimate obscurity. One might argue that the physical, continental limit faced by Calvin is the spatial analogue of the temporal destination of prophecy: neither "end" reveals itself upon arrival but is instead newly obfuscated. As "St. John" winds down, the logically affiliated "presence," "world," "non-force," and "*Kinder-Scenen*" remain veiled.

As a self-aware mind, the Back-Ache attempts to know presence discursively, to delimit and thereby to define it, but its method precludes its grasp of a state of being beneath the reason and resistant to it. Presence lies "far too deep" (39) for access to the effect of pain upon it, and its reaction is thus judged to be "irrational" (40). As Emerson tells us, pain is a shallow stream (472), all the more so as it is prologue to the all-inclusive depths. By the poem's end, the self-conscious, aching mind—the subject as discrete from its object—bars its own admittance to a state of being conceded, in the humble musings of dénouement, to outdistance its reach. A symptom of the loss of unity, of the dis-ease of homeostatic imbalance, indeed of *duality*, pain cannot grasp presence because it is itself the product of its disintegration, of the Cartesian separation. Pain cognized, perhaps more so than other conditions, points back toward the memory of its infliction, perhaps forward toward the hope of relief, however vaguely. The discrete knowledge of the reactive capacity of presence the Back-Ache seeks is available only upon the "rational" inscription of cause-and-effect and subject-object duality, which effectively prevents an unmediated experience in which world "fills the being before the mind can think" (12). As the poem concludes, its dialogic structure maintains the presence-erasing objectification the Back-Ache cannot overcome.

Resting with its failure, the Back-Ache resigns itself to its lack of access to presence. Nevertheless, the poem enacts presence after a fashion through the voicings of St. John. It may be argued that the experience of imbibing its elusive metaphors induces the state experienced by Emerson before his landscape. St. John's speech deploys a panoply of techniques, including negative constructions, irreconcilable images, and nonsensical sounds ("ti-rill-a-roo") that render the exposure to the incomprehensible and the unanalyzable that is often experienced as beauty. Stevens's coy phraseology, his aphoristic encoilings give off the commingled odors of irreducibility and profound depth. Their calculated obscurity seduces, stranding one precipitously, blissfully, on the verge of discovery, before the fragrant portal of the divine, serving as a vehicular technique by means of which a sense of presence, a concept I shall argue bears ecological significance, is imported into the poem.

Stevens, by his own admission, drew inspiration from Simone Weil's mystical theory of "decreation," the transition from the created to the uncreated that was, in his estimation, necessitated by the stresses of modern reality. Like Emerson, Weil embraces the present as a means to the self-annihilation that bestows the key to divine access:

> We must … renounce the past and the future, for the self is nothing but a coagulation of past and future around a present which is always falling away. Memory and hope destroy the wholesome effect of affliction by providing an

> unlimited field where we can be lifted up in imagination (I used to be, I shall be ...), but faithfulness to the passing moment reduces man truly to nothing and thus opens to him the gates of eternity. (21–2)

Weil's asceticism courts and endeavors to sustain affliction without succumbing to the temptation of hope. Her renunciation of the selfhood the personified Back-Ache cannot transcend effects a regression to innocence, a value-laden station in and from which spirit may be fully realized. "Decreating" one's self by retreating to a state that precedes creation, however one construes it, returns one, inevitably, to a point of origin (76–86), to the possibility of the "nest" (*n'est*), the abode where one is not, but might yet indwell.

The idea that self-effacement returns one to one's source is a core tenet of both Buddhist doctrine and Judeo-Christian mysticism. Significantly, Weil depicts this regression in organic terms when she writes, "We must go down to the vegetative level" (83). Stevens once again plays the role of demystifier. His version of innocent presence, *Kinder-Scenen*, makes the Romantic move of invoking a developmental phase to epitomize a decreated state: "Much of the poetry of the whole world is the poetry of children ... as if they were the creatures of a dimension in which life and poetry are one" (*Angel* 159–60). Yet he foregoes Romantic yearning after the lost "hour of splendor in the grass" and rather matter-of-factly assumes that this state of poetic origin is not only available in adulthood, but relatively natural, pervasive even. The passage continues, "The poetry of humanity is, of course, to be found everywhere" (160). Elsewhere, he maintains the theoretical identity of the poetic and cognitive realms: "The theory of poetry is the theory of life" (*Opus* 202). By way of naturalizing both theory and the poetic vocation, Stevens explains, "The theory of poetry is not abstract ... but is a normal activity of the poet's mind in surroundings where he must engage in such activity or be *extirpated*" (*Angel* 173) (emphasis mine). Preserving his attention to the common etymology of "theory" and "theater," it is possible to begin to unwrap the central metaphor of "Of Modern Poetry" in which life is a stage on which the human mind's dual functions of mediating and enacting play out. Poeticizing, theorizing, then, is an enactment on the part of the mind through which it maintains the embeddedness from which, like Weil's vegetables, it cannot be uprooted. The threat of deracination harrowing Stevens's passage carries overtones of survival: the maintenance of the poetic state of presence (which the poem's suggestion of stage presence also evokes), it would seem, forces recourse to basic skills. Although life-or-death situations are not run of the mill lyric grist,[17] the natural necessity of the poetic enterprise is here thrown into relief. That lyric is a mode marked by some urgency is evinced by the poem of the mind's propulsive series of mandates, the "it musts" of "Of Modern Poetry," and by Frye's insight that the poem arises from a compulsion to interrupt the daily course of things in order to write ("Approaching" 32). Staying rooted for Stevens is a function of instinct, the transfer of agency not to God, but to "the precious portents of our own powers" (*Angel* 175). His alliterative phrase is not merely a slogan for the whelming Romantic imagination: as for Weil, the goal of an innocent state (one of "unknowing") is attainable only by the irrational surrender of agency to the nonself (82, 83), a sentiment Stevens expresses in his wished-for "cure of ourselves, that is equal to a cure/Of the ground."[18]

In "St. John and the Back-Ache," the fluent turning of metaphors in the mouth of the saint of apocalypse predicts, however tentatively, an ur-prophet figured as the invisible but possible serpent carping within our hymns (32–3), "whose venom and whose wisdom will be one" (34). In ecological terms, Stevens here closes in on his own version of innocence. "Venom" is a member of a class of healthful preservatives that effects a "mindless," species-specific participation in an ecosystem; its use is equivalent to the assumption of a felicitous role therein. The poison marks a regression to a phylogenetic base because it affords the snake the ability to survive by virtue of what it does. Presence, then, entails a recursion to being that fosters right becoming through the recuperation of species-specific, instinctual skills. The not-knowing that venom figures enables a purity of action that maintains oneself and an ecosystem through the maintenance of one's place within it: the behaviors that maintain an individual also maintain the whole—and thus the health—of the system. Its release effects what Heidegger calls a return to the salutary.

As complement to venom, wisdom emerges through the accumulation of experience; unlike venom, it is innate only potentially. Wisdom assumes the ability to engage the world prophetically in a sense, to envision what is by necessity posited in the future—the knowledge of "that day"—and to act accordingly, as a wise choice of action presumes a forecast of its consequences. Dependent upon a gathering of perspectives, it demands an understanding of the tendency of the whole that precludes the assumption of one's vegetative or species-level position in it. Yet, wisdom is also indebted to the culling of experience that position affords. In revealing what is inaccessible from a local perspective, the wise only appear to rise above their situation. The prophet prophesying must be all knowing (the wise serpent) *and* limited to a specific situation (the venomous serpent). The release of venom is also predictive, but simply so. If it were possible to synthesize venom and wisdom, the calculations of wisdom would resolve into a single, unambiguous action (as the drive to poison), a clear path forward, an accessible prediction. "We shall be heavy with the knowledge of that day" ("St. John" 36) because it is the knowledge of the realization of all possibility shouldered by the one, who must, from his limited vantage point, reveal the whole of which he is a part without deranging it, a sheer impossibility that is nevertheless the poet's charge.

While Simone Weil's mystical end is the comfortable resting place of self-abnegation, Stevens recognizes that the mind is intractably dualistic. He further understands that its poetically enabled pursuit of "reality"—of its revelation—is doomed because a fluent *mundo* includes the mind, preventing its ascension to a bird's-eye view without the enabling artifice of a supreme fiction.[19] Revelation is always a self-violating verbal act: the dilation of one vantage point in order to enclose all vantage points assumes no less than an apotheosis and the replacement of the usurped Hindu turtle that now bears the weight of the world ("St. John" 35). Yet, the coordination of an instinct below the will with the self-assertive exercise of wisdom as a member of the "sapient" species is an earthy and earthbound, animalistic feat. What exists at the juncture of the possible impossible but the poet, whose brute and best instinct is to accumulate wisdom, the far-reaching predictive skill that constructs its "dwelling" on earth? Enacting the poetry of life is the means by which a being functions at its full capacity; enacting a life of poetry is the means by which it poeticizes.

Both poetics and poetic lore recognize this tension and thus tend to situate themselves at one end of the paradox of human existence or the other, though in its fullness, poetry, as life, preserves the paradox. At one extreme, insuring naive functioning by positioning lyric at the point at which doing and being are one and the same, at the point of metamorphosis to *the* singing bird, marks the recursion to a phylogenetic (and by extension an ontogenetic) ground that is also the point of seamlessness of individual and species. At cursory glance, this understanding is at odds with the time-honored view of the lyricist as an exemplary *sapiens*, as far-seeing citizen *Vates*, the Romantic figure who "doth grow in effect another nature" (Sydney, "Defence" 113). Yet, even Romanticism may be defined as the attempt, however cumbersome, to marry instinct with the visionary powers of the human mind, if one that elevates the natural activity of the mind more than it naturalizes the poetic imagination. In this tradition, Emerson's poet "stands among partial men for the complete man" ("Poet" 448). Stevens's "major man" of "Notes toward a Supreme Fiction," his abstract "exponent" of "the idea of man" ("Abstract" X.1–8), is also representative based on his ability to transcend his situation and to impart the commonwealth he perceives to others. However, to do this, he must be like his peers, "In being more than an exception, part,/Though an heroic part, of the commonal" (6–7). He must sing as "the bird" if his poison is to be toxic to all.

Hegel also recognizes the paradox inherent in the idea of exemplary locality when he makes the lyric poet the subjective unifier of the universal (*Aesthetics* 1114), but does not resolve it in a way that might satisfy the nonidealist. That the poem of the mind is both particular and universal, individual and species is precisely what allows one's fellows to enter into its space, to cohabit comfortably within its crevices. One is made welcome in the house of lyric because another has successfully homesteaded in the cognitive wilderness, taming it to some degree. "Apotheosis is *not the origin* of/The major man" ("Abstract" IX.5–6) (emphasis added): his origin lies rather in the symbolic breadth and depth of the idea of theatricality. Particularly in the context of a mandatory scene shift, "theater's" cognation with "theory" begs further consideration. In admitting the etymological splendor of the Greek-derived word, Stevens sought to recover perceptual origin, what he elsewhere calls the "first idea" ("Abstract" II.2). The word's root—*thea*—denotes a view, a sight, a new sight, an original sight, the place at which an idea is based in sight, and eventually, an idea, or theory, itself. The casting out, the disorientation, and Calvinist vertigo that follow from finding oneself "in the wrong play," so to speak, give rise to the necessity of sensemaking in situ; they induce postlapsarian vision, the inevitable and primary means of negotiating the new milieu, making sense of it by "theorizing" it sensorially. All lyric is in this sense Edenic, that is, pervasively originary to human conduct and, as it were, continuance. The endeavor lyric initiates serves to recover Adamic experience. A return to a hypothetical point of origin in innate human behavior, which is necessarily cognitive in the full sense of the term that subsumes perception, action, and emotion, is then the premise of a naturalized poetics.

What may be interpreted as presence in these several works grounded in perception is not, then, the Western concept valorized in relation to absence. It is rather the state in which one might relinquish one's painful self-awareness, an attentiveness (presence) to that which is before one (in one's presence) underset by one's physical connection to, or rootedness in, the proximity it is now safe to call an environment. Being-present-to is an implicit acknowledgment of the presence of the other in the apolitical sense of the term pertinent to embeddedness. The condition is both font and product of the interactions, including perceptual interactions that co-construct actor and environment. Entities in embedded systems "mutually co-construct," that is, they inform and form one another in a qualified "dying into" that effects the emergence of mind. Reactions are undetectable, then, given the continuity of organism and environment that enables their mutual co-construction. The Back-Ache cannot access the presence that is world because it seeks to comprehend the world's *reaction* to the goad of pain remotely, a reaction it deems "irrational" because it exists in the main beyond (below) the inscription of cause-and-effect relations within the discrete terms of the reason. A character and not a lyric singer, the Back-Ache attempts to know the world as it is on its own terms, a feat it cannot ultimately achieve. Presence as construed in the poem is illogical in the terms of Western metaphysics (more accurately alogical) because it is resistant to the dualism upon which logic depends. The Back-Ache is solely subject, and subject cannot sing. "To sing the song means to be present in what is present itself. It means: *Dasein*, existence" (Heidegger, "Poets" 137–8).

The physical connection assumed by this double sense of presence as an awareness and a productive contiguity—an awareness that what is proximate to oneself is potentially of one—is realized in part perceptually. As Emerson underscores, attentiveness to that which is in one's presence is necessarily a perceptual act. In fact, the alliance of presence and perception is so strong that Charles Sanders Peirce defines the latter in terms of the former: "That universal conception which is nearest to sense [impressions] is that of *the present, in general*" ("List" 1). Necessarily "of the moment," perception as presence is essentially resistant to the duality that is the past and the future, and exists only in the absence of the Cartesian split. It implicitly collapses subject and object, and not only theoretically, that is, as concepts. Perceptual processes proceed from continuity: they are initiated as the object present to the subject becomes a part of it, as aspects of the physical environs are imported within organismic borders. Yet, as the Back-Ache realizes, the immediacy perception assumes is elusive: at the same time it blurs the distinction between the subject and the object physically, it registers their detachment, culminating in the distinguishing on a mental level of the subject and object forms. The faculty subsumes both an instinctual, venom-like mode dependent upon the embeddedness in an environment to which the organism must be present and an objectifying capacity that abstracts the organism from its environs, permitting the wisdom dependent upon the recognition of one's experience as one's own, as an objective possession of sorts. Perception as predictive of sufficient action is a naturalized form of prophecy.

In deriving from perception, lyric engenders this same sense of presence. The genre's native co-propensities to self-abnegating surrender to an other, and to self-asserting distance from it, derive, I propose, from those of basic cognition. As will be demonstrated, in acknowledging a continuity with an embedding environment, lyric renders it inaccessible, both blinding one to the nest of possibility and intimating that it exists, invisibly, beyond the limits of what is perceived. While Adorno claims that the immediacy lyric effects is illusory ("Society" 41), it is equally valid to assert that the genre's mediacy, the duality it seems to create in mediating organism and environment, is spectral, more precisely, a construct. In the manner of perception, lyric gives rise to the appearance of duality it resists, effectuating it in the form of the pronouns "I" and "you."[20] What Stevens grasped in making the poem "of the mind" is that it is situated at the point at which venom and wisdom are co-activated, precisely the point at which perception, the instinctual, wisdom-enabling faculty, transpires.

In the end, versions of lyric abandonment come to figure an exile into self-awareness that is perceptually derived, the entropic, isolating pain of which must be overcome through the surrender to an environment that embeds one in the ongoing act of finding. Stevens's poem of the mind is suspended in the present act of "*satisfying*" itself, to use the term he possibly borrowed from Alfred North Whitehead, who also found it necessary to eschew predication in order to create an anti-dualistic process philosophy, what he calls a metaphysics of event.[21] Enactive without predicating, "finding" is enfolded in what must be an ongoing search for sufficiency. To suggest that a satisfaction has more than a momentary extension would be to implement predication, to say "I am satisfied," and thereby to obviate the search. And as Stevens tells us elsewhere, "It can never be satisfied, the mind, never"[22] (17). Embeddedness cannot in any ultimate sense brook predication, which rebuffs, in fact, undoes it: it is maintained by an open-ended process, continuous in a temporal as well as a material sense, refusing the stability from which identity may be objectified and hence secured.

The Presence to Potential: Lyric Obscurity

Alfred North Whitehead emphasizes that because "actual entities," the basic unit within his monism, are formed of other actual entities, they are constituted of a sheer multiplicity that is their vital source (24). It is in the nature of entities that they are potentially of other entities: the existence as potential of what might come to constitute an entity is a given in systems presuming the embeddedness of their elements. The mind-poem is then *constitutionally indebted to* (i.e., composed of), rather than merely "about," a potential multiplicity of events. Such potentiality conditions the "deciding" that determines the entity by selecting from and thus realizing potential (23). This ontology of potential assumed by co-constructive interactions is one Emerson explores, if only indirectly. On the surface, his rhapsodic and symbolic death back into nature may be taken to be a mystic surrender, or a yielding to the fate that has betrayed, but upon closer look, it is a submission to invisible, coextensive causality. For the sage, the deeper nature of causal relations is ungraspable because causes are not singular, but multiple and contemporaneous: many converge to precipitate a single effect ("Experience" 482). It is altogether too tempting to live by the superficial certainty of the "multiplication table," but the hardiness of the present, its health, Emerson tells us, depends upon one's ability to renounce "the perfect calculation of the kingdom of known cause and effect" (482) and to embrace what is undetermined.[23]

Because causality is simultaneous and far-reaching, we cannot access it in its totality without the broad lens of omniscience; we can only remain cognizant of its presence. The network of multiple and coextensive causes darkened to the view of the individual is akin to the invisible source that is Stevens's mysterious nest/*n'est*. As Emerson beams, "God delights to isolate us every day" (483). Such unenlightened causes are designated "fate" in the latter's lexicon, "a name for facts not yet passed under the fire of thought;—for causes which are unpenetrated" ("Fate" 958). But the latency of causality—a latency that is ontological as well as epistemological—allows for the patent exercise of free will, as one's free agency is a player effectuating the grand plan to the extent one's aim is refined and attendant, as much as it can be, to a multivalent relationship to nature.

> But to see how fate slides into freedom, and freedom into fate, observe how far the roots of every creature run, or find, if you can, a point where there is no thread of connection. Our life is consentaneous and far-related. This knot of nature is so well tied, that nobody was ever cunning enough to find the two ends. ("Fate" 961)

Within an ecological system, one is ultimately linked to all else.[24] Because what one is connected to is in turn present to what is in *its* vicinity, and so on, influence is practically untraceable given the extensive effects of a single ramifying event. According to transcendentalist tenets, the intellect is properly embedded within a causal network that eludes its apprehension, an insight not exclusive to the philosophy. In defining the set of factors in the environment influencing an organism as an *Umwelt*, the biologist Jakob von Uexküll explains, "The rule of causality is a poor guide: causal relationships deal only with antecedents and consequences, thereby completely concealing from us broad biological interrelationships and interactions" (43). Causal agency must be obscured because one is constrained by one's *Umwelt*, though connected broadly: embedding systems thrive upon this veiling. Given an ecological infrastructure, knowledge of reaction is not available in any full sense to an organism because it is largely obscured from his vantage point, particularly one bent on objectifying said knowledge. This is not to badger the weary notion of an alienating cage of consciousness, but rather to stress that understanding the nature of embeddedness, neglected until rather recently in approaches to both literature and the sciences of cognition, is necessary to understanding how the dynamics of both the poem and perception, as the basic activity of the mind, obfuscate potential relationship while deciding it creatively.

In his investigation of the role of art, Friedrich Schiller identifies two sorts of indeterminacy: the indeterminacy of nothing (the homogenous) and the indeterminacy of everything (the heterogeneous). The latter he dedicates as the fertile soil of the aesthetic (100). Rooted within the sensory, the aesthetic is the response to potentiality conceived as all-inclusive, a view Emerson espouses in noting that we too easily assume the opposite, that all is impossible until realized ("Experience" 483). The embrace of possibility is necessary to effect the communion with nature Emerson attains through the creative activity he calls *thinking*. As potentiality exceeds the limits of the self, he seeks to access it by embedding himself within nature in order at once to rid himself of the crutch of past-referencing pain and to maintain God's grand plan, amplifying, indirectly, the function of social death as prod to lyric. If lyric, in its execution, amputates its spawning context, in so doing, it disables determined causal efficacy and the mastery of the same: the past cannot bear, or support, the future; the future can no longer bear, or sustain, the past. The rupture of the predictable alliance of cause and effect results in a hiatus, a suspension in a hypothetical interstice in which habit and individual history have been rendered passé. Exile as trope also accounts for the need to be receptive to alternative causes. In positing a wholly other locale, an asymmetry is wrought within the poem between language's habitual usage and present necessity. In the initial, responsive state in which one cannot infer causes from effects and call it a day because experience remains untested, language becomes a repository and a vehicle of potential meaning. Lyric is the linguistic usage that introduces this fresh potential available in the immersed state of childhood, the unencumbered present tense Stevens calls *Kinder-Scenen*. Arriving at a similar insight, James Longenbach borrows child psychologist D. W. Winnicott's term "potential space," that which is idealized to exist before accumulated use value, to claim it as the proper domain of poetry:

> Children spend most of their time in a psychic space that is neither completely internal nor completely objective—the "potential space" of play. Adults may too readily capitulate either to a world of inanimate objects or to a world of uncontested fantasy, but the healthy adult continues to live in increasingly complex and tenuous versions of potential space. (*Resistance* 56)

The adult trained in the dialect of cultural interchange, in conventions that entail given relationships of cause to effect, must contrive to maintain the access to this invisible, potential space that is granted to children and poets.

To establish the homologous ways potential is activated within poetry and perception as a consequence of embeddedness and a means of nourishing prophecy, I refer to Charles Sanders Peirce's sign theory built upon a pervasive triad sporting the names "first," "second," and "third." Forming what he calls a genuine trichotomy, one irreducible to dichotomies ("Relatives" 183), these categories give rise to mediation, which emerges from an inaccessible realm of firstness through secondness to thirdness. (The latter two categories will take on significance later in this text.) The scope of Peirce's system is wide-ranging, compassing both the physical and cognitive realms, permitting each to be broached in semiotic terms. It is, as such, a basis of biosemiotics. In describing both physical and mental semiotic processes, it is apposite to perception.[25]

What Peirce designates "first" is a "mode of being" ("Principles" 75), or an attitude of immediacy, what exists but is not (yet) mediated ("Guess" 250):

> It must be initiative, original, spontaneous, and free ... It precedes all synthesis and all differentiation: it has no unity and no parts. It cannot be articulately thought: assert it, and it has already lost its characteristic innocence; for assertion always implies a denial of something else. Stop to think of it, and it has flown! What the world was to Adam on the day he opened his eyes to it, before he had drawn any distinctions, or had become conscious of his own existence—that is first, present, immediate, fresh, new, initiative, original, spontaneous, free, vivid, conscious and evanescent. ("Guess" 248)

Peirce elaborates upon his description of this ephemeral state by explaining that as it is neither differentiated nor integrated, it is composed of a variety that is in his word *virtual*, that is to say, not definite and not definable ("Guess" 257). In other words, firstness is what is *potentially* heterogeneous. That its variety is prospective aligns it with the all-inclusive indeterminacy Emerson and Schiller privilege in relation to the homogenous indeterminacy characteristic of a void (140–1).

Peirce ascribes an inceptive role to firstness, a developmental priority, when he writes, "The indeterminate first of anything is the *material* of which it is formed" ("Guess" 257) (emphasis added). In his piece "Lyric Substance: On Riddles, Materialism, and Poetic Obscurity," critic Daniel Tiffany alights upon the same term, "material," in the same sense of raw material, in attributing a primacy to lyric obscurity: "What precisely does obscurity yield in the act of reading—in the absence of clear, cognitive meaning—if not a sense, strange indeed, of poetic *materials*" (83). Analyzing the prototypically lyrical form of the riddle, he notes that its "formal sophistication and delicacy … coupled with its inherent obscurity, points to an 'unresolvable'—and *productive*—ambiguity in its literary character" (78) (emphasis added). It is exactly as obscurity that the inscrutable yet fecund quality of firstness, the possibility within which Emily Dickinson wished to dwell,[26] manifests poetically.

Tiffany's contention that this early Anglo-Saxon form is the principal forebear of the English language lyric expands on Frye's identification of the lyric with the "radical," or root, of its presentation (*Anatomy* 246–7). Tiffany recurs to the subgenre because it inscribes as fundamental the lyric paradox of coextensive self-assertion and self-disintegration, exility terminating in silence. (His case is buttressed by the lucky survival of the transitional poem "The Dream of the Rood," a full-fledged lyric whose objectified speaker preserves the riddle's presentational mode.) In meeting the form's often explicit (and always implicit) challenge "Say who I am," the goal is to transition from the silence of a Keatsian "wild surmise" to a single, certain response, the distilled new name that Hart Crane will much later declare to be the inexpressible heart and residue of the poem (221). In presenting a speaking object, the riddle claims subjective agency for "it," yet the "being" in question is inert and rendered in the accusative case.[27] Riddles operate in this morphological grey area, simultaneously evolving ontic status by means of the attribution of feature and function and undermining it by making such ascription equivocal, deferring the predication that secures identity. In his essay "Lyric and Modernity," Paul de Man frames this opposition in terms of the lyric's inbuilt literal-figurative duality that "reveals the paradoxical nature of a structure that makes lyric poetry into an enigma which never stops asking for the unreachable answer to its own riddle" (186). Reference objectifies in endeavoring to stabilize features, rendering them apprehensible, while figuration tends to obscure the features of its objects as such (185). Per de Man, each diametrically opposed trajectory within the genre is an extension of its intrinsic riddling mode.

Elucidations of the subject-rendering tendencies of the lyric abound and will be set aside for the moment. That the lyric subject must face effacement is a rather less thoroughly hashed-out aspect of the genre picked up, for example, in the conceit that the courtly subject "pines" or "wastes away" for an unrequited love. The idea of exilic dislocation in which the coherence of the subject is altered almost catastrophically when subjected to a strange new world with which it is forced to contend must be reconciled with Romantic theories, which if they do not wholly identify lyric with a cogent subjectivity, classify it according to this feature, for poems subject their speakers to this tug of war.

Here and in his book *Toy Medium*, Tiffany analogizes this core poetic tension to the conundrum faced by philosophical materialism: the dilemma that the fundament of the physical world is imponderable except through representations that obscure its direct perception, rendering its substantive essence invisible. By way of explanation, he proposes a bidirectional analogy:

> A riddle is essentially an allegory, though, unlike conventional allegory, the phenomenon veiled by the dark or enigmatical description is not a metaphysical entity (an abstract concept or a divinity), but a physical object or being. A riddle, because it is obscure, is a *materialist* allegory (as well as an allegory of materialism). (79)

Drawing on Blanchot, who in turn tows Heidegger, Tiffany goes on to claim that lyric substance is situated between the idea of the thing and the thing itself (83–4), between its phenomenality and its materiality. Blanchot's suggestion that poetry is the medium of the *postmortem*, a body as decomposing corpse, is yet another version of the lyric mythos of disintegrating subjectivity that parallels a coming into "being" in the emergence from obscurity. Blanchot's "radiant cadaver" comes to symbolize the kind of matter the lyric embodies and in embodying obscures (85). For all three thinkers, lyric ambiguity acknowledges the imponderable basis of what, intuitively, should be eminently ponderable[28] (94).

Obscurity in the lyric has been viewed as a deliberate and sometimes an exclusive effect of modernist and/or postmodernist technique, a reflection of a culturally induced state of detachment responsive to overwhelming change, a kind of balm through coma blunting painful sensation. (I do not confront, so I do not feel.) As proposed in Chapter 1, modernist alienation so registered may be argued to be another version of the forced departure from the ordinary. The slant of much recent thought attributes the shrouding of reference to the poem's struggle to fix meaning as against language's inherent fluidity. Obscurity, as many postmodernist theorists would have it, is a textual function arising from the resistance of language to the stasis interpretation inflicts. Paul de Man's notion of "undecidability" as between "rhetorical praxis" and "metalinguistic statements about the rhetorical nature of language" (*Allegory* 98) and Derrida's anti-theory of the irrepressible, upending motion of *différance* are among the more well-known renditions of this stance stressing the bent of language to forestall its own transcendence in stable reference.[29] Yet, post-structuralism is remiss in dodging the question of the function of such resistance: lyric releases the obscuring tendencies of language to a specific end, troubling subjects and objects in the process.[30] To a significant extent, the binary logic Derridean deconstruction abstracts and motivates lacks a historical sense, and thus the capacity for origination. While it implicitly acknowledges that the power of evoking meaning attaches to the signifier at a point in time, and it explicitly concedes that meaning lingers as trace, the semantic inversion driving this theory is not cumulative. In fact, it denies the possibility of emergence, stalled as it is in the repetitions of the obsessive-compulsive: the brain is not permitted to register and to integrate the completion of the deconstructive action, which would afford it a subsequent perception.[31] Yet, actions, including semiotic actions, are irrevocable, constructing not only their objects and their enactor but also an arrow of time, and it is by virtue of their irrevocability that they become functional. If life were a play of reversible, flip-flopping motions without historical consequence, no one action would bear significance to future survival because it would immediately be negated. If an organism is to contend with newness, a mode through which meaning is renewed must obtain at the intersection of observer and fresh scene. Accounting for lyric obscurity is never simply a matter of pointing to semantic play, but rather one of recognizing the way that that play realizes potential constituent causes and eventually irrevocable meaning. It is not necessary to conceive of language as autonomous and unearthly to account for its tendency to obfuscate.

Furthermore, obscurity in lyric clearly preexists self-conscious movement-making in art, even when allowing for the fact that its effects may be partially a product of the cultural and temporal distance of a reader from a poem. In "Lyric and Modernity," Paul de Man finds in lyric—paradoxically, he notes, in light of its aboriginal qualities[32]—an innate tendency to obscure. Interpreting modernity as a descriptive rather than a categorical, and ultimately rather than an historical term, he rejects the criteria for the onset of poetic modernity proffered by various critics who credit the pivotal shift from a representative to what he calls an "allegorical" (hence obfuscating) use of language to the French *symbolistes*.[33] Both modes, de Man claims, enjoy an ambivalent presence in lyric poetry; indeed, their copresence all but defines it. Surveying the ways in which the language of Mallarme's "*Tombeau de Verlaine*" may be read literally, he opines of the poetic that it is "language that is representational and nonrepresentational, or allegorical, at the same time" (185), the former in that it refers externally and the latter in that it gives rise to meaning by means of self-generated structures. By inquiring into the historical phase of modernity, he finds that the dual, enigmatic nature of language has been the stuff of lyric poetry all along (185).

Indeed, the phenomenon of obscured or disintegrating subjectivity finds an even earlier incarnation than that of the Anglo-Saxon riddle in the self-shattering motions of Sappho's fragment bearing the *incipit* "In my eyes he matches the gods." In the surviving lines of this poem, estrangement from a beloved, through her marriage perhaps, causes a concatenation of dissolutions of autonomous and autonomic functioning, including visual and aural obfuscation and the muting of the speaker, who by poem's end purports to be "little short of dying":

> My tongue breaks down, and then all at once a
> subtle fire races inside my skin, my
> eyes can't see a thing and a whirring whistle
>   thrums at my hearing. (Powell 23–4)

The disintegration of Sappho's subject, one might argue, is described rather than enacted here, but the poem both acknowledges a decomposition counteracting her verbal self-assertion and obscures overall context. As is common in the lyric, the poem's rhetorical situation is vague. We do not know who speaks, or to whom, nor are we privy to the events giving rise to the utterance. The "I" is presented as an isolated series of untethered perceptions and actions directed at no clear addressee. This run-of-the-mill lack of rhetorical clarity inspires Mill's quasi-caricature of lyric as an "utterance that is overheard" (46) implying that the genre encompasses even inarticulate mumblings, to invoke the ideological extreme that is the expressionist reduction: an overheard utterance need not be endued with the clarity of a direct address. This is not to imply that the lyric shrinks from an audience or insists upon its secrecy as a matter of course—it clearly does not—but that in deriving from a perceptual event, it does not always find it necessary to acknowledge witnesses.

It is not in any event controversial that lyric skews toward the nondiscursive, the nonexpository, and does not, as a rule, stoop to explain itself. As noted, the indeterminate quality of the semantic unit in poetry is often lauded, especially by poet-critics, as an innate attribute, one they choose to exploit. Obscurity-producing techniques vary and are valued differently by different poetics, and I will not here attempt to compile an exhaustive list, only to distinguish general types.

1. *Contextual Obscurity.* The lyric often obscures context as a matter of course, including the identity of the speaker[34] (undermining his subjectivity) and the locale, which appears as the generic "here." This is one of the most salient of the genre's characteristics, a marker defining it as against fiction especially.
2. *Figurative Obscurity.* As de Man argues, figuration obscures by representing something as what it is not, most often substituting a concrete entity for one that is abstract or unfathomable. This is in part why attempts to comprehend the spiritual almost always involve troping, and ultimately obfuscation. Endeavors to represent the intangible in material terms have given rise to the notoriously obscure hermetic and hermeneutic traditions.
3. *Linguistic Obscurity.* The "out-of-the-ordinary" quality of poetic language is often attributed to the flouting of linguistic convention. Enjambment, line breaks in general, juxtaposition, ambiguous diction, vague antecedents, mixed discourses, disarranged syntax, repetition, and subject-object confusion comprise a partial compendium of techniques productive of ambiguity, which obscures by invoking more than one potential meaning.
4. *Sonic Obscurity.* Poetry's musical elements, whether literal or linguistic, whether voiced or not, themselves obscure due to their overlaying of nonreferential sound onto language. This category of obscurity is treated more fully in the section below dedicated to song.
5. *Affective Obscurity.* The emotional content associated with lyric (itself an essential element of perception) also serves to obscure, especially in the absence of an identifiable referent.

It would seem to follow from the given of social estrangement that the genre's indulgence in obscurity simply registers the initial unfamiliarity of the environs into which the singer is plunged within the encounter "come upon" but not yet grasped. Conversely, the poem's fuzziness might suggest a bewildered subject, one whose ability to express himself is temporarily confused as a result of the shift of ground. What might be termed "first experience" is certainly locatable (or is at least alluded to) in lyric thematically; in addition to the advent of the vista from a mountain top, it takes the form of the confrontation with death, religious communion, and of course love, which is most often initially fresh, laden with potential, and, it would seem, withheld. It appears in the medieval trope of vernal rebirth evoking the seasonal juncture that promises the revelation of new life. If the modernist iconoclasts and masculine detractors of Romanticism (Pound and company especially) claimed responsibility for the historical swerve away from some of these themes to a hard-edged, no-nonsense poetics, the belief in the inexhaustibility of the state of firstness new love confers was earlier spoofed by Sappho in the self-deprecating, invocatory "Ode to Aphrodite," in which the summoned goddess inquires of her, "Whom *this* time should I persuade to/lead you back again to her love?" ("Aphrodite" 3–4). Old tropes bow to the new, and are at times revived to star in subsequent scenes. Yet, stopping at this representational account of obscurity amounts to resting with a mimetic view of poetic language and an inappropriately stable concept of subjectivity and objectivity within a genre that consistently destabilizes said terms. What this pervasive set of master tropes serves to do is to direct focus to the physical *presence* to one's environment that is thrown into relief by early, unobjectifying contact with it, and thereby to reinforce, at the level of content, the initiation of the processes of embedded perception the lyric enacts through its deployment of the raw material of obscurity.

Though Tiffany does not explore the perceptual dynamic active in the confrontation with the material world, he grazes the subject in probing matter's core invisibility: the essence of the material is fundamentally imperceptible, yet it is productive of an allegorical sort of envisioning. In order to yield physical vision as a synecdoche of the sensorium—and the vatic sense of vision is salient here—what is obscured must be potentially visible and is thus not an essence in a subatomic or any other sense, but rather that aspect of the material world compatible with the organism's sensory systems. The term "obscurity" is itself a perceptual term implying a darkening. As if to allow the basis of all knowledge in perception, criticism has evolved further terminology denoting perceptual occlusion, chief among them the close cousin "obfuscation" and the contemporary favorite "opacity" (meaning not transmitting light). The store has been supplemented with vocabulary designating the logical effect of perceptual impairment—disorientation. William Empson's "ambiguity," Bernadette Mayer's "bewilderment," de Man's "undecidability," the lingering modernist "indeterminacy," and the general "equivocation" further embroil perception because they imply a hesitation to act and thereby to realize the perceptual process.[35] In a rare structuralist account devoted wholly to lyric, Jonathan Culler adopts the aforementioned term "resistance" to describe this quality:

> "The poem must resist the intelligence/Almost successfully," says Wallace Stevens; and its distinctiveness lies in that resistance: not necessarily the

> resistance of obscurity, but at least the resistance of patterns and forms whose semantic relevance is not immediately obvious. (*Structuralist* 178–9)

In other words, what resists interpretation must at length yield to some degree of meaning, what Stevens would call a "satisfaction," and not the "unsatisfying" end of irresolvable obscurity, or obscurantism. As Bernadette Mayer muses, "The poem may have to mean nothing for a while or reflect in its meaning just the image of meaning" (658). With its complement "recuperation," "resistance" is a defining lyric criterion within this first of Culler's codifications of the genre's central features. Together the two form a concept of lyric becoming: the making up of a semantic deficit through a reorganization accomplished within the structures of the poem, an event that, as will become clear, is dynamically homologous to perception.

That poetic obscurity inheres in the perception of novelty in particular, and that lyric subjectivity and objectivity are equally tenuous, is accounted for in the lore of *poiesis.* In mythical portrayals of reembodiment in which the poet-figure decomposes to become simply a singing being superseding a socially constructed self (or the suggestion of such in the case of *Orpheus*), the fiction of phylogenetic devolution serves to force a beginning within an existence in which discontinuity is artificial. The conceit of the eradication of even the possibility of a facilitating cultural and biographical past entrains a hypothetical moment of original perception conferring primordial being. (That this erasure is practically impossible is beside the point.) As the significance of what is to be *envisioned*, literally or figuratively, cannot simply be recalled, it is necessarily obfuscated. The mythological frame of lyric fictionalizes a circumstance in which reference is interrupted: language imported into an adopted homeland is not immediately responsive to unexplored circumstances. The poem thus resists a prepackaged system of signifieds, automatic or facile categorization, habitual usage. Lyrics are obscure, then, by virtue of their compromised ability to fall back on remembered significance, to integrate it seamlessly into present circumstances. As perception relies on memory, the genre reaches toward the ideal of original vision in minimizing the relevance of what can be recalled, a fact the myths account for in laying inordinate stress on the respeciation of the singer, and thus the early phases of perception in which obscurity inheres as a registration of potential.

The Presence to Potential: Perceptual Obscurity

In order to lay bare the perceptual foundation of lyric, it is necessary to outline the dynamic by which the displaced mind begins to reorient itself sensorially.

It bears reinforcing at this point that perception is a physical process, an actual—and not a metaphorical—site of organismic embeddedness. Perception presupposes the physical contiguity of the perceiver to what is perceived. As such, it is a border function, the cognitive means by which physical embeddedness within an environment is effectuated. Perception is instigated at the periphery when external stimuli in the form of energy or matter, depending on the sensory system, are selected from the physical environment by receptor organs based on a preexisting compatibility with them. For instance, visual perception is triggered when a photon is captured by retinal receptors to which it is adapted.[36] This process by which stimuli are apprehended is to some degree stochastic, a function of their chance distribution and capture.

A second basic point to highlight about perception is that once stimuli are captured by receptor neurons, they are transduced into electrical impulses, adapted, if you will, into a medium compatible with the body, and thereby embodied as a prerequisite to their comprehension. In converting stimuli to a form consistent with itself in order to perceive them, the nervous system renders them unknowable as they are. Prior to their transforming, the raw materials of perception take the forms of electromagnetic radiation, scent and taste molecules, the pressure of sound waves, or the direct pressure of touch and thus exist in a state unperceivable to organisms endowed with sensory apparatuses in the absence of the amplification afforded by technology, in some cases even then.

In their native, objective states, these raw materials of perception are themselves mutable, maintaining a versatility that is physical, though not necessarily cognitive. As entities within embedding systems, even while they are temporarily realized (or per Whitehead, decided) as stimuli, they exist in a state of potential. For instance, the particle prevailing objectively as electromagnetic radiation, a photon, may be transformed into chemical energy through the process of photosynthesis, eventually becoming of a plant (sugar); it may give itself over to another end as thermal energy that sparks fire, becoming of the fire; and it may inform vision once it is captured by a retinal receptor and transduced into electrical energy transmitted as nerve impulses, becoming, in the process, of a visual system.[37] An initial sense of firstness inheres within, and is a condition of, physicality within embedding systems because said physicality exists simultaneously as potential physicality, what might be thought of as an immanence or a latency, an "invisible tree" of ramifying possibility obscured by a patent manifestation. What I call "physical firstness" is a preliminary stage of physical emergence, what an entity might itself become.

In relation to the system it may inform (including a nonsensory system), a stimulus exists in a state of as-yet undifferentiated, virtual variety, that is, as a "relational" kind of firstness, the set of what it might become once incorporated into the subject entity. The transformability of the stimulus into the neural substrate of the percept that is enabled by the physical continuity of organism and environment implies that prior to the selection and transduction of the stimulus, it exists as undifferentiated potential with respect to the organism, unknowable within the nest of possibility by force of its invisibility, invisible in its possibility, a thing that from the perspective of the percipient *is not*. The transduction of stimuli to a form compatible with the organism, the making them of itself and knowable through itself, renders them ontologically inaccessible. Prior to its transformation and encoding as an occluded physical reality, the fodder of perception exists as what might become of an entity and is thus "first" in relation to it.[38]

A further sense of firstness is recapitulated within perception qualitatively. When perception culminates in the formation of a percept, the tableau presented to the mind is first encountered as an undifferentiated whole, its elements distinguished immediately afterward. In the phenomenon explained by "Reverse Hierarchy Theory," visual percepts are experienced first as integrated wholes and only subsequently differentiated within consciousness (Hochstein et al. 791). As dramatized in the aforementioned poems of Keats and Stevens, firstness is a phase of the emergence of the percept itself, a kind of felt sense of its potential. To broach the ineffability of firstness, Peirce conflates it with feeling, and explicitly the feeling of what he calls the *toute ensemble*, the tone, or mood, that accompanies, indeed describes, the immediacy of the content of consciousness ("Principles" 81).

> By a feeling, I mean an instance of that kind of consciousness which involves no analysis, comparison or any process whatsoever, nor consists in whole or in part of any act by which one stretch of consciousness is distinguished from another which has its own positive quality which consists in nothing else, and which is of itself all that it is, however it may have been brought about. (81)

This "feeling," experienced but not cognized, is not itself representable. In consisting of a featureless whole, the type of consciousness Peirce qualifies as first, and thus imbues with potential, is itself a sign, or representamen[39] (what Saussure calls a signifier), but one lacking an object. A percept cannot signify an object until it is sufficiently differentiated to make its identification as a sign possible. Such an objectless sign is first, as is an unsignified object, which exists in a state of physical and relational firstness (my distinction) with respect to the sign.[40] (If the sign had an object—an identifiable provocation—it would be "second" to that object.) This qualitative version of firstness, the temporary suspension of the perceptual process in unresponsiveness—in inaction or speechlessness—is, as all firstness, fleeting and all but abstract. The poems' extension of it is therefore an artifice, but one that draws attention to the potential lyric poems entrain.

The rendering of an object inaccessible through its conversion poses a dilemma for perception as its end would seem to be the apprehension of objects as objects. Stimuli, unknowable as they are, are further not objects perceived, but rather the potentially perceivable correlates of them, what living organisms can interpret of the objects with which they are associated. Stimuli bear a metonymic relationship to the objects they effectively index: sound waves emanate from their shaping sources, scent molecules are released from odiferous objects, light is reflected off of what it renders visible.[41] In perception, the object qua object is understood through and as the selection, transformation, and interpretation of mere indices of itself. In contrast to the stimulus, the object is not first in the sense that it may be realized by becoming of the percipient, but rather because it may be realized epistemologically as the referent of perception. This conferring of the status of referent through the determination of the object's meaning is secured for the object as it is acted upon in consummation of the interpretation. An object may then be said to exist as a set of potential uses to the organism, which potential is determined once the organism makes a decision by acting upon it.[42] Successful action secures the identification of an object referent, realized not as an object per se, but as the meaning of that object for the organism. Perceptual identification is always a form of use, a finding of sufficiency, even when said use is strictly cognitive as opposed to overtly physical. In a third perceptual instantiation of firstness, the object as it is exists in a state of functional potential realizable epistemologically in a process that includes acting upon it. If a percept is regarded as a sign, the entity to which it refers (what Peirce calls its "object")[43] exists as a possible set of uses from the standpoint of the percipient, if not that of the scientist.

Each of these forms of firstness I have delineated depends upon the previous. Physical firstness, the ability of material to realize its potential, permits relational firstness, the realizing of that potential by another entity; the two in turn permit the realizing of qualitative firstness within perception and thus the potential use of the object as functional firstness is determined in action. This codification of potential marks a casual gesture toward a biosemiotics of perception and a step within an argument holding that perceptual dynamics linger as residue in poems. In suggesting that the experience of embedded organisms may be characterized in terms of sign relations, it grants biosemiotic significance to both perception and the lyric. As a full semiotics of either meaning-making enterprise, much less one uniting the two, would no doubt be vast, I shall only sketch one here as a means of calling attention to the significant overlap between the two experiences and, eventually, of accounting for the functional consistency, and interdependency, of the lyric's generic traits.

The Semantic Potential of Lyric

Within a revision of the dualistic and reductive methods of biology, the biologist Jakob von Uexküll first theorized that the activity of life (including, but not limited to, the activity of perception) is primarily semantic. Uexküll devised the concept of the *Umwelt*, the subjective or self-centered universe consisting of an organism's significant experience of the environment based in the capacity of its sensorium to select from it in order to meet its biological needs (29–34). Subsets of objectively delineated habitats (36), *Umwelts* may be defined as closed, unified networks of meaningful physical relationships between a "meaning receiver" (an organism) and "meaning carriers" (27) (here, stimuli), the compatible aspects of a habitat with which a meaning receiver interacts by perceiving and "operating" (or acting) upon them (27, 31). Though circumscribed with respect to a particular organism, an *Umwelt* is "a biologically instantiated and causally efficacious set of agent-object relations reducible neither to the organization of the subject nor to the organization of the environment but always as the product of the interaction between the two" (Favareau 83). It is the domain of meaning-making created as an organism perceives and acts, what is therefore present to it. "All else is neglected" (Uexküll 31), occluded as the extremes of Emerson's stair.

It is useful to think of a poem as the construction of an *Umwelt*. For the poet, the speaker, the voice, or the text, as one's poetics allows, the poem becomes the co-constructed middle ground to which the meaning receiver is present, the registration of what is seen, as it is seen and the efficacious verbal-musical action, or utterance, toward the same.[44] By way of pregnant example at the level of content, in the courtly tradition, the beloved is described as she is wooed, wooed as she is described: the portrayal of her beauty is at once an acting by persuasion upon a meaning carrier to which the lover is attracted due to a preordained compatibility or likelihood of attraction. Acting into the environment positions an organism to attract what is "stimulating"—the perceptual stimuli that index the desired object. Conversely, the reception of a poem constructs an *Umwelt* for the listener it creates: love poetry, as a verbal-musical act, is also a luring or a seduction of a beloved for whom it itself becomes a meaning carrier. Orpheus's summoning of flora and fauna with his song may be said to offer his unlikely auditors such a meaning-laden experience: his poetry takes on import for them as they hear and are drawn to it. This overt awareness of perception and action, indeed its fusing, with the potential for the bidirectionality of *Umwelt* creation (the relationship between the bee and the flower inhabits the *Umwelt* of each) is among the reasons the courtly dynamic, exhausted as it now is, remains central within the lyric tradition.

Remarkably, Uexküll conceives of an *Umwelt* as a "building," as both an edifice and the process of its raising. He redundantly names the space contiguous to the organism in which meaning carriers "bustle about" a "dwelling house" (33). The domain of significance the percipient shapes in inhabiting it is, I propose, consonant with the home the poetic subject makes in dwelling within the poem. As noted, it is commonplace to conceive of poems architecturally: Dickinson is hardly alone in figuring the form as a house, as she does in Poem 466, but she further grasps that such an edifice requires ventilation. The house of poetry stands "More numerous of windows—/Superior—for doors—" (3–4) and features "for an everlasting Roof/The Gambrels of the Sky" (7–8) to allow for the entrance of possibility in which to dwell. It is opened to potential in the form of its relationship to the informing environment (which environment in poetry is perforce linguistic). Uexküll is aware that meaning carriers are objects of potential significance to percipients: he writes that their meaning is "*realized* through perception and operation" (36) (emphasis added). Lyric acknowledges the potential implicated in the relationship of perception to reality, I argue, by means of its obscurity, the expedient admitting linguistic potential, the locus of the origin of poetic meaning.

An understanding of the function of firstness in semantic emergence constitutes the first bit of evidence supporting the claim that the lyric not only represents but also models and perhaps adapts perceptual processes, as it is the undifferentiated potential for meaning that obscurity evokes and welcomes into the poem. Lyric obscurity inheres to a great extent in what is referred to as the materiality of language, a designation that is half figurative, half literal. The physicality of language is double, existing as ink on a page (or pixels on a screen) and as sound, manifestations that are slight, but physical nonetheless. Of the two, lyric's orality, its persisting, aboriginal form (as is well known, even written lyrics are intended to be heard) manifests most ephemerally, as voice originates in a body emitting energy in wave form pulsing through a medium, perhaps exciting an auditory nerve. David Nowell Smith characterizes primal vocalizations, cries, as "raw, quasi-bodily *matter* from which language will be made" (28) (emphasis added), invoking a double significance for the term while stipulating that this so-called matter is also a medium (28). Matter in the sense of substance becomes for Nowell Smith something like a figure (it is "quasi-bodily"), as it does for Tiffany and Blanchot. Blanchot's figuring of poetry as a decomposing corpse suggests that it transpires at the cusp of the conversion of matter to energy or to other matter, at the point of its evanescence. Sound is in fact physical as it is energic, but it is not technically matter since it has no mass. As Nowell Smith suggests, it feels substantive nevertheless in issuing from and impacting the body.

The materiality of language, whether written or oral, its so-called "privileging of the signifier," was a pet if not an original focus of twentieth-century poetics: de Man, Blanchot, and Tiffany are representative in viewing the poetic word as physical or embodied, a quality that correlates with its lack of transparency.[45] The word that is not an unclouded window on to a referent commands attention, becoming, by virtue of its opacity, a thing unto itself. By way of its widely noted resistance to reference, lyric foregrounds the "substance" of its medium, matter on the verge of transforming to energy. As a "physical" system, language, like the physical world within which perception transpires, is an embedding system featuring, indeed dependent upon, the dynamic of mutual co-construction through which entities (for the sake of simplicity, words) are constituted of other entities (other words), of "matter" that is in a sense transformed into themselves in the process of signification.[46] As words are informed by their denotations and connotations, they are made meaningful by entities that are potentially of the same stuff. They consist of constituent elements transformed, alchemically rather than physically, to become of themselves, elements that are then unrecognizable within their transformed state, but denoted, indexed by it. One needs only a dictionary to evince this claim. If language is conceived of as material in this sense of mutable, its ability to mean assumes the transformation of what it means, and with it a kind of continuity. The word, as sign, is in a sense continuous with the linguistic units it denotes, and by which it is informed, in the same way that sensory systems are continuous with informing matter-energy, the reception and conversion of which is the catalyst to the construction of perceptual meaning. The words with which the words of the poem are continuous are, in the manner of sensory stimuli, the spur to the composition of poetic meaning.

As a percipient consists within itself of other constituting and in a sense extant entities, by simply existing—that is, by perceiving—it gestures beyond itself to what is potentially significant, to what has not yet been but might be transmuted and thus signified—in other words, to relational firstness. A word, analogously, is composed of denotative and connotative significance that takes the form of other words, and thus points beyond itself to a complex of potential lexical meaning. Words, like percepts, radiate outward toward the entities by which they might be defined, that is to say, granted meaning and contour, words that are in turn formed of others in a continuum mirroring the physical world. (Defining by informing is literal in physical processes such as perception and figurative within language.)[47] What renders this potential significance *present*, and thus realizable, is the poem's disposal of obscurity, particularly in the form of ambiguity. Lyric expression makes present, and makes itself present to, the fullness of the linguistic context it implies rather than ignoring it. What renders this set of potential significance inaccessible, and its variety indistinguishable or virtual, is the materiality of the sign (percept, word) that has transformed and obfuscated it merely by existing. Poetry liberates this predisposition of language to indeterminacy. Its verbiage shimmers with a foreign patina: a repertoire of potential meaning hovers over the poem like an aura that is visibly indistinct. The poetic word strives to release the fullness of its evocative power, the totality of its as-yet-undifferentiated valence of accruals and purgings, expansions, revisions, and scars. Chafing at stable meaning, the poem puts potential meanings into play, airing them, and in so doing, acknowledges that the environment extends beyond the shallow focus that is the predicament of the fallen human. As lyric poetry reflects as well as effects this potential for connectedness in a replication of the same, its obscurity may become practically inexhaustible—the *raison* for its durability. As Shelley tells us, "All high poetry is infinite; it is as the first acorn, which contained all oaks potentially. Veil after veil may be undrawn, and the inmost naked beauty of the meaning never exposed" (327). In implementing a directionality outward into language as a whole, the genre foregrounds systemic connectivity, and in so doing, competes with and downplays language's aptitude for determined reference. It manifests a lexicality that resonates as a signifying physicality, a physical system of signs. At the back of opacity is capacity, what extends beyond one's curtained station on the stair.

This condition of potential connectedness, active while it is masked, must remain unseen since seeing, poetic and otherwise, determines, lopping off ramifying potential. Both Adorno and Heidegger stress that the immediacy of poetic engagement is less than fully conscious. Adorno in fact equates "the unself-consciousness of the subject submitting itself to language as to something objective" with "the immediacy and spontaneity of that subject's expression" (43). Heidegger claims that the nature of one's attachment to the Open is necessarily unconscious, for consciousness coevolves with the representation that distances one from it ("Poets" 108). The physical connectivity that is the basis of the perceiver's relationship to its environs is likewise unconscious: points of organism-environment connection within perception are themselves unperceivable. This unseen affinity is all that is enjoyed, in an alternative interpretation of Dickinson's poem, by being as a detached ear, one capable of the physical processes of perception but, in the absence of the brain and the remainder of the body, not the perception of sound, and certainly not the perception of itself as distinct from what it perceives (neither awareness nor self-awareness). As she understood, this state is foundational to lyric utterance and lyric reception at the same time it is one from which the genre inevitably emerges, maintaining its linguistic embeddedness all the while. Potential meanings remain even as interpretive acts decide them. (These unconscious mechanisms of perception are semiotic in their engagement with an environment, the first stage in a process of meaning-making. Biosemioses depend on the conscious registration of neither signs nor objects.) Lyric returns one to this basis, to a physical groundedness in and through which a perceptual means of meaning-making, mediated in language, emerges. Poetic utterance flirts with obscurity, then, not simply because its object is obscure (travel writing and teenage journals would then pass as lyrical), but because the poem of the mind's contention with the strange is accomplished by evoking the immediate, healing state of presence to potential. The lyric in effect embeds itself in a linguistic environment by remaining receptive to the role of that environment in the emergence of meaning. To cope with the estrangement to which we are all subject, to act wisely within a new situation, one must, as Emerson reasoned, be present to unconscious points of connection to the extent possible within the act of thinking.

The types of firstness inhering in lyric semiosis and correlating with those of perception may now be distinguished. (1) All language, as a physical medium, houses an immanent, physical type of firstness, a latency consisting of the possibility of other words into which it might be transformed. Language's mutability is an effect of the fact that it gives meaning to instances of language with which it is, in a sense, continuous. Text considered to be autonomous correlates with an extracognitive, physical reality, the fluctuations of which presume firstness. (2) Corresponding to the potential significance of stimuli to the organism, firstness manifests in the poem relationally as the potential meanings of the linguistic units of which it is composed, the specific words defining the chosen words of the poem. Said potentiality is released through ambiguous constructions and other aforementioned obfuscating techniques and is differentiated only virtually prior to its determination by the perceiver constructed by the poem, or the receiver of the poem. (3) Firstness may also be experienced consciously in the form of uninterpreted first exposure, that unspeakable registration of the as-yet-undifferentiated, still to be comprehended whole. The firstness instantiated in and experienced upon the exposure to novelty may be represented within the poem itself. It may also inhere in the immanent potential conferred by the irreducibility of lyric language during the phase in which poetry impacts the reader but has not yet been differentiated and grasped, the phase of the extension of its resistance. (4) Firstness in lyric exists in the potential form of the objects of the stimuli-like words that index them, the often nebulous referents of lyric utterance made so by generic conventions, including the apparent extrapolation of entire utterances from contexts that are thereby concealed. As objects are realized when acted upon—the lover by her wooing, the ideas of the poem in their interpreting—functional firstness exists as the set of potential actions responding to referent objects.

Obscurity is then a symptom of an embedded form of signification the lyric adopts, of the sign's potential constitution by other signs that may potentially constitute still others that at any point may designate potential objects, physical and intellectual. The genre's exploitation of this proclivity may be demonstrated by a glance at the calculated use of ambiguity in the famous opening of "Leda and the Swan," William Butler Yeats's sonnet about the mythohistorical ramifications and theological implications of the rape of Leda by Zeus. The line reads, "A sudden blow: the great wings beating still" (1). The framing of the opening action to convey its suddenness replicates the experiential firstness of the assault upon Leda, prompting it, to some degree, for the reader, as does the poem's rather succinct depiction of the event and its consequences. One lacks adequate information upon immediate exposure to the poem to delineate a comprehensible image. Obscurity is further created by the choice of the ambiguous word "beating," which gives rise to the potential, informative senses of "flapping" or "hitting," and the likewise ambiguous "still," which permits the denotations "without motion" (oxymoronic in light of the Swan's moving wings) and "even now." Each inherent alternative meaning buzzes about the poem as a virtual option, feeding potentially into interpretive acts. Verbal alternatives to these words that are perhaps less apt also intrude; however, as synonyms bearing less obvious significance, they are less likely to be captured by "sense receptors," if you will. For instance, the word "beating" evokes "whisking," a particular violence done to eggs, as well as the contraction and release of the heart muscle that is directly mentioned later in the poem. Last, the potential objects of the poem are inscrutable at this early point, especially in the absence of an acquaintance with the myth. What kind of blow? What great wings? Even when the poem has transpired, its objects, in whole mythical events and the theological queries they prompt, remain unknowable in and of themselves by virtue of their verbal representation, yet graspable as the interpretations they trigger, themselves the counterparts of physical actions.

The obscurity endemic to lyric utterance hence betokens the genre's understanding of language and its users as embedded, a condition for which lyric signification accounts in exploiting what might safely be called the nature of language. In restoring language's full functional, that is semantic, potential into the milieu of the poem, poetic obscurity puts language into ontological and epistemological alignment with an embedded, embodied understanding of cognition. "Poetry can be defined as that language in which a world (of unfolded meanings) opens up, and in which our terrestrial essence as mortals reverberates" (Vattimo 72). Lyric technique maintains the fluid preconditions of linguistic decision, which mirror, and possibly arise from, the fluid preconditions of perceptual decision. Presence is the openness to what "being" might implicate of the environment (or earth, or world) with which it is continuous but which it cannot perceive because, as will become clear in the next chapter, perception determines potential. The admitting of obscurity as a semiotic component also acknowledges that local interpretive freedom is constrained by events determined beyond the interpreter's ken. Its use invokes the set of implicit possible, but not illimitable, relationships between poeticizing organism and environment—and by extension between reader and text—in order to elongate the chaotic, messy activity of recuperation and allow one to decide wisely.

In the practical terms of poetry, the airing of potential allows lyrics to render the process of decision making in which all options, or at least all best options, are entertained and preexisting sets of connotations shuffled so that best matches may be constructed to restore an efficacy in context to words, an end that has been staked as the *raison d'etre* of the major poet. That active potential is requisite to the fabric of lyric is dramatized in the Orpheus myth when Eurydice is forced to follow the poet during their single-file ascent to the upper world, to exist potentially to him for a space while obscured from his view. The trust that her potential state will be actualized, that the poem only resists the intelligence "almost successfully," is essential during the phase of poetic emergence into the daylit world of comparatively stable signification, the earthly realm in which Eurydice *is* Orpheus's wife. Because the poet cannot tolerate his beloved's indefinite existence, he turns. As he does so prematurely, she recedes, remaining eternally unrealized, forever muse, source of his never-ending, always recallable song.

To prophesy demands that the prophet access things as they are in order to project futurity from present tendency, to foresee the simultaneous "irrational reactions" that determine potential. To understand how potential will be determined, one must understand the potential, which is neither cognizable nor effable. If reality were directly accessible, the prophet-percipient would function as a mere mouthpiece, funneling the world, or the world to be, in lucid fashion. Prophecies articulated with such clarity would not be prophecies per se, but direct communiqués from a godhead obviating the prophet. As this figure of interest is not a mouthpiece but a mediator, or, per Hegel, a unifier (an incomprehensive but not inaccurate term for what the poet and the percipient do), he alters what he delivers of the world, thereby obscuring it in determining its potential. He speaks not only what is necessarily an interpretation, an individual perspective, but one that is literally, physically, of himself. Given that what is uttered has been transformed and adapted, the unperceived material object remains in a state of potential significance that contrasts with the mediating "percept." The complex act of interpretation that is perception renders the object obscure, consigning it to a state of epistemological potential.

The ur-prophet St. John imagines to be both venomous and wise would seem to transcend this difficulty. The venomous serpent, ever of its niche, entertains potential locally, realizing it through survival-enhancing action. The release of toxin decides possibility by killing it—literally. Wisdom, which is also predictive, depends on less proximate knowledge, knowledge that is beyond the reach of a situated organism, evaluating potential on a larger scale to determine it systemically: in its ultimate form it instigates apocalypse. Remedying the venom-wisdom split, making the global local—the task Hegel arrogates to the poet—would inflict a burden so debilitating that the Hindu turtle or Christian serpent shouldering the heft of the world would "grow limp from age" ("St. John" 35), yielding to a new world order. The unification of venom and wisdom posits a god-like human, one who acts on a grand scale with the accuracy of instinct, the figure poets of the ilk of Sidney, Shelley, and Wordsworth aspired to become. But as poets and prophets are finally human, in mediating coextensive potential, they reinscribe its obscurity, preserving the "little ignorance that is everything" (29) in forming (and in informing) the percept or the poem that "is not" its object. Perception, together with the action it subsumes, is itself a form of prophecy, a guess at what might happen as one acts.

It is now possible to begin to account for the riddle's central position within the genre as conflater of the subject and object of the poem. The adulteration of subject and object alike is attributable to the poem's status as perceptual residue, its implicit recognition that the percipient is composed of its mediations of objects, the presence of which undermine, even as they constitute it. Each "actual entity," each percipient, is both a subject and its embodiment of the object(s) of which it is composed, materially and as qualia. The lyric-perceptual event, as a physical event, entrains connections that cannot be completely circumscribed and absented as *other*, even as a contingent or relational object-other. In acknowledging an expanded version of perception, one that reaches backward into the obscurity of what might be termed the pre-perceptual, the lyric speaker (more tenuously, the voice indexing a speaker, still more tenuously, a free-floating text indexing a voice) invokes the raw materials of itself, decentering itself in introducing a centrifugal momentum toward the environment into which it is in danger of dissolving. Concomitantly, the object is obscured because it is known only through the subject prophesying it: it too is compromised, diluted. The riddle, as a seminal form, destabilizes subject and object in overtly fusing them, deferring their identification—or ultimate predication—to the interpretive process, content, in the meantime, to subsist in the act of finding.[48] The riddle's "I," as a lyric "I," is self-assertive in its self-portraiture at the same time it speaks into existence the objects (in the broad sense) it appears to reify. Walt Whitman stands out in his acknowledgment of the extremes of an overbearing and a retiring subject, an "I" that is both all-encompassing and the dust beneath one's "boot-soles" ("Song" 52.10), anaphorically insistent, yet concealed amid lists of objects. The paradox of the decisive yet compromised subject, the subject on the verge of silence as it recognizes that it is comprised of the presence of others, is the crux of lyric.

A Lyrical-Perceptual Semiosis

As Peirce's category firstness is generative in both physical and cognitive sign processes, it may be seen as the basis of the biosemiotics he foresees. In addition to a phenomenal sign in the form of a percept, the brain generates a physical sign in the form of the neural substrate of a percept. The two types of sign systems (unconscious/physical and conscious/mental) are coactive in perception, with physical signification continuing to drive the process at all points. As a result, the activity of signification is layered, involving a doubling of the sign, although it is, ironically, the qualitative sign that is in some instances gratuitous: the sign that takes the form of neural patterns within the substrate may be interpreted unconsciously, through acting.[49] That said, given consciousness, the physical sign also affords the conscious enjoyment of a percept. In poetry, the foregrounding of the material status of words—their sounds, their opacity, their simultaneous constitution by and indication of other words—acknowledges the word as a physical sign composed of what it signifies, that then exists mentally as it is interpreted. Of course, all language use deploys material signs and assumes their conscious registration, but lyric poetry, in modeling a perceptual dynamic, stresses the material foundation of signification.

It is further possible to claim that in poetic language, as in perception, the physical entities of which signs are composed (other signs) are indices of the objects to which they refer. As perceptual stimuli index the physical objects from which they originate, words, once learned (once they are words and not mere insignificant sounds) indicate, analogously, the objects they reference.[50] This indexical relationship of words to objects is also a function of physicality: indexing presumes a physical connection or correlation arising from proximity, forging an association that may be learned. In lyric, words evoke the other words of which they are constituted in the process of referencing objects metonymically. Terrence Deacon in fact attributes this ability of words to index objects to the primary relationships of words to one another, a relationship that for him is indexical rather than constitutive:

> This [referential] ... relationship between the words—words systematically indicating other words—forms a system of higher-order relationships that allows words to be *about* indexical relationships [to objects], and not just indices in themselves ... we use the sense to pick out the reference and not vice versa. (83)

Ultimately, the percept is an emergent mix of all three types of signification: it is indexical in indicating objects, which gesture extends to its action upon them; it is iconic in mirroring some aspects of reality;[51] and it is further symbolic as a construct taking its shape to a large extent from the medium in which it is formed, that is, the embodied history of the organism. (Iconic and symbolic signs, based on the resemblance of a sign to its object and its lack thereof, respectively, do not depend upon physical contiguity. The former relationship is imitative and the latter arbitrary.) At present, I am concerned primarily with the fact that what indexes an object (a photon, a word) comes to inform the sign (the percept, the word), and in so doing acts as an intermediary effectuating embeddedness, a fact poetry, in owning the materiality of its materials, foregrounds.[52]

What is finally *signified* in each semiotic process inheres in the impactful action back into the environment integral to the perception of the object acted upon. (The relation of action to perception will be treated in detail in Chapter 4.) The action that is the writing of the poem is embroiled with a hypothetical perception to which it responds. The verbal actions instantiated in the poem are entangled with the verbal percepts the poem registers. The interpretive action of a reader or listener emerges in tandem with her perception of the poem. Each action arises as what Peirce calls the "interpretant," the effect of the sign on the perceiver-interpreter, and as such ultimately narrows potential by determining functional and, with it, physical, relational, and qualitative firstness.

The following chart sets forth the correspondences in signification between perception and the lyric poetry that models it.

Phenomenal Sign	**Physical Sign**	**←MATERIAL CONTINUITY→**	**Index of Object Informing Percipient**	**Object**	**Interpretant**
Perception					
Percept	Neural correlate of percept		Stimuli	Physical object	Action upon object
Lyric Text					
Represented mental experience	Materiality of poetic language		Senses of words evoked (other words)	Objects, physical or cognitive, represented in the text	Linguistic action of the text upon its objects
Reception					
Mental experience of the poem, itself perceived	Materiality of poetic language		Senses of words evoked (other words)	Objects, cognitive	Interpretive action

Note: The correspondence of the two types of signs inhering in the text to that of those inhering within perception is probably inexact. The material poem may be regarded as a "substrate" of the conscious experience encoded in the poem in a sense only loosely analogous to the relationship of the neurological substrate of a percept to its phenomenal experience. It is not yet possible to draw a better analogy as the relationship between the brain and the mind awaits further explanation.

The ultimate significance of this alignment in which perceiving minds and brains are seen to correspond is that the "perception" of each is properly material fodder for a new perception, thus effecting a nesting of perceptual events: as the poem as text "perceives," it registers and reframes what it implies as an original, most likely hypothetical, percept. The reader in her turn "perceives" the text of the poem. Each perceptual event "assumes" in the Whitmanian sense, or takes on the perspective, the situatedness, of the previous one in reperceiving it: "And what I assume you shall assume" ("Song" I.2).

Song as Lyric

As the term "lyric" derives from the lyre that accompanied the singing of early poems, it subsumes, historically and etymologically, the separate and severable forms of poetry and song. Yet no matter how high a fence one stakes between the forms, it is all but impossible not also to regard the two as continuous. As such, I will here emphasize the resemblances rather than the antagonisms born of their kinship, as each medium replicates the perceptual dynamic I am limning. This emphasis accords with Steven Mithin's neuroevolutionary defense of Stephen Brown's claim that music and language diverged from a common ancestor the latter names a "musilanguage" (Mithin 26). In contrast, Jahan Ramazani explores what he terms an "affectionate contention" (222) between the two forms arising from their discontinuity: for him, song functions as a foil against which modern and postmodern poetry self-define (188–9). "Contemporary American poetry often represents song not only as its lost beloved origin or vital intergeneric twin or ego ideal but also as an antagonist" (211). It is not without a degree of ambivalence, however, that he concedes that the genres also fall on a continuum (200), with song positioned as poetry's limit: "Song is poetry's *arche* and its *telos*, what is was and what it might aspire to be" (210).

As Ramazani observes, setting written poetry to music often distorts its sound and its tempo, "obscuring the text's intricate semantic networks" (189). It may indeed be challenging to introduce music posterior to the writing of a poem because each medium employs its own means of obscuring.[53] The layering of a technique specific to one upon that of the other may muddle, but it may also prove productive. In any event, each "twin" features and foregrounds a vital ambiguity it achieves via special means, and in so doing invokes potential. In song, the presence of instrumentation, vocal or otherwise, obscures. It is by now a cliché that music is an—if not *the*—"abstract" artistic medium, one dominated by nonreferential sound patterns that check the referential thrust of language. Even within the most lucid of lyrics, the music intrinsic to the genre itself obscures, as much (if not more) so as a present and literal accompaniment as it does as a derivative, verbally wrought effect. It is worth mentioning that poetry becomes linguistically "difficult" at the point it is written, at the moment it divests itself of live musical accompaniment and assumes the task of generating an atmosphere of firstness verbally. As lyric language absorbs and adapts the music that had previously accompanied it, generating a sonic architecture to do the work—including the obfuscating work—of music, it is imbued with a greater structural complexity. In obscuring, music makes the invisible present: "The world, music reminds us, inhabits while extending beyond what meets the eye, resides in but rises above what's apprehensible to the senses" (Mackey 88).

Vocalization techniques further obfuscate by opening up the semantic potential of words. The effect of elongating vowels in their singing, for instance, is to suspend the listener in an inter-referential extension of sound, a pre-morphemic, pre-analytic spell in which consonants do not intrude to demarcate and to impart significance. Instrumental interludes depart all but entirely from denotation. Nonsense refrains and pre- and quasi-linguistic fillers (what has come to be known as the "Hey Nonny, Nonny" phenomenon, the vapid "yeah, yeah, yeah" of popular songs) serve to install intervals of minimal meaning. (As Ramazani notes, the lyrics to rock music are often purposefully obfuscated (191).) These interpolations, along with the pervasive presence of instrumentation, infuse song with potential, as do the aforementioned techniques of poetry; they offer fodder for meaning—albeit differently. Music's methods of invoking firstness tend to be nonlinguistic, and thus the sets of potential it summons are more open, more rawly emotional in their derivation. Song—"air"—is airier, not only more ephemeral but also better ventilated. The possibility it admits is thus vaguer and more primal, less potentially conceptual. As if to balance this musically derived openness, song lyrics in isolation tend to give rise to potential interpretations to a much more limited extent than do their poetic counterparts.

As an emotional vehicle and prod, music is popularly thought to be universal and to bridge, in hyperbolic accounts, not only species boundaries but also the gap between the inanimate and the human. William Congreve grants it the "charm" "To soften Rocks, or bend a knotted Oak" (*The Mourning Bride* I.1.2). Music's universality has often been said to inhere in its emotional efficacy, and lyric is thought, reductively, to be at heart a medium of emotion. It is the prevailing bias of specific movements in art, such as that of sensibility, that artistic product is a consummate emotional vehicle, and no literary form shoulders the task in reputation of communicating emotion to the extent that lyric poetry does. The most infamous simplification of the genre is no doubt the philosopher Carnap's relegation of lyric expression to an emotional ejaculation categorizing it with laughter and other primal forms of outburst (17).

As it is a means of encountering a context, of registering a sense of it, emotion can also be argued to be a technique by which lyric occasions firstness, one intimately bound up with its penchant to obscure. Not all emotional experience is first, only that which is problematically obscure, as it may be within life, especially in its vague incarnation as mood. Very often, the musicality of poetry generates this vagueness: as the sounds of music are most often disassociated from object cues, from objectifiable referents, the emotion they elicit appears to be without object as well; it is therefore first, apparently sui generis, the phoenix rising.

The primacy of lyric emotion, its apparent lack of reference, suggests that it is somehow fundamental to the compositional process as well as to the generation of meaning within the poem. In a nuanced and often misunderstood treatment of the subject, Wordsworth illuminated its priority when he rooted the compositional process in the seeming "spontaneous overflow of powerful feelings" ("Preface" 260). Spontaneity is associated with firstness because it is acausal, that is, undifferentiated from its cause. As Peirce asks, "How is variety to come out of the womb of homogeneity; only by a principle of spontaneity, which is just that virtual variety that is the First" ("Guess" 257). Although one might note that the onset of Wordsworth's powerful feelings is not, strictly speaking, impromptu, originating as it does in the pondering of "emotion recollected in tranquility" (271), by labeling it so, Wordsworth secures the importance of emotion as a source of the poem, attributing the genesis of his art to its unmotivated appearance. He thereby marks off the poem as an emergent process of its own: tranquility evaporates to make room for not the same, but a "kindred" originary feeling, an analogous but separate point of origin (271).

Inhering in lyric poetry, then, is what may be separated out as another source of poetic firstness, that provided by the emotional timbre of the poem. It is linked to obscurity in the source of musicality, although neither emotion nor obscurity is dependent upon music—or even sound—for its livelihood: these springs of firstness tolerate disentangling. However, that linguistic and emotional obscurity may be indebted to, and intensified by, poetic musicality suggests that music is part of the *res* of lyric and not embellishment to it. Stevens's and Heidegger's claims for the health-giving properties of poetry can be interpreted to mean that poetry's soundness is maintained by the regular relaxation into the convalescence of sound within a genre that nourishes its representations.[54] Yet, the music of lyric also looks forward. By virtue of its versatility, it is not merely an escort to poetry, but a vital immanence, a matrix of determination and a means of determining through the secondness toward which it gestures, the subject of the next chapter.

Notes

1. Stevens's preferred title for his *Collected Poems*, *The Whole of Harmonium*, was rejected by his publisher, Knopf.
2. Although Keats's substitution of Cortez for Balboa as the European "discoverer" of the Pacific is usually considered to have been an error, the possibility that it was intentional is suggested by the name's resonance with the word *cortesia* and its subtle invocation of the courtly gaze.
3. This almost fractal-like accretion of "C" in its many guises, including that of the aural pun "see," is a key to Stevens's opus. These meaningful minutiae are announced in the poem "Comedian as the Letter C," although they appear previously within *The Collected Poems*.
4. I refer the reader to the full texts of this poem, as well as those other poems of Stevens treated in this chapter, as I am unable to reprint them.
5. I am indebted to Joan Richardson for the interpretation of Calvin's use of his handkerchief as a stoic suppression of tears.
6. My premise, as yet undeveloped, is that this embedding of a rupture in the act of its repairing is a feature of perception, which remediates the exile it also effects.
7. "Animadversion" derives from the Latin phrase *animum advertere*, meaning "to turn the mind toward."
8. That "On First Looking into Chapman's Homer" and "The Doctor of Geneva" are written in the past tense fits with their initiatory content.
9. Culler further ascribes lyric presence to its privileging of *melos* (its orality), experienced in the fleetness of the moment, over *opsis* (its visual aspect) (*Theory* 252–8).
10. The lines are from the poem "The Death of the Hired Man" (38).
11. The sanctity of this custom is exemplified by the host-guest contract that codifies it. In his *Inferno*, Dante accords the crime of its breach a penultimate gravity, second only to the betrayal of one's God.
12. It is no surprise, then, that disinheritings are often ritualized as deaths.
13. The phrase is a section heading within "Notes toward a Supreme Fiction" (*Poems* 380). Stevens's ubiquitous, significant "it," which must also change and give pleasure, is grammatically neutral, and its neutrality not only opens reference but also permits it to refer to either an entity or an event.

14 Homemaking also enjoys traction as a metaphor for perception, the essential first activity of a displaced mind. In an argument I make elsewhere, Henry David Thoreau figures perceiving as house building, as the erection of the three-dimensional space contiguous and fitted to the perceiver, what Gaston Bachelard calls "a garment house" (Lattig 441, 443–4).

15 In Schopenhauer's view, willing comes to blend with this unwilled state within the poem (250).

16 Paul de Man dissents from this view, positioning trope in a position anterior to the lyric itself, which is by his definition anthropomorphizing. See "Anthropomorphism and Trope in the Lyric."

17 "The Seafarer" is a notable exception. One thinks also of Chidiock Tichborne's "On the Eve of His Execution" and the urgent life-and-death topos of courtly love poetry.

18 The lines are from "The Rock" (II.3–4) (*Poems* 526).

19 "Supreme Fiction" is Stevens's term for the belief in a fiction one knows to be a fiction (*Letters* 430).

20 The mechanism by which poems realize duality is addressed in the forthcoming chapter.

21 As predication confers the exclusivity and relative permanence of the object, it correlates with and enables an ontology of substance. When Whitehead proposed his syncretic process philosophy, a philosophy of *finding*, he found it necessary to discard the subject-predicate concept as an untenable abstraction, indicting it in the downfall of all previous metaphysics (7, 13, 30, 44, 51, 145). He remedied this philosophical impasse by developing an alternative metaphysics of event circumventing subject/object duality.

22 The line is taken from "The Well Dressed Man with a Beard" (*Poems* 247).

23 Emerson draws upon the then new field of statistics to explain how unpredictable local variations nest within the tendency of a whole that for him was divinely determined, an assumption that must be jettisoned as an unverifiable ideal, to focus on the significance of the veiling of potential meaning within the poetry of life.

24 This idea is given early voice by Alfred James Lotka. See Sharon E. Kingsland's chapter "The World Engine" in her volume *Modeling Nature*, pages 25–49.

25 Early on, Peirce explicitly designates thought as a semiotic system: "Every thought is a sign" ("Meaning" 213).

26 See Poem 466.

27 The manufacture or acquisition of objects—their coming into being and/or into possession, and thus object status—was often, Tiffany notes, the occasion for the writing of a poem commemorating them (73–4).

28 See also Northrop Frye's "Charms and Riddles" in *Spiritus Mundi*, especially pages 141 and 145–6, for an earlier, less developed version of several of Tiffany's insights.

29 Derrida's theory is first set forth in his early writing, "Structure, Sign, and Play in the Discourse of the Human Sciences."

30 One could make the argument that the purpose of linguistic resistance is political subversion, but per Derrida, this is more properly a result of a dynamic that is, regardless, already in motion.

31 The completion and integration of an action also affords learning.

32 The case for the primordial status of lyric was largely a Romantic argument made separately by Vico, Herder, Rousseau, and Bovet. See footnote 5 of the Introduction. It is, however, widely accepted that the lyric was an early form of linguistic expression that emerged from religious ritual. In "Why Lyric?" Earl Miner notes that it is a "foundation genre" in all non-Western cultures (579).

33 De Man responds to Hugo Friedrich's *Die Struktur der Modernen Lyrik*, Hans Robert Jauss's "*Zur Frage der Struktureinheit alterer und modernern Lyrik*," and Karlheinz Stierle's "*Moglichkeiten des dunklen Stils in den Anfangen moderner Lyrik in Frankreich*."

34 I do not generally espouse this term. It is, however, useful to designate a more rather than a less fully evolved lyric "I."

35 It is the premise of my argument as well as the neuroscience it draws from that this sequencing that sees perception culminate in action is at best partial. The role of action in perception will be discussed in Chapter 4.

36 For example, retinal receptors are specialized to attract radiation hailing from a specific range of the electromagnetic spectrum.

37 In an obvious example on a larger scale, an acorn may become food for a squirrel, it may grow into an oak, or it may decompose into the soil.

38 Even in breaching the percipient and becoming fully present to it, stimuli remain potentially knowable for a time pending their contextualization neurologically. They literally "fill the being before the mind can think" ("St. John" 12).

39 Peirce's terminology for the signifier is notoriously fluid, bearing, as it does, the alternate names of "representamen," "sign," "sign-vehicle," "representation," and "ground." I use "sign" throughout this text.

40 Peirce thought of the sign (here the percept) in isolation as first. (It is second to its object.) Since sign and object are second to one another, the unsignified object is also first. The corollary obtains within perception: unperceived objects lack a sign and are thus first.

41 Photons may be said to differ from other forms of stimuli as they qualify as separate objects of sort; nevertheless, their distribution is given by the topography of the object itself, making their relationship one of causality and thus indexical. As patterned physical entities, stimuli also bear iconic relationships to reality: light is patterned by the objects off of which it bounces; and it is this pattern, or form, that becomes available to perception rather than the materiality of the object

itself. Certain aspects of the object, such as location, timing, etc., are preserved in perception. Reality is both qualitatively inaccessible and yet interpretable to a degree of accuracy, a functional necessity insuring survival.

42 Objects can be identified below the level of consciousness, as in the phenomenon of blindsight. In this instance, the identification of an object is clearly identical to acting upon it.

43 In Peircean terms, an "object" can be either a physical entity or an idea. The term collapses Saussure's concepts of the "signified" and the "referent."

44 It goes without saying that such action-utterance is literal in the case of oral poetry. As will be addressed in Chapter 4, written poetry encodes actions.

45 The identification of language as substantive of course precedes modernism. See, for instance, Roland Greene's "The Lyric," in which he reveals early modern lyrics' awareness of their materiality.

46 One might argue that, strictly speaking, this is a mental embedding of meaning rather than a material embedding and thereby foreground a limitation of language. However, connectivity ontology grants ontic status to the points of connections or relationships within ecological systems, providing further evidence for the materiality of the relation-intensive medium of language.

47 Saussure, of course, was seminal in pointing out the relational nature of meaning, made in his theory between the units of the language within a system of difference (165–6). However, he did not take the critical step of claiming that words embody what they signify by altering it.

48 Tiffany offers the fascinating detail that riddles were sometimes inscribed directly on the objects themselves, allowing for the simultaneous perception of poem, speaker, and referent (73).

49 It bears noting again that perceptual signification can play out in the absence of consciousness, as in the condition of blindsight, or while executing customary actions, such as driving inattentively.

50 Deacon argues that indexical signification marks a stage of learned association based on "inferential or predictive powers" following the iconic and preceding the symbolic comprehension of language (78).

51 There is a quantitative correlation, and thus an iconic one, between sense modality, the location of the stimulus, the intensity (energy level) of the stimulus, and the timing (duration) of the stimulus in the environment and within sensation.

52 It may be argued that a key difference between language and perception is that the former is precoded in agreed-upon, socially significant ways. Yet, this coding must be learned, as must the significance of percepts. Sense data may be precoded in the sense that an organism remembers its interaction with similar data and applies this meaning in formulating a response. Percepts are regularized, fit into preexisting categories where possible. Each code is learned through individual experience with

it and reinforced through social interchange. Coding is fluid and subject to revision in each case.

53 Ramazani notes exceptions to this basis for a distinction between poetry and song, citing, specifically, the work of Bob Dylan (191).

54 Jonathan Culler characterizes obscurity as a psychiatric rehabilitation of sorts in calling it a "freedom" from the "compulsion to signify" (*Theory* 304).

3

This Is "Where the Meanings Are": Lyric Disjunction and Perceptual Shattering

We can find no scar—
But internal difference,
Where the Meanings, are—

—Emily Dickinson

Jonathan Culler muses of the lyric that it is "a place where enchantment and disenchantment, opacity and lucidity are negotiated" (*Theory* 352). The former terms of the two dyads he regards as seductive ploys, pleasure-giving preludes to the elucidation that disenchants, regretting the lack of a better term than "enchantment" to describe the genre's "visceral appeal" (352). Lyrics vary in the quality of their fogs and the extent to which they dissipate to disclose their latencies, but while fog lingers, it serves to ease one into the unknown. This further role played by tones of firstness in their various incarnations finds a neurological parallel in the brain's tempering of newness. The neuroscientist V. H. S. Ramachandran chronicles the case of a patient with a version of the disorder anosognosia (the pathological inability to admit the presence of a disease) that casts light onto the intact nervous system's ambivalent tolerance for novelty.[1] The brain, he theorizes, maintains discrete mechanisms for preserving the status quo and for admitting challenges to it, mechanisms that are localized hemispherically. This particular form of the disorder is suffered by paralysis victims whose left side is afflicted as the result of an injury to the right brain. Remarkably, these patients disown their paralysis through elaborate confabulations, rationalizations concocted in order to deny to others, and by extension to themselves, that an immobilized limb is in fact their own (130–1, 153–5). (Ramachandran observes that the techniques read as pure Freudian defense mechanisms.) Deducing that the right brain admits radically new concepts, Ramachandran suggests that the paralysis-inducing injury also damages the mechanism via which it does so. As a result, the efforts of the left brain to inhibit the integration of the new condition go unchecked. Curiously, when paralysis is presented to these anosognosia sufferers as a passing condition, they are able to accept it, leading Ramachandran to conclude that the less unsettling prospect of short-term incapacity does not trigger the left brain's defense system and galvanizine it to protect the reigning order (151). The brain accepts newness if it is tempered, qualified, or minimized—if the lily is gilded, so to speak. The right brain's silence prevents gilding, allowing the left brain to conserve unchallenged.

It is perhaps significant that the right brain processes music and figurative language, sources of obfuscation that ease the induction into the exotic.[2] (The conservative left brain, it is speculated, attends to syntactical information and literal meaning.) One softens to the novel if one is lulled into it, if it is elucidated *gradually*. Obscurity both resists and promises its complement—revelation—the disclosure mystery anticipates. Within the ethos of lyric, the predicament of a mismatch between the language one has at one's disposal and the environment before one forces poetic utterance to become functional—to recover meaning. To accomplish this, lyric stresses pre-semantic division-making, thereby facilitating entrée into the new order lurking within the obscure as an immanence and an imminence. More than ornamental, more than emotive, the sounds of poetry are instrumental within this pre-referential process of marking significance in order to determine the firstness lyric airs.

Determining Potential: Perception and the Operation of Secondness

As a font of meaning, firstness in its sundry forms gives way to Peircean secondness, the principle of condensation into distinction afforded by the conventions of the lyric poem, among them its music. Within Peirce's trichotomy, the potential of firstness is actualized through the contrastive principle of secondness. Realizing the virtual variety of the first, every second is second to some thing against which it is defined ("Guess" 248). Secondness is an operative mode of constraint, a bringing into relief through the contrast that delimits and thereby defines "the sense of … an external fact, of another something" ("Principles" 95). Effort and resistance, cause and effect, and brute factuality inhabit this mood ("Principles" 75, 79). A fragile, ephemeral stage, it will evanesce as soon as the duality it effects is mediated by thirdness; its ephemerality in fact vitalizes the culmination of semiosis in semantics. What is strictly inapprehensible because potential as firstness, becomes suggestively significant by means of immediate, proximate contextualization.

While perception has been regarded as an interpretive, indeed a creative act, it has been consistently seen as one that integrates environmental input, regardless of the fact that in selecting stimuli from an environment, the sensory systems initially disintegrate it. The legacy of empiricist philosophy—especially the theories promulgated by Berkeley and Locke holding that simple ideas of sense originating in the environment are combined in the mind to produce complex ideas formed of combination, relation, and abstraction (Locke 129–32)—has proved a hindrance to fully understanding the perceptual mechanism of an embedded organism. The atomistic and inductive assumptions of empiricism were adopted by neuroscientists, who for decades ascribed to a model in which discrete stimuli transduced by receptor neurons are eventually unified into a percept that represents an object in the world. In his landmark 1906 text, *The Integrative Action of the Nervous System*, Sir Charles Sherrington lays bare the discipline's inductive bias: "If the nature of an animal be accepted as that of a whole presupposed by all its parts, then each and every part of the animal is integrative" (xiii). This supposition has given rise to one of the most intractable conundrums to beset the field, the "binding problem" so-dubbed by Sherrington himself. Perceptual systems are organized hierarchically, activating larger, more interactive neuronal networks as input proceeds along afferent pathways, and their anatomy and physiology do in fact enable the integration of diverse input. For instance, cortical neurons along visual pathways respond to progressively larger and less definite receptive fields, the sets of conditions that potentially activate them. At the level of experience, perception would also seem to culminate in an integrative action, as consciousness itself is most often integrated, possessing, as it does, the property of unity, the sense that it harbors a single event. But an exclusive focus on this trajectory leads, predictably, to the positing of a site of integration within the brain, an executive office, if you will, where a neural correlate of the percept is assembled to correspond to the object in the world it represents. The resulting need for an ur-intelligence that must not only synthesize the percept but also judge its representational accuracy—and must therefore have an alternative, that is, non-perceptual means of access to reality—is spoofed in the figure of a resident homunculus, the personification of transcendent subjectivity that must exist in order to ascribe meaning to arrangements of neurons. As the central unresolved problem of neuroscience, the binding problem expresses a dilemma of representation that harkens back to philosophical empiricism.

Yet the neurological processes that integrate percepts also involve disintegrative action, permitting the inference of a preexisting whole. That integrity precedes the making of distinctions is a tacit assumption of embeddedness, and thus a precondition for much of the thinking adduced herein. (The inductive methodology of empiricism obviates this presupposition in positing the binder as a separate entity assembling discrete data toward the end of representing reality as it is.) Whitehead names the determination of actual entities a "deciding" in order to evoke the word's root sense of "cutting off" (43), here of a process of which the entity is a part. For the late neuroscientist Francisco Varela, distinguishing an object from the continuity in which it is embedded is an act of interpretation he describes as the realization of "a domain of distinctions" that have been "selected" (155) from a "background" of randomness (156). His designation of perception as a hermeneutic activity determining randomness[3] accords with the idea that basic organismic functioning realizes the *potential* inherent in a connection to an environment. His understanding of cognition is thus "enactive": "Perception is not simply embedded within and constrained by the surrounding world; it also contributes to the enactment of this surrounding world" (174). Secondness, the making real of virtual distinctions, is a response to the maker's relationship to wholeness.

Collaborating with Walter J. Freeman, neuroscientist cum philosopher Christine Skarda elucidates the contribution of systemic wholeness to perception at the level of the physical substrate.[4] She, also, begins with the assumption that a functional integrity preexists perception: it cannot therefore be the end of perception to mend what is not rent. An integral relationship between an organism and an environment is a given; the perceptual processes expressive of that relationship must proceed from this integrity. Adopting a radical stance that obviates integration as a process aligning an organism with its environment, she argues that perceptual flow proceeds unidirectionally toward articulation, dividing components in the manner that a limb is articulated at its joints (83), that is, creating disjunction that preserves points of attachment. This jointure underlying disjunction is a key property of secondness. By way of example, the relationship between a sense receptor neuron in the retina and the spectral range of electromagnetic radiation located so as potentially to trigger it (its receptive field) assumes, she argues, a preexisting relationship governed by causality. Her pregnant assertion, "To be subject to causation is to be related from the start" (82), displaces that causal relationship to a potential state, consigning it to firstness. Connections exist as unrealized (receptor neurons and their potential activators, words and their potential senses) *and* as realized: a photon causes the activation of sense receptors, realizing difference while preserving relationship.

In a thoroughgoing pragmatic argument, Skarda defines perceptual processes as " 'uses' that progressively articulate the interactive organismic events taking place at the interactive interface between the organism and its environment into percepts" (81–2). One notes the effort extended in expressing the fact that articulation does not efface integration (especially in the phrase "interactive interface") as well as the inveterate tendency of the English language to sunder subject and object she has difficulty skirting. Perceptual events are like the affairs of the littoral that belong to both the shore and the sea but may appear as one or the other. Assuming the mutuality inherent in perception, Skarda then rather boldly refutes the neurocentric doctrine, the tenet that neural activity is the sole creator of the percept (83, 85), a move that allows her to claim that sense organs themselves contribute to the percept prior to neural engagement by cocreating, with the environment, what she calls a "phenomenal fabric," the basis for subsequent neuronal functioning (83). Within the visual system, the lens (with, one assumes, the cornea and the vitreous humor) creates a "complex light phenomenon," a tapestry of structured electromagnetic energy[5] that is then projected to the sense receptor neurons of the retina. Echoing Peirce, perhaps unwittingly, she describes the phenomenal fabric as a "complex, but as yet undifferentiated, sensory content *directly apprehended by the organism* without the intervention of neural activity" (83). In other words, the complexity of the phenomenal fabric—"directly apprehended" in that it is embodied—is latent, virtual. As the shared construct of the organism and the environment, it is a narrowed set of potential constituting a point of immediate attachment she calls an interface, a physical incarnation of unity that preexists its disintegration.

In order to construct a percept, the sense receptor neurons of the retina onto which the phenomenal fabric of patterned electromagnetic energy is projected then proceed to "fragment" it, Skarda's term analogous to Whitehead's "deciding" and Varela's "enacting of distinction." In the earliest stages of perception, neuronal activity (what Walter Freeman calls "Level One activity") is parallel: in visual perception, neurons do not initially interact with one another, but rather isolate their triggering stimuli along pathways into what will become the features of the percept. Receptor neurons specialize, that is, they respond maximally to the limited range of energy within their receptive fields. The brain then engages in a series of compare and contrast mechanisms in order to tease out information from the energy it has segregated. For instance, the post-receptor ganglion neurons, which receive input from the retina, specialize for center and off-center location. Each cone in the retina attaches to one ganglion neuron specializing for the detection of light at the center of the field and one specializing for the detection of light in its surround. On-center neurons fire rapidly in intense light, while off-center neurons fire slowly, and vice versa. The excitation of one type results in the inhibition of its complement. This dynamic is further exemplified in the early stages of color vision, in which a three-cone system gives rise to the sensation of color by a simple mechanism of secondness. The three types of color receptors, the S, M, and L cones, respond preferentially to the small, medium, and large wavelength portions of the color spectrum, respectively.[6] Each color receptor neuron responds to a range of electromagnetic radiation. It is not possible to discern simply from the activation of a receptor neuron whence in its dedicated slice of the spectrum a captured photon hails. The electrical response following transduction is consistent across variations in the wavelength triggering it. Upon the firing of the retinal receptors, the photon detected continues to exist as a potential set of qualia in the form of colors inherent within the signal. The brain commences to create the information that is color by contrasting the signals emanating from the three cones, employing a simple mechanism of secondness that first calculates the arithmetical difference between the long and medium wavelength receptors (L – M) and then contrasts the subtractive difference (the variation between them) with the signal from the short wave (S – (L – M)). Via this mechanism, the system begins to make distinctions within its visual field, resolving detail from out of the broad swath of the phenomenal fabric by bringing borders and edges into relief. Contrast is the larger principle of secondness, the enactment of which makes oppositions patent.

In order to facilitate the recovery (or the preservation) of bearings, perception realizes virtual variety, animating it through an articulating mechanism. Information comes into being through a process by means of which the sensory systems begin to make the distinctions that bring the borders and edges of the features of a percept into relief. Secondness is a necessary intermediate phase in which relation is precipitated, indicated but not yet confirmed through the mediating activity of thirdness. What is unknowable, because potential, becomes suggestively semantic by means of local, proximate contextualization, a process transpiring in the encounter with a riddle during which juxtapositions delineate first small and eventually larger features from which an object may be inferred. As sense data are encoded neurally and begin to ascend the brain's dynamic hierarchy, they continue to be governed by a differentiating mechanism: secondness is a recursive strategy of the bottom-up processes of perception. As Freeman makes explicit in his theory of olfaction, systemic behavior involving globally distributed neural networks continues to make use of this contrastive activity, as progressively larger groups of neurons oscillate synchronously, distinguishing the neuronal correlates of progressively larger features, until a neural correlate of the self is articulated from a neural correlate of the non-self. Ultimately, organismic functioning creates from the phenomenal fabric what Skarda calls "the subject-object form of use" (90–1) to stress both the functional and constructed nature of these concepts.

These mechanisms of contrast instigate a process by means of which the organism contextualizes perceptual knowledge within its history, one that will eventually lead to decisive categorization, a hermeneutic and a functional necessity. As it actualizes potential in selecting and then differentiating what it selects, the operation of secondness is among the mechanisms responsible for the perceiving entity's distortion of reality as it is. For example, the datum that is the wavelength of electromagnetic radiation does not continue to exist beyond the retinal cones. As cones are activated by a particular range of electromagnetic wavelengths and maintain a probabilistic relationship to photons of light, there is no consistent correspondence between wavelength and a color perceived. Color qualia are rather *created* and regularized by means of the aforementioned contrastive techniques, a discovery Edward Land exploited in developing the Polaroid process ("Retinex"). In its relationship to physical reality, the perceived greenness of the leaf becomes a sign, which is in itself stable but which corresponds to a fluid array of indices of objects (as does a verbal sign). Percepts are presumably regularized in this way because they are constrained by the value that the organism attaches to them. Perceived consistency amid inconsistency facilitates categorization and thus the advantageous use of the object whose properties are regularized.[7] Secondness is, among other things, a mechanism creating the appearance of stability that leads to the illusion that our objects are unmediated. It is the means by which the shattering of environmental unity gives rise to the qualitatively different, internal unity of the percept, a unity the organism remembers.

As William James argues in "The Stream of Thought," empiricism's approach is curiously anti-empirical as one does not experience sensations discretely, but rather in relation to one another (171–2). On the qualitative level of James's investigations as well, induction is compromised as an exclusive method of perception. Supporting his claim and extending it, recent studies suggest that the integrity of consciousness precedes and survives its attention to specificity rather than emerging from it. The aforementioned work of Shaul

Hochstein and Merav Ahissar on reverse hierarchies in the visual system implies that explicit perception, defined as "stimulus-driven experiences that are accessible to conscious identification and recognition" (in other words, percepts), is experienced initially as already-integrated wholes (794). In the phenomenon Hochstein calls "vision at a glance," consciousness registers a field impressionistically and only subsequently focuses in on details by enacting "vision with scrutiny" (791). One does not experience a visual tableau by making the acquaintance of its individual elements and subsequently uniting them: the whole is registered as such despite the fact that its parts are as yet undistinguished. A movement toward disintegration is possible in the experience of percepts because the conscious apprehension of a whole does not depend on the conscious integration of its components (791). "Reverse Hierarchy Theory" posits that, while implicit (unconscious) processing progressively integrates neural input (input it has previously disintegrated as described above), explicit (conscious) visual perception occurs in reverse hierarchical order as percepts register to consciousness only after implicit processing has ascended the hierarchy (794). The first exposure to a scene amounts to a loose or "crude" binding, what might be called an obscure one. Hochstein refers to the impressionistic unity yielded by "vision at a glance" as a "hypothesis" about the whole. (Such an as-yet-undifferentiated whole would seem to be itself a version of firstness in that its inherent variety is potential.) Reentry, the process of scaling down the hierarchy to focus in on details, functions subsequently "to confirm or refute such initial guesses" (794).

This analytic orientation shared by the initial physical processes of embedded perception and the conscious experience of perception is acknowledged in a number of pertinent evolutionary and developmental theories of language. For example, Allison Wray and Michael Arbib have proposed separately that language as we know it evolved from a proto-language in which complete utterances were the primary unit, not the words or the phonemes and morphemes that are their building blocks (Wray 50–2; Arbib 185). According to Wray, the segmentation of the message into smaller meaningful units that can then be recombined marks the advent of language proper (53). The absence of articulation within the messages posited by the "whole utterance" model would seem to entail their ambiguity. Stephen Brown's theory that music and language diverged from a common form of expression likewise posits an evolutionary trajectory toward articulation. His hypothesis that early language was musical (a "musi-language") would seem to accord with the speculations of Rousseau, Herder, Vico, and Bovet as to language's aboriginally poetic state.[8] The experience of lyric poetry recapitulates and foregrounds this directionality because it also transpires as an event that initially disintegrates. Though a poem must be experienced sequentially, whether it is read or heard, a sense of the whole of it nevertheless precedes, to a great degree, the resolution of the provocative obscurity that is a product of its self-awareness as embedded, an awareness reflected, at times, at the level of content.

Logically, the disintegration enabling contrast at progressive levels of perception within the neural substrate would necessitate integration. Percepts are unified, and their congealing depends upon progressive recombination pursuant to the distinction making the brain enacts. Skarda's theory, it should be stressed, does not obviate the directionality of integration: her emphasis on the "shattering" function of peripheral neurons would seem rather to underscore the subsequent need to integrate what has been shattered. What perception unifies, however, is a materially and qualitatively distinct percept private to the organism and its history. The hierarchical dynamics of the brain imply both analysis and synthesis, but not the simple reassembling of what is, as Skarda says, already integrated (80). This integrative function of perception is constructive—creative—because percepts are functional in that they are confederated with action. As she puts it, use correlates with creativity (84)—what the brain creates is the way it will use the percept. As neurological constructions are functional and not veridical, they do not need to be exhaustively correlated with things as they are by means of retrospective synthesis; rather, their accuracy is tested and refined prospectively, through their correlation with subsequent input following action.

Such internal building of meaning is carried out within the poem as well. With this understanding, Culler follows Empson in making the claim that "the poem's organization ... absorb[s] and restructure[s] meanings" (*Structuralist* 185). When Frye opines of lyric language that its "words do not resonate against the things they describe, but against other words and sounds" ("Approaching" 35), one takes this as a relative statement meaning that they do not resonate against the things they describe to the degree that words deployed differently do. Reference is inevitable, tied, as it is, with action, verbal or otherwise, toward the object referenced. The relocation of the emergence of meaning to the poem's interiority where it is made in the relations between linguistic units, in acts of secondness, even as a relocation of emphasis, betrays an assumption that the construction of significance takes place within an alternative medium whose arcane organizational principles are specific to itself, as neurological processes are to the brain. Features created in contrast are created in a context, in a private context in which they gain significance when encoded within preexisting structures. In lyric, then, privacy is a function of the adaptation or transforming of matter or material from the source that is the environment, the larger, enveloping natural or linguistic system. Intimacy is not simply situational or thematic, the personal content of a love affair or a lament, but the result of a self-contained semiotic strategy dependent on a larger, informing context from which the raw materials of its content are derived.

Neither, however, is either of these two private enterprises entirely subjective. The claims that perception is a subjective faculty and the lyric a subjective genre most often attribute subjectivity to the coloring of bias, motive, and belief. But what is private in the sense outlined above is not subjective but rather "of the subject." That the organism is informed by indices of objects it transforms and obscures as objects, in the process making its access to them less than objective, has been discussed. Yet, if objects were to be thoroughly personalized, perception would hardly be adaptive. As the object yields to the subject, becoming of it, the subject retains aspects of the object. For instance, although the retinal image—the pattern of activated neurons over the retina—is not a spatial correlate of either the phenomenal fabric or the percept, receptive fields within vision (as well as touch) correspond to the topographic location of stimuli and thus enable the brain to encode information about an object's position and size from the get-go. The brain maintains this information, constructing the more unverifiable features of the percept, such as color, tone, smell, and taste. "Perceived objects are not located outside of the perceiver any more than subjectivity is localized within the organism" (Skarda 92). Clearly, perception is both of the subject and the object, as is lyric utterance: the lyric subject decomposes to become object; the lyric object speaks.

The assertion that distinction must follow from indistinction, the differentiation of parts from a preexisting whole is logically unassailable: secondness permits the inference of firstness; distinction, indistinction; realization, potential. Skarda is on target in proposing that there is an as-yet-undiscriminated structure apprehended bodily at the point of contact between organism and environment that points back toward external stimuli and forward toward the percept. The phenomenal fabric is a boundary condition (84), a parameter shaping the realization of potential in the subsequent event of its shattering. As an effect and a subset of an ecological holism, a momentary manifestation of connectedness, it is as-yet-unrealized. Yet, it is also an already-bound structure that will be preserved through the articulation of its features, and in this sense also, it is directly accessible to perception[9] (82).

The Play of Lyric Seconds

The attribution of semantic efficacy to form is a common, even a characteristic, maneuver of poetics that precedes the advent of formalism proper. Form becomes a valuable concept for poetry the moment it is regarded as dynamic, that is, as productive of meaning, and not merely as its vessel or mirror. An understanding of the logic of the apparatus of the poem as a self-consistent logic of secondness grants it this dynamism. Among the characteristic tendencies of lyric is its naked exploitation of secondness, an instinct to which it gives wide rein. Poetic obscurity differs from the narrative technique of withholding information in the degree and kind of its participation as potential determined through contrast operations. There exist intrinsic lyric techniques by which obscurity is resolved into features in the manner in which firstness precipitates into secondness. The genre's musical elements offer instances of what is perhaps the purest form of secondness in creating prosodic distinctions that are not in and of themselves semantic, but, as the gradations of color on an object, foster apprehension. In speaking "below/the tension of the lyre" (22–3), the prophet of "St. John and the Back-Ache" seeks to collapse these distinctions and thereby to deliver presence unto his acolyte. The tension born of the tuning of string instruments permits the manipulation of vibrations to produce the discrete tones upon which secondness depends and is, as such, a means of realizing firstness. Devices such as alliteration, assonance, rhyme, meter, and rhythm rely, in one way or another, on the establishment of distinction (or its enhancement) as against similarity. What is paired sonically is also brought into contrastive relation, creating significant disjunction at points of jointure within the poem. For instance, alliteration, in focusing attention on initial sounds and thereby isolating them, creates local islands of order, clusters of consonants that contrast with the nonrepeated portions of the words, articulating words internally, as well as one from the other. In metered verse, patterns of stressed and unstressed syllables (or syllabic lengths within quantitative verse) create borders that highlight the differences between them and between the metrical feet they compose. In both its literal and derivative forms, music effects the division-making from which the features of the sonic landscape emerge, and thus offers a form of secondness indebted to its compeer musical firstness.

Aside from sonic structuring, the form of secondness in which relation is least overtly semantic because it does not depend upon determined senses of words is deixis. Deixis, understood properly, is a means of negotiating a lack of customary significance. Like secondness, it begins in the here and now, in what Peirce calls "haecceity." As language's orienting function, deixis involves the making of spatial and temporal relation through the deployment of shifters,[10] words whose referents can only be understood in context. As contrast has its limit in indication, deictics most often operate in accordance with a contrastive principle: most shifters entail an opposite. As such, they are the first resort of one for whom the sheer chaos of novelty impinges on the senses and threatens comprehension, a quasi-gestural linguistic strategy in which tentative or preliminary designations establish proximity: the "there" takes on significance in relation to the "here" with which one is newly acquainted. Deixis speaks to both an exoticism and an immediacy of locale. Dickinson's nebulous "here," where "I" and "silence" are wrecked, would permit situational inference, becoming a basis of incipient knowledge, if the unchristened, contingent "there" were allowed to materialize. As "I felt a Funeral, in my Brain," is abandoned at the point it is, a precise location cannot be conferred, and the result is a state of limbo.

Culler is one of the few, if not the only critic to make deixis a basic lyric principle, and his work is unusually incisive for this fact (*Structuralist* 164–70). Although deixis and resistance comprise two of his original four criteria for the genre,[11] he considers the former to be productive of the latter: deixis intensifies a sense of presence in constructing an immediate locale, an unidentifiable "here and now," that strengthens the poem's resistance to interpretation (*Theory* 16). A sign of the fictionality of lyric, the technique is a means of coercing what he calls an "enunciated posture" for the poem (170). I would like to argue that deixis is also a *response* to resistance, as he defines it, one that, in indicating context, occasions a recuperative strategy and, further, that its vagueness is symptomatic of its nascent emergence from the obscurity of potential meaning.

As the effect of deixis is to render meaning nascent, to mark as potentially significant pending the emergence of certain reference, this elementary mode of ordering must not be foreclosed upon prematurely, but allowed its full breadth if one is to glean accurate meaning and act appropriately. It demands an extension that is often met with frustration: "If we had world enough and time," pens Marvell, "this coyness, lady, were no crime." (50). The lady's conditionally decriminalized posture gives rise to what is a central metaphor for the extensive play of secondness, the approach and recoil, the here and there of courtship responding to an ultimately unyielding, virginal firstness. Lyric invites lingering in this yet uncertain phase where there is, as Keats would prefer, no "irritable reaching after fact & reason"[12] (*Letters* 167). It is this intuitive stage of relation that Orpheus aborts in breach of the condition that he not look upon Eurydice prematurely. Not content with vague, relative knowledge, faithless that the "here," the "this," and the "I" entail—are trailed by—the "there," the "that," and the "you," he turns to "see," to know her presence, reaching after fact and rushing on, unwittingly, to thirdness, the mediation of seconds ("Guess" 249) by the creation of her image. (As I shall argue, to mediate the gap paradoxically and ineluctably expands it.) The courtly figure dares not consummate his courtship, for such a lucky end would desiccate the courtship lyric in drying up its fancied forms of secondness and firstness. (The latter for Orpheus occurs as the regenerative potential of the underworld.)

The range of deixis knows no bounds and may extend indefinitely. "Here" and "there" may exist as the extremes of Arcadia in the past and Utopia in the future so that deixis is not merely local and localizing, but scales to the poem's unknown, elastic extremes. Deixis also temporalizes as it does in Wordsworth's separation of the "here" of a diminished present from the "there" of an idealized past. This temporal expanse opens space for the vatic mediation of "now" and "then" at the same time the referential postponement deixis effects defers revelation, and therefore closure, maintaining the uncrossable interval between prophecy and its fulfillment. Culler explicitly associates deixis with vision, calling it an "invocational-prophetic mode … an instance of the energy of anticipation that characterizes the poetic spirit: a spirit which can envision what it calls for" (*Structuralist* 166).

Gaston Bachelard captures the drama of poetic anticipation, as well as the psychic danger, trauma even, experienced within the fragile, in-between phase of secondness when he writes,

> The poet has brought us to an extreme situation beyond which we are afraid to venture … The slightest sound prepares a catastrophe, while mad winds prepare general chaos. Murmur and clangor go hand in hand. We are taught the ontology of presentiment. In this tense state of fore-hearing, we are asked to become aware of the slightest indications, and in this cosmos of extremes, things are indications before they are phenomena; the weaker the indication, the greater the significance, since it indicates an origin. (175–6)

As Bachelard suggests, poetic images are "images of the first time," because they picture the faintest of indicia and in so doing prioritize the incipient. The primary is the sphere of the poetic and distinctly not the scientific: "Observation," he writes, "belongs in the domain of 'several times'" alluding to the experimental requirement of repeatability (156). It is intrinsic to the "ontology of presentiment"—here a learned and not a divinely bestowed mode of existence that is at the same time an epistemological stage—that it exist a shade past firstness. (The "mad winds" that ready a "general chaos" bespeak a Dionysian version of potential.) Sensitive attention to indication evades the impasse that is the inexpressibility of the first. Presentiment is an anxiety-ridden, egalitarian (or "commonal") styling of the early phases of prophecy; it narrows by selecting virtual potentiality, discerning hints of meaning and "articulating" them along the way to forming a guess at the future, preserving firstness all the while: the future remains lodged within the present as potential, always. The experience of presentiment, commonplace in lyric, commands indication as a tactic to initiate the bringing into relief of features, a precondition for determination. It points toward what can only become certain once events have attained translucence in evolving the apparent clarity of thirdness.

Deixis then functions as a method of "finding" in which the poem is embroiled. It is the ineluctable next step, the means of emergence that depends upon the continuation of firstness. As if in acknowledgment of this fact, the deictic play of seconds as against the pull of firstness within the poem "St. John and the Back-Ache" is ingeniously dense. The Back-Ache's audible musings first divide mind-as-force from world-as-presence, clearly delineating a relationship of secondness that in creating "presence" as an object of inquiry second to the mind renders it inaccessible and thus recognizes the persistence of an ontology of potential. The strategy of naming presence paradoxically defines the indefinable and does not, particularly as St. John withdraws "presence" within his speech, substituting for the name the shifter "it." This technique of unnaming (one Dickinson was prone to draw upon) may be construed as an attempt to undo mediation, devolving the thirdness that is the representation of firstness as "presence" into the secondness via which "it" is contrasted with the figures "it is not." The anaphoric repetition of the assertion "it is not" echoes as the converse (and thus second) of an implied "it is," the third-person version of the riddle's "I am." This riddle-like technique that is also the technique of prophecy, the listing of features that precedes identification and gives rise to it, is therefore simultaneously disqualified. The subject within St. John's tropical oration is then slyly switched from "presence" to "the effect of the object," a coy way of saying "the subject"—and of turning the object (presence) into the subject—in a doubling that serves to stress the dependence of these terms one on the other. A more straightforward example of deixis in the poem is found in the use of the modifier "*That* big-brushed green," which, by virtue of its negative qualifier "it is not," may be taken to mean "*This* big-brushed green." Deictic pairs are both established and not: their negation pulls the poem back into the potential of firstness, into the overwhelming obscurity of the lines Harold Bloom has identified as among the most difficult in all of Stevens (298), even as ever-emergent couplings countervail it. It is easy to see how the deictic play the poem releases might be interpreted to be a deconstructive exercise, the poem an artifact receptive to such an exercise, and deixis itself merely subversive.

And yet, "it is not." The truism that the meaning of poetry is made in the gaps might be revised to read "by means of the gaps," or disjunctive joinings the lyric incarnates diversely. Secondness is a chiaroscuro technique, the fine-grained play of light and shade bringing detail into relief. The genre's arsenal of techniques for creating spots of secondness is well supplied, enjoying broad implementation within dissimilar poetics. That lyric poetry emphasizes the word more than its fellow literary forms is not simply a function of its brevity, but of distinctive means of isolating the unit, setting it against, rather than—or in addition to—seamlessly linking it to other units. The artifice of the line break (manifesting as a pause in oral presentation) is perhaps the most representative and central instance of the lyric's tendency toward granularity. To the extent that it affords a point of hesitation, a brink where meaning is multiplied and made ambiguous, the juxtaposition lineation creates prompts a dynamic that begins to realize the potential so generated. An obscure line, especially one rendered so by its ending, may be defined as against what follows it. The opportunities for such larger-scale instances of secondness abound and can be created, for example, by the caesura between the hemistiches of the Anglo-Saxon line as well as by stanza and section breaks. To offer a highly touted example of the workings of juxtaposition, in Pound's ideogrammic method utilizing "superpositioning," the meaning of a unit is delimited by an ensuing unit. As exemplified by "In a Station of the Metro," each line is intended to signify the same abstract concept in the manner of the Chinese ideogram (*ABC* 21–2), a mediating idea reached through the inference of their similarity, which, to reiterate, arises pursuant to the resolution of their difference. Peirce categorizes this type of secondness as degenerate, that in which the first and the second do not depend on one another for their existence, in order to distinguish it from the true secondness, the relationship of interdependence, or dichotomy, that characterizes most deixis ("Guess" 253–4). This is not to simplify units that in themselves may be quite complex, or the diversity of their engagements, but rather to point out that, as in perception, the dynamic of secondness between units does not fade as they grow larger and absorptive of meaning.

Nor is the genre dependent upon formal discontinuity to engender secondness. The tension de Man explores as between the literal and figurative uses of language reveals the tropes standard to poetry to be inductive of secondness. The interpretation of metaphor, a figure broadly associated with the lyric, is a prevalent recuperative tactic deployed against resistance in collocating the seconds "tenor" and "vehicle," or "target" and "source."[13] In the same manner, the tension-producing devices to which the New Critics were partial—irony, paradox, and ambiguity—furnish opportunities for contrast, and thus the means by which ambiguity may begin to resolve itself.[14] Secondness may also operate at the level of content: Culler notes that the emotional vacillations endemic to the courtly dynamic, the wild swings from exultation and praise to despair and complaint (*the* lyric emotional polarities) create "inner divisions" within their subjects (*Theory* 316). These affective extremes native to the genre as a whole are authentically second to one another. Such content may offer an isolated opportunity to engage the technique, or it may align its divisions with formally molded seconds, thereby buttressing them.

It is in this overlapping and cumulative plethora of significant division that the lyric distinguishes itself most clearly from other genres. Because it breaks down into units, or self-shatters more extensively than other literary forms, multiplying borders in order to exploit them, the poem motivates secondness at multiple stages of one's encounter with it. We tend to think of discontinuity, with obscurity, as a contemporary phenomenon, yet this estimation proves equally untenable. By way of example, one of the oldest extant verses in modern English veers from its opening, "Western Wind, when will thou blow,/the small rain down can rain?" to the ensuing lines "Christ if my love were in my arms/ And I in my bed again!" (68), exhibiting a discontinuity of content and tone that is strikingly modern in its presentation. The lyric has been continuously discontinuous, and its discontinuity is indigenous to its formal radical.

Among the techniques producing discontinuity, the line resonates as the most distinctive feature of the lyric genre[15] because it generates both ambiguity (particularly when enjambed, but also when end-stopped) and the distinction that begins to resolve ambiguity. And yet, lineation as such remains under-theorized. T. V. F. Brogan argues that the primacy of the line is evidenced by the use of the plural form of the word as a metonym for verse and by the fact that the unit "generates" and thus precedes its subunits (in the form of feet, words, and phrases) rather than the other way around (694), a contention that assumes a deductive movement from the whole to its parts. The claim that the unit is fundamental to poetry is bolstered by Turner and Pöppel's finding published in "The Neural Lyre" that the approximately three seconds it takes to process a line of verse (an extension standard throughout the world) coincides with the length of time the brain attends to aural input before its attention is interrupted to process it (286–8). A "bundle" of auditory information is sent to the cortex every three seconds or so in what Turner and Pöppel call a "parcel of experience." The line break thus reflects the point at which the brain naturally pauses before cognizing input (296–8). James Longenbach speaks to the tension within a unit subject simultaneously to a stasis (a staying within the line) and the motion propelling one forward beyond it (*Line* 20). These conflicting impulses to self-containment and to self-transcending connection are most pronounced in this most basic of lyric elements with respect to which jointure clearly undergirds disjunction. Often doubly stopped, by white space and by structuring devices such as anaphora, epistrophe, and rhyme, the line break is a brink where one might tumble headlong into firstness if its articulation did not also afford secondness.

Given the line's centrality, one is obliged to address nonlineated lyrics. Prose poetry, rather than eschewing disjunction, devises other ways to institute it. As Longenbach observes of this relative newcomer, "The effect of our more typical notion of a prose poem depends on the deletion of lineation from the formal decorum of poetry, and the absence of the line would not be interesting if we did not feel the possibility of its presence" (88). Jahan Ramazani considers oral poetry, a fellow outlier, not be lineated (3), and in a strict sense it is not. Yet, oral renditions of poetry indulge in distinction-making, and thus secondness, courtesy of the pause, a convention pure song preserves (in all likelihood originates) and more often than not exaggerates: the interlude between lines sung often extends beyond the length of the pause observed as poetry is performed and the pause one permits oneself when reading silently. If there is no detectable surcease of voice in singing, a stop is often effected by the elongation of a line's terminal syllable, especially its vowel sound.[16] That the line breaks of written poetry derive from the breaks of lyrics spoken and sung is evinced by the lineated format used when transcribing song lyrics.

Hierarchies of Seconds

It is central to my argument that within poetry, as within the brain, a hierarchy of scale exists along which secondness is enacted between increasingly larger semantic units. This modular "nesting" enables the modules to enter into relations promiscuously by participating in both horizontal and vertical, proximate and distant contrast behavior. For example, a line may be set against the sentence that contains it as well as a stanza that does not. The disposition of the poem becomes an invitation to read nonsequentially and against the forward flow of language, to notice relationships between spatially separated elements, rhyming words, repetitions, and so on. Units existing at a different level of scale can offset and constrain the meanings of others, including those at a distance, in the forging of significant disjunction. Brogan notes that as part of the reading process short-term memory repositions what is perceived, allowing for the "synchral (aserial) recognition" of units extracted from the flow of language and thus the making of connections across space and time (696). Poems then share with the brain a structure permitting the ascension along scale and complexity to larger and larger contrasting units, together with an ability to reverse the directionality of influence and modulate a smaller unit with a larger one. The segments of poems are intricately interconnected in the manner of the brain's neural networks. Reading them may involve bottom-up, top-down, and lateral processing.[17]

The particular instances of secondness the brain mediates are selected when they exceed a threshold level of detectability. This is true within the encounter with a poem as well. A reader might not concern herself with the differences within a customary grammatical construction such as occurs within Wordsworth's line "It is a beauteous evening, calm and free" (1)[18] and treat the report instead as a unity. In contrast, Donne's line "Batter my heart, three-personed God, for you" (1)[19] introduces several points of discontinuity within a roughly equivalent number of syllables that may constitute difference that matters. To echo Gregory Bateson, every opportunity for difference is not significant (78). The capacity to select stimuli emanating from the plenitude of Darwin's entangled bank, or information arising from the brain's intricate differential calculi, bestows a freedom of thought vital to the composing and recomposing of novelty.[20]

To instance such multiform occasions of secondness, I turn to Gerard Manley Hopkins's poem "Spring," reproduced here in full:

Nothing is so beautiful as Spring –
When weeds, in wheels, shoot long and lovely and lush;
Thrush's eggs look little low heavens, and thrush
Through the echoing timber does so rinse and wring
The ear, it strikes like lightnings to hear him sing;
The glassy peartree leaves and blooms, they brush
The descending blue; that blue is all in a rush
With richness; the racing lambs too have fair their fling.

> What is all this juice and all this joy?
> A strain of the earth's sweet being in the beginning
> In Eden garden. – Have, get, before it cloy,
> Before it cloud, Christ, lord, and sour with sinning,
> Innocent mind and Mayday in girl and boy,
> Most, O maid's child, thy choice and worthy the winning. (1–14)

This early sonnet touting nature's ideality begins with the poised, if pedestrian, iambic line "Nothing is so beautiful as Spring –" (1). Offsetting its sense of containment faintly, the endash at line's end predicts a forthcoming rupture that arrives in the form of the contrastingly exuberant dependent clause of line two: "When weeds, in wheels, shoot long and lovely and lush;" (2). This ordering brings into relief an opposition between the generic comment on spring and the less conventional image of unkempt, rambling excess. The poem's third line then serves up a picture of containment abutting the excess of the second: "Thrush's eggs look little low heavens, and thrush" (3). Within the line, the infinity of the heavens appears to overtake the shells of enclosed and therefore finite eggs (which themselves enclose unrealized potential). The line contrasts excess and containment, giving rise to each as a concept as it does the corresponding opposites "infinite" and "finite." Within the preceding line, the alliteration and assonance linking the words "weeds" and "wheels" highlight their discrepant terminal sounds, thus throwing their differing meanings into relief, saliently, the dissimilarity in the shapes of the objects they signify: one typically thinks of weeds growing upright, bending perhaps, but not curling round to form circles. Roundness thereby becomes a feature of these weeds "in wheels," highlighted as against their typical verticality. By means of contrast, the elements of spring are discriminated, reinforcing the season's rank luxury.

In the second line's alliterative trio of adjectives, "long and lovely and lush," "long" is both allied with and distinguished from the following two words, as "lovely" and "lush" are themselves coupled by the added authority of assonance. As such, the concepts of length and width (or outspreading) given by "lush" are juxtaposed. The coupling of "lovely" and "lush" is in turn uncoupled by their distinct final sounds, permitting their contrast (they seem to correlate with and reinforce the first and second lines of the poem, respectively) and serving to distinguish the members of this polysyndetic grouping as particular features of spring's overgrowth (as does the use of polysyndeton). To adduce a further example, the rhyme scheme of the sonnet's octave allies the words "lush," "thrush," "brush," and "rush." As the middle two terms also encase the latter one, they provide a further opportunity to distinguish it from its sound-alike hosts, emphasizing the fleetness of the literal and metaphorical season that is the poem's topic as against the concrete nouns "brush" and "thrush," suggesting the ephemerality of what is so provocatively present. The aural pun offered by "wring" (fortified by the embedding of "ring" within "wring") in line four evokes an ambiguity of meaning resolved through the contrasting of the constituent concepts (one is a motion, one possibly an object) that are allied in their shared quality of circularity (the concept evoked as mediating third). ("Ring" also harkens back to "wheel," affiliating two similarly shaped objects disaffiliated by the latter's ability to effect motion and the former's typical immobility and association with permanence. One might mediate this difference in arriving at the interpretation that seasons are perennial in their fluid circularity, a fact that itself contrasts with the fleetness and linearity of the human lifespan. What contrast affords is grasping, literally in perception as the edges and features of objects are brought into relief, and figuratively, conceptually, in poetry.

To indulge a larger-scale example of secondness, the poem's turn juxtaposes the octave's description of spring's riot with the sestet's analysis of its significance. The warning to partake of the season before its excesses "cloy" introduces the thematic opposition that sees innocence tainted by experience, by sin. This moment of thematic fixing resolves the ambiguity of the repeated word "rush," which in the octave refers both to movement with haste and the wetland plant, in favor of the former, at least at this moment. The internal rhyme nestled within the opening line then takes on retrospective significance: its yoking of "Nothing" and "Spring," the idea of spring's rarefied beauty as well as that of its absence affords the same cause and effect sequence instituted by the turn (if in reverse order), reconfiguring the oppositions "excess and containment," "infinite and finite," "circularity and linearity." The mediating term in each case is the idea of the seasonality of spring in its literal and broadly figurative, Edenic sense. All of this is by way of noting a small sampling of the play of secondness within this poem, which, like spring, abounds, exceeding the ambit of this glance.

In "Spring," the final invocation "O maid's child" serves to position a "you" as against the "I" that advises it. The ultimate deictic negotiation within the lyric poem transpires between these complementary pronouns the utterance constructs, a dyad often adduced as the crux of lyricism, and not necessarily one inclined to the Romantic. In "Personism: A Manifesto," Frank O'Hara describes his anti-metaphysical approach to a poem: "One of its minimal aspects is to address itself to one person (other than the poet himself). ... [Personism] puts the poem squarely between the poet and the person, Lucky Pierre style, and the poem is correspondingly gratified" (634). O'Hara's choice of the word "gratified" would seem to echo Stevens's term "satisfied," and is certainly reminiscent of it. A poem can culminate, or appear to culminate, in the separation of the self from the nonself the "you" comes to figure, forming true seconds that are not only interdependent but also mutually co-creative. Culler lists this arrival among the factors creating the "complexity of the enunciative apparatus," the lyric habit of "invoking another and the self-reflexive putting-into-play of the status of that other"[21] (*Theory* 16).

This intimate sort of relation-making inhering in poems, what Isenberg calls a "relational concept … of personhood" (22, 28), also emerges within perception. Indeed, the culmination of the poem in the deictics "I" and "you" reflects the terminus of human perception in what Skarda calls the "subject/object form of use." As Walter Freeman details in his theory of olfaction set forth below, as sensory input is processed at successively higher levels of the brain, contrast mechanisms continue to play out between populations of neurons along afferent pathways and are triggered, finally, with respect to the neural correlates of the self and the nonself (*Brains* 105). The contrasting of global neural networks serves the same function as lower-level contrast mechanisms, but it is implemented differently, by means of the alternating synchronization and desynchronization of the networks caused by negative feedback between excitatory and inhibitory populations of neurons (101). This outcome of perception in the large-scale play of seconds grants an object status as an object, defining it against the percipient in a process that does not necessarily entail self-consciousness, but is intensified by it.[22] Perceiving an object as distinct facilitates strategic action toward it. In order to act into the world, the organism distinguishes itself neurologically from what it is not, filing it in the complementary folder "you." Objectification is an effect and not cause of the organism's engagement with its environment, or, as de Man put it, "Seeing creates the dialectics of seeing."[23] The fundamental subgenre of the riddle employs this directionality, the conferring of adjusted contrasts in the form of features results in the naming that enlivens the named as it enlivens the Genesis namer, the interdependent entities collapsed within this representative species of poem.

The movement toward objectification is the making of *poiesis*, the vital and fictive business of Stevens's *finding* (construed as a process) of a "satisfaction," Whitehead's term for the culmination of finding in "concrescence," the emergence into concreteness that abstracts entity from process (84), and subject and object from embedding environment. Satisfaction is the decisive separation that circumscribes, and thus concretizes, entities.

> The notion of "satisfaction" is the notion of the "entity as concrete" abstracted from the "process of concrescence"; it is the outcome separated from the process, thereby losing the actuality of the atomic entity, which is both process and outcome ... the "satisfaction" ... closes up the entity. (84)

This "closing up" that generates the self in contrast to its own percept of the object other occurs within perception in defining a perceptual event systemically and distinguishing it from the rest of the organism's functioning. The ability to perceive distinction suffices the organism, and is thus pragmatic: "Perception is a process by which perceivers use the seamless state of their embeddedness in physical reality as if they were independent of it" (Skarda 81). As mentioned, this view diverges from both naive realism and the subjectivism with which the lyric is both casually and systematically allied. The percept is not a pure creation of the perceiving subject because it is causally embedded within the system from which the subject co-emerges with the object. Neither is the percept objective: because derived of organism-environment co-construction, it does not mirror the noumenal object, but rather "construes" it, to borrow Varela's term. After breaking down input from the environment through its selection, isolation, and configuring, the brain dynamically merges it with the other sources shaping the percept, including organismic history (memory), motivation (emotion), proprioceptive information about the body's location in space (embodiment), and information from the other sense modalities (perceptual reinforcement), generating chaotic feedback and feedforward loops in order to create something serviceable (*Brains* 33, 108). The organism thereby forms percepts in accordance with the way it is equipped to use them.

As if in acknowledgment that the perceiver as subject and the percept as object are engendered of the same process, the lyric's co-animation of an "I" and a "you" gives rise to an anthropomorphizing tendency that apostrophe and prosopopoeia distill. The often-noted prevalence, indeed centrality, of apostrophe in particular to the genre is stressed by Culler, who describes it as the lyric's "characteristic trope": "An O, devoid of semantic reference, is the very figure of voice" ("Reading" 99). The "O"—as image and as vehicle of voice—it should be noted, at once asserts itself and initiates the invocation of an addressee, and it is this forming through invocation and not the addressee's preexisting character that is significant. The gesture of speaking to the insentient as if fully present amounts to a *fiat lux*, a calling into existence that, in the manner of perception, brings the object "you" into coextensive emergence with and as against the "I" that asserts it: the two delineate and define one another. Culler refers to apostrophe as "a mark of poetic vocation" absent from other discourses (*Theory* 216). Poetic vocation *is* invocation, and the word's dual meanings of "personal mission" and "vocative act"—its conflation of a calling and a calling into being—may be said to recognize that what the subject is compelled to act toward (here by invoking it), and thus perceive, is necessarily an object, a bearer of meaning in relation to it, whether or not it is potentially, in some other context, a subject. Even when explicitly configured as a human being, the lyric "you" rarely assumes the status of subject within the poem's rhetorical exchange. And when the "you" is overtly an object, it tends to enjoy Martin Buber's feeling-based I/Thou relationship in contradistinction to an impersonal I/it relationship (Buber). "In an operation that sounds tautological, the vocative of apostrophe is a device which the poetic subject uses to establish with the object a relationship that helps to constitute the subject itself as poetic, even vatic" (Culler, *Theory* 216). One might invert the ending of Culler's statement to read, "to constitute the poetic or even vatic figure as subject." Each declaration rings true.

In describing such anthropomorphism as "an identification on the level of substance" ("Anthropomorphism" 241), de Man speaks to the nature of the practice as an imaginative appropriation that is subsequently naturalized. His well-known analysis of Baudelaire's sonnet "*Obsession*" as a self-described lyric reading of the earlier poem "*Correspondances*" centers the genre around the figure of prosopopoeia (literally, "face-making"). A prosopopoetic gesture, he writes, must be taken for "granted," because it is "not given in the nature of things" ("Wordsworth" 91), by which, it is fair to assume, he means the objective nature of things. The lyric constructs objects by means of an internal dynamic enabling what one might without reservation call an appropriation precisely because objects are not available objectively, but in a form fit for the subject's use. That unlikely renditions of "you" populate lyrics, including song lyrics, may be explained by the fact that the subject and object at length arise as neurological, perceptual complements: the "you" co-emergent with the "I" is to some extent the latter's creation, fantastical or not. An intimate exists at the boundary of the self as an other, one that is also of that self. Such an intimate may manifest as the otherness of the self. John Stuart Mill remarked, famously, that "poetry is feeling confessing itself to itself in moments of solitude," securing for it a rhetorical posture that necessitates its overhearing (95). That the "you" of lyric may become a construct of internalized otherness, an objectified half of a divided self,[24] is a recognition exploited frequently within Shakespeare's sonnets. Joel Fineman asserts that the bard's ambivalent presentation of the figure of the Dark Lady deflates a visual ideal, creating a temporal gap between the poet's "ego ideal" and its loss, and thus a self-image that resists identification (22–5). "His identity is an identity of ruptured identification, a broken identity that carves out in the poet's self a syncopated hollowness that accounts for the deep personal interiority of the sonnets' poetic persona" (25). One might argue that the division of the self from the self is also generated by the complex and manifold instances of secondness afforded by the elaborate structures of the sonnet form, not incidentally the preferred lyric vehicle of Renaissance "self-fashioning." Regardless of form or period, this tendency to objectify the self is the origin of the terror wreaked by the "terriblest force," the severing mind that must come, ironically, to its own defense if the rupture into deictic, pronominal points is not qualified as apparent. On a somewhat lighter note, Ben Jonson pays tribute to the coevolution of the "I" and the self as "you" in penning "An Ode to Himself," a pep talk aimed at overcoming his writer's block that opens by lamenting the frustration he hopes to allay in taking up his lyre:

> Where dost thou careless lie
> Buried in ease and sloth?
> Knowledge that sleeps doth die;
> And this security,
> It is the common moth
> That eats on wits and arts, and oft destroys them both. (1–6).

Whatever fictional status the poem grants its object "you," anthropomorphizing it recognizes that one's knowledge of it is cut of the same cloth as one's knowledge of oneself. Thus, as the lyric "you" is made other, it may be reflectively animated and granted self, or soul. By anthropomorphizing, the genre fosters the tandem emergence into what Culler calls "commensurability" ("Reading" 101), a term evoking, once more, the archetypal status of riddles, a subgenre in which the "I" and the "you" are concededly of the same stuff. Tiffany stresses that the identity of the riddle straddles the border between not only the subject and the object but also between the human and the nonhuman, making them substantively coextensive (74). The understanding of perception as creative of an apparent dualism of equilibrated seconds frees these figures of the egocentric charges levied against them and naturalizes, even normalizes them as the cognitive products of a perceptual act.

Embedded and Disembedded "I's": The Limits of Perception and Genre

Needless to say, the figure of apostrophe does not grace every lyric poem; when it does, it is not always clearly delineative of subject and object both.

Poetic presentation may skew toward the subject or the object pole, implying the absent term rather than realizing it. For instance, Keats's ode "To Autumn" does not announce an "I" but instead focuses on the object season by means of the prosopopoeia that enlivens it. Modernist movements such as imagism and objectivism made overt their quest for the thing in itself, the desire to lay bare unmediated "reality," emphasizing what they saw as concrete detail and rejecting the co-emergence of a subject (Zukofsky 12). Yet despite best efforts, the spareness they espoused tended to emphasize disjunction and thereby enabled the emergence, however imperfect, of an object, implicitly mediated by a subject. In poems of this sort, the "I," though silenced, is implied, clearly as in H. D.'s "Oread" with its direct address to the sea, or more obliquely, as in most haiku or Baudelaire's sonnet "*Correspondances.*" Indeed, certain poetics suppress the subject's emergence more forcefully than others, striving at times to avoid even an intimation of its presence. In a key justification of this emphasis, Charles Olson argues that Romanticism flounders in refusing to concede that self-consciousness inhibits the creative act in distancing one from, rather than reuniting one with, nature. In his view, high Romanticism in particular suffers from its failure to revisit the lost "hour/Of splendour in the grass" (Wordsworth "Ode" X.10–11):[25] though its goal may have been to reenter a natural state, it can be seen as an ambivalent attempt to sacrifice ego in order to recover this embedded, instinctual mode of being, an uncertainty secured for it when Coleridge collapsed the conscious faculty of the will into the imagination ("Biographia" 263). By way of correction, Olson sought to purge poetry of the presence of the ego (24) in order to restore the human to what he calls an object status, that is, to a state prior to his co-emergence with, and separation from, nature, one in which he is an object in an absolute sense. If he can poeticize as if propelled by the automatic, unself-aware mechanism of the breath, the poet will remain "contained within his nature as he is participant in the larger force" (25). Perception-action events may and often do occur in the absence of conscious control, resulting in the instantaneous, unquestioned recognition of an object and an appropriate action toward it. This unself-conscious level of perception is evolutionarily primary: it exists in organisms that are not self-conscious, and it constitutes the better part of the experience of organisms that are. Our feeling that we are consciously controlling our actions is mostly illusory as the coordination of action and perception is primarily an unconscious event, the assignment of causality to the will retrospective (Freeman, *Brains* 17–18). Another way to think of this is that cognition happens. As William James puts it succinctly, "*It*" (the object, the brain as object) "thinks"[26] ("Stream" 224) (emphasis added).

It is precisely this pre-attentive level of functioning that Olson aspires to access in order to register perceptions poetically. He wishes to position writing on the back of the perception-action event by recording each perception as soon as its predecessor is enacted (i.e., given verbal form), before a self-aware "I" can intrude upon an unwavering attention to the voice as registrar of perceptual flow and ponder its efforts—or worse, its existence (17). The speed and attentiveness required in subserving the movements of perception are bulwarks against interruptive self-reflection, what Allen Ginsberg called the "feeding back" that distracts the attention from the object at hand (147). Indeed, Freeman describes self-consciousness as a mechanism of delay inserted into the uninterrupted flow of preconscious organismic functioning: "Perception is a continuous and mostly unconscious process that is sampled and marked intermittently by awareness, and what we remember are the samples, not the process" (*Brains* 18). The state of being that the projective poet seeks to tap into and to convey is more connected and more capacious than that accessible to a consciousness conscious of itself.[27]

Olson is not alone in regarding the compositional process as unself-aware. If his poetics is of a certain ilk, his understanding of the creative act is decidedly more catholic. For example, Northrop Frye describes poem-making as a compulsive act, one the poet is drawn to perform though unaware of the source of his motivation, one that "blocks" quotidian self-inquiry ("Approaching" 32). We find further evidence that poetry is generated at this instinctual level in the mystifying and divinizing of the inspirational source: the visitation of the muse is often thought to be a fortuitous occurrence beyond conscious awareness and control. Attracting her involves a dynamic receptivity to what is apparently external, an active attention, or a listening, in Emerson's notion, for the poem that will arise in spite of one's bumbling interference ("Poet" 449). The poetry Olson seeks to create, like much of what follows in the postmodern era he helps to inaugurate, has as its goal the manifestation of this objective process. It presents a voice in its physical, object state, before it gives rise to a subjectivity, subduing any sense of personal identity by emphasizing the early stage play of secondness within perception. The poem in the end situates itself among natural objects (25) by recapitulating perception's unconscious beginnings. That poetry as a whole both embeds and gives rise to a self-aware "I" is the paradox of this genre that, like perception, exiles by means of its articulating directionality. The gap it creates may be resisted, or it may be mediated as the chasm over which desire, unquenched and enduring, is perpetuated. The conceit of the transmogrification of the poet further recognizes that perception is a primal, animal activity originating in an embedded, self-compromising state situated at the opposite end of the spectrum from the self-awareness that gives rise to self-assertion. That perception culminates in objectifying self-awareness is recognized by the cyclical ejection of the poet, who must, in lyricizing fully, endure the correction that is his expulsion into an original state. What is reprised within myths of poetic origin and in the lyric genre as a whole is the arc of perception itself, a faculty that obscures as it clarifies, embeds as it disembeds.

It is in the nearing of the divisive, relational destination of perception that the odic and elegiac modes invest their energies. Among lyric subgenres (with, perhaps, the poetry of courtly love), they concentrate most intensely on the negotiation between the subject and object forms they precipitate, reacting, in principal, to the emergence of this breach. As a formal expansion of apostrophe, each subgenre invokes a "you" with which it contends on the scale of the poem as a whole. Basing the ode, specifically, in the trope, de Man rather astutely makes the form exemplary of the genre: "The figure of address is recurrent in lyric poetry, to the point of constituting the generic definition of, at the very least, the ode (which can, in its turn, be seen as paradigmatic for poetry in general)" ("Hypogram" 32). (He of course refers to the kind of lyric that situates itself at the terminus of the perceptual process.)[28] The elegy is likewise central in elaborating a "you" it invokes. Once a generic song of praise concerned predominantly with love, elegiac verse was recast in the seventeenth century as a form dedicated to the honoring of the dead. In lauding the deceased, it too posits an absent object of address as present, employing apostrophe to this end, a technique that consoles by revivifying. The anaphoric "ubi sunt" structure common to the lament marks yet another elegiac means of rendering absence, in this case through rhetorical inquiry into the location of the absented. Orpheus's emblematic turn is a literal attempt to make present that in its failure necessitates the resort to poetic invocation.

The object of odic and elegiac address is by convention, indeed by definition, an object of exaltation. To elevate an "object" through praise is another way of summoning it. As all such summons, it betrays existential anxiety: the vocative is intimately intertwined with the fear of the loss of the object invoked; the object is reinforced as object in order to prevent the mutual and contemporaneous dissolution of its complementary subject. What strikes one as overreach is rather an attempt to fix the object as a means of self-preservation. Praise and its suasive motions are one of many lyric exertions that function—as all actions do—as a form of thirdness, bringing the organism into a more salutary alignment with its environment. Action toward an object adjusts the subject's relationship to the object, furthering their connection at the same time it maintains the fiction of their separation. The plethora of poems (courtly and non-courtly) fueled by desire, the fundamental optative mode of lyric,[29] also betray this preservationist motive in their reliance on encomium to [re]mediate, as do prayers, which propitiate, praising to effect an immortalizing reunion with God. In the psychology of perception, behind the awakening effected or intensified by praise, behind every elegy, ode, prayer, and love song loiters the fear of one's own death, a fear that is perceptually rooted and spawns the intense reaction of venturing to forestall self-loss by preserving, if only by proxy, the presence of the other.

To avert loss, praise may aspire overtly to eternalize the other: Horatian odes thus secure the "divine" status of exalted leaders; earlier Pindaric versions of the form deify nonpareil athletic prowess in forging (in both senses of the word) a divine lineage for the hero at the fleeting moment of youthful excellence as a stay against its certain decomposition. Courtly love enshrines an instance of supreme beauty in paying worship to a beloved who "holds in perfection but a little moment" (2).[30] Paul de Man captures both the poetic means of forestalling self-loss and its motivation when he opines that the hermeneutics of lyric is distinguished by "the uneasy combination of funereal monumentality with paranoid fear" ("Anthropomorphism" 259). Heidegger saw the poetic word as initiative of death in its "shattering" of earth into world. In interpreting his theory of this inevitability, Gianni Vattimo urges that this transition to the point of tragic separation instituting morbidity (68–9) occurs for Heidegger not, as is commonly thought, at the moment the word surrenders its innate earthliness to reference and discloses the world, but rather at the point it *evokes* world from earth, achieving a relational "positioning *in proximity*" (69) (emphasis added). The functional concepts "I" and "you" are artificial, worldly, as it were; their scission purchases autonomy, a condition that, per Gregory Bateson (whose work is addressed below), is paired with death (117–18) in introducing its inevitability. This shattering into pronominal fixities is the point at which identification becomes possible: "*Ein 'ist' ergibt sich wo das Wort zerbricht*" (An "is" arises where the word breaks up) (Heidegger qtd. in Vattimo 65). By its nature, it is the point of prophecy's realization (68), the end of the poetic foreboded by Bachelard's presentiment. Poetry lives in fear of what it exposes, a fear it simultaneously assuages: lament consoles—praise celebrates, and thus consoles.

The making permanent of the other through praise and/or the other's identification with longed-for ideals is, then, a means of safekeeping that attempts to remediate solitariness. Yet, such moves also jeopardize the co-constructed society. One praises to lure and to hold, yet paradoxically fortifies a stubborn duality in the tacit admission that it demands mediation, whether by praise or by gaze. In consoling himself by turning to see Eurydice, Orpheus objectifies and loses her, which proves to be his undoing. Simone Weil cryptically reassures us the object is constant in spite of the unbearable absence of the possessing gaze to which he succumbs: "Attachment is no more or less than an insufficiency in our sense of reality. We are attached to the possession of a thing because we think that if we cease to possess it, it will cease to exist" (59). Eurydice continues to exist, but in Hades, within and of the earth, unavailable to sight. As a result of Orpheus's banishment from his marriage, he will sing into being a new "you," which will prompt his own death, continuing the cycle of poetry. Exile and its repetitions are folded in to the poetic-perceptual dynamic.

So-called private odes often strive to secure immortality, or at the least an extension of mortality, for their poet-speakers by alternative means, pursuing merger with the object as a means of repairing a perceptual breach. Keats's speaker of "Ode to a Nightingale" yearns to identify with the unself-conscious, undying bird while ruefully conceding the futility of his quest. Wordsworthian Romanticism bends the form, making the child's first experience praiseworthy in a psychological attempt to recover a past, unself-aware "you" ("thou happy Shepherd-boy"[31]), yet ends resigned to the impossibility of reconciliation with an earlier mode of being. The courtly lover pursues a quasi-physical, quasi-spiritual union with his beloved. Neither are these framings atypical: the apostrophic object is of necessity unself-conscious and, as such, represents not only an elusive "you" but also one less removed from a state of embeddedness a speaker might wish to emulate.

Even at the quintessentially Western end of the spectrum in which independence is privileged over interdependence, poetry understands that the "you" is constructed as the "I" is constructed and vice versa, not simply as byproducts of one another, but as vital, codetermined consequences of the brain's and the mind's fracturing of a continuity. Lyric gives rise to a homologous process, or at least some phase of it, bringing the two limits into mutual relief. In each case, useful distinctions permit their mediation in the form of acting: praising, grasping, singing, and so on. The ability to distinguish the self from the nonself facilitates the self-sustaining actions of the organism into the environment that in negotiating the relation between the subject and object forms, bridge them. (The nuances and relevance of the neurology of action and the action of lyric will be addressed in the final chapter, but for now I return to the supposition of Varela's enactionism, that percept and action are folded into a single event (173).) Though lyric is compelled toward this division, the complete severance of entities that are materially embedded is, as noted, illusory. Yet, the stubbornness of these eventual destinations is evidenced in the set of drives that attempt to span the "dumbfoundering abyss" to maintain the object's continuity with the subject, to remain present with the object in order to remedy isolation and to ward off death, attempts that in the end ensure the confrontation with it. Or as de Man asserts with the aphoristic profundity often reserved for the footnote: "We do not see what we love but we love in the hope of confirming the illusion that we are indeed seeing anything at all" ("Hypogram" 33fn.).

The Nesting of Lyric "Minds": Poet, Poem, Reader

Thus far in this chapter, I have been concerned with the emergent play of secondness within the poem and its possible culmination in the distinguishing of the first- and second-person pronouns as an analogue of the activity of perception. (Although the poem may assume this ultimate distinction from the get-go, it nevertheless enacts its emergence, which the reader may encounter subsequently.) Yet, the lyric impulse gives rise to another entity, and that is the reader, who may or may not be considered in the critical lingo to be "ideal." Beyond the poem lurks another presence critical to the genre's dynamic. As T. S. Eliot asks,

> Who is the third who walks always beside you?
> When I count, there are only you and I together
> . . .
> —But who is that on the other side of you? (*Waste Land* 360–1, 366)

These lines from *The Waste Land* enacting—one might say willing—the transcendence of aridity, spiritual and otherwise, may be interpreted to express a central problematic of the genre: the role of the reader within a complex system of address, the triangulation born of her discrimination from the fictive addressee that is the lyric "you." The receiver of the poem, the "eavesdropper" onto Mill's overheard utterance, is a ghostly third, present but not countable, integral, but not integer, a figure implied by the poem's private, pronominal interchange, but not of it. Even in those rare instances in which a reader is addressed directly and thus conflated with the "you," he or she becomes the object constructed by the poem, and not its actual, or even its implied, reader. The reader figured as "you" must be construed to be different from the receiver of the poem.

To bring this spectral yet essential figure into the dynamic of lyric and to extend the claim for the layering of poetic perception onto perception proper into one for an homologous relationship between perception and poem, I turn to the work of Gregory Bateson. In his *chef d'oeuvre, Mind and Nature*, Bateson calls for an understanding of systems as derivative of the larger systems they constitute. Positing an origin and a dynamic common to mind proper (and its implicate, the brain)[32] and the encompassing system of nature within which it nests, he defines "mind" broadly, forging a grand science, ecological in its essence: "It is the Platonic thesis of the book that epistemology is an indivisible, integrated metascience whose subject matter is the world of evolution, thought, adaptation, embryology, and genetics—the science of mind in the widest sense of the word" (81–2). The pervasiveness of the dynamic Bateson defines as epistemological, along with its ability to embed subsidiary epistemologies, accounts for the lyric's intimation of a "mind" beyond—yet enfolded into—its own. In so doing, it explains why the confrontation with the lyric invites something of a lopsided *ménage à trois*.

For Bateson, nature (whose dynamic is evolutionary) as ur-mind and its constituent minds are defined based on two criteria: (1) that they are stochastic systems, that is, subject to statistically analyzable chance events, and (2) that said events are ordered subsequently by selective processes that constrain randomness (139). For instance, random processes induce mutations in nature that may be subsequently selected for as a phenotype interacts with an environment[33] (45). As with respect to the mind proper, the randomness driving evolution is generated at the interface of organism and environment: "In sum, the combination of phenotype and environment thus constitutes the random component of the stochastic system that *proposes* change; the genetic state *disposes*, permitting some changes and prohibiting others" (168). Selection is then the mechanism through which proposed or potential changes are actualized, for instance, in the genetic preservation of a mutation.

If the chromosome is the gateway of chance occurrence within evolution, the place where mutations are admitted as difference through their genetic coding, the point of initial registration of new sensory input is its homologue. Within both the system of nature and the subsystem of the mind proper, the registration of difference triggers a threshold-dependent operation of secondness[34] (27). As Bateson puts it, *the difference must matter* (78) (emphasis added), that is, its admission must prompt interaction among the mind's components (85). The registration of *significant* difference is in each case the first step in the creation of information, which in a physical system incurs the literal meaning of "formation within."

> A world of sense, organization, and communication is not conceivable without discontinuity, without threshold. If sense organs can receive news only of difference, and if neurons either fire or do not fire, then threshold becomes necessarily a feature of how the living and mental world is put together. (189)

Difference so-registered must then be assimilated into a system. The next of Bateson's criteria for mind is the coding, or transformation, of the difference initiated within what becomes in consequence an information-processing entity (64, 66). Difference is converted to information once it is incorporated into a circuitry in which it sets off "trains of consequence" (102). Bateson cites Alfred North Wallace's example of a steam engine governor in which the input entering a circuit creates information within the circuit. The governor serves as a simple example of a positive feedback system, one that generates its own parameters and is capable of incorporating them into its subsequent functioning.[35] In nature, the encoding of genetic difference triggers a consequence manifesting as an altered phenotype, which then inhabits its environs differently, altering it; in the brain, the encoding of difference in the form of a receptor neuron firing activates trains of consequences through the invigoration of neural pathways that influence the progressively more complex networks activated in turn. In the like-minded system of poetry, precipitating difference is admitted as the chosen senses of language that repercuss within the poem's progressively larger units, informing them.

The final piece of Bateson's theory mandates a "hierarchy of orders of recursiveness" that permits the emergence, and at length the preservation, of the change that is the mutation or the new percept, the "learning" in which epistemological operations culminate (188). (The species-level equivalent of the learning enabled by neuronal plasticity is the preservation of genetic change.) Each level of the hierarchy through which information ascends sees a shift to what Bateson calls a different "logical type," a metamessage "about the coding" of its predecessor that is a means of interpreting a received message (106–7). For example, a phenotype is a means of interpreting a change in a genotype that is typologically different from it. The dynamic by which the brain forms a coherent sense of a subject and an object is just such an emergent process: subsequently, more complex neural nets congeal as they interpret the significance of the input received from lower-level neuronal activity. To enable the emergence into a new logical type, Bateson mandates the following additional criteria for "mind": (1)

it must involve vast numbers of interconnections between functionally heterogeneous units; and (2) the connections themselves must be reciprocal, enabling both top-down and bottom-up functioning (167). Embodying a much more complex, distributed system of connectivity than Wallace's illustrative governor, the brain's perceptual hierarchy fulfills these requirements, enabling a myriad of top-down and bottom-up interactions. While a lesser number of opportunities for reciprocal connection is given by the segmented and scaling units of lyric, the genre's architectures also permit the creation of new "logical types."

Bateson explicitly confirms that perception fulfills the requirements of "mind" in and of itself: "The thrust of my argument is that the very process of perception is an act of logical typing. Every image is a complex of many-leveled coding and mapping" (178). To elucidate the means by which information ascends through a hierarchy of logical types within perception, I turn to the understanding of olfaction cultivated by the hybrid field of neurodynamics founded by Walter Freeman. Informed by nonlinear dynamic systems (i.e., chaos) theory, Freeman's work elucidates the co-constructive mechanism by which the sensory systems engage the world. His studies are illustrative for present purposes because olfaction is both analogous to the other sensory systems and simpler than they. It is also evolutionarily primary, the system upon which the intentionality of the other sensory systems is built (*Brains* 67), and close to the memory loops of the limbic system, making smell an especially evocative sense modality. Finally, olfaction implicates the poetic medium and vehicle of the breath, thereby explicating the inextricability of poetry from sensation.

Freeman's theory of the workings of olfaction reproduced here exposes the dynamic manner in which the brain creates metamessages as it ascends a hierarchy ranging from the firing of a single neuron to the mass action of cortex-wide neuronal assemblies. In the earliest stages of olfaction, sense receptor neurons lining the nose are engaged as they capture a scent molecule for which they have a preexisting affinity. Here, as in general, neurons specialize: each has evolved to detect the particular range of odors that is its receptive field. The relatively few neurons activated by a given odorant form a pattern over the closely packed sheet of nasal neurons that Freeman calls an "aggregate" (*Brains* 67). Due to the turbulent flow of inhaled air and the highly individualized repertoires of the receptor neurons, each encounter with a stimulus, no matter how ideal the conditions under which it is generated, produces an entirely new aggregate pattern formed in part by chance as air currents swirl unpredictably within the nose (68). The quantity of energy transmitted by the nasal neurons following contact with an odorant, however, remains proportional to the quantity of energy absorbed from the environment (67). (One hears echoes of Olson's pegging of energy as the consistent, highly transferable medium of what is in consequence a physical act of poetic creation: "A poem is energy transferred from where the poet got it ... by way of the poem itself to, all the way over to, the reader" (16).) The pulses the receptors will subsequently transmit to the brain carry neither information nor meaning, which, as Bateson also notes, will emerge in time, and in no way represent the odorant (*Brains* 67). From this early stage in sensation, there is no consistent correlation between odor and aggregate pattern, and thus no firm basis for a correspondence theory of truth (67).

The sense receptor neurons comprising the aggregate then transmit the energy they have organized via their output arms, or axons, to the next way station along the olfactory pathway—the olfactory bulb—where they excite awaiting bulbar neurons (*Brains* 68). This juncture sees the ascent from a microscopic dynamic involving the activity of single neurons to what Freeman calls a mesoscopic level, a critical shift to an intermediate phase of neuronal interaction involving population behavior. The aggregate pattern is transported from the nose to the bulb on the breath; as it is relayed, it is met by "background" activity generated by the random firing of bulbar neurons from which it elicits a bulb-wide burst of synchronous oscillation (*Societies* 59; *Brains* 71–2). If exposure to an odorant is sufficiently sustained, the elevated activity level induces the preexistent nerve assemblies of the bulb to exhibit a common waveform called an "amplitude modulation" or "AM" pattern. The oscillating motion of the AM pattern is born of the synchronized alternation of the excitation and the inhibition of bulbar neurons. (Excitation occurs when neuronal outflow increases the activity of a receiving, or postsynaptic, neuron, inhibition when neuronal outflow decreases or suppresses the activity of a receiving neuron.) An increase in gain—the ratio of output to input at a synapse—tends to occur at synapses between neurons that excite one another preferentially as a consequence of past learning.[36] In other words, these synapses and clusters of synapses, or nuclei, generate output that is disproportionate to the input received as a result of previous exposure to it, thereby increasing efficiency. The gain in output then prompts a positive feedback cycle—a progressive amplification of input—that generates the pervasive AM patterns, as different frequencies from the bulb, nucleus, and olfactory cortex interact (69–81). The AM patterns—a new logical type in that they interpret the aggregate pattern—graph as a chaotic attractor, that is, they are attracted to a limited, coherent (and thus identifiable) range of behavior that is nevertheless unpredictable within said range (Crutchfield et al. 50–2, 53).

Freeman interprets his findings to signify that what gives form to the AM pattern is not the scent molecules themselves, but individual history written in synaptic assemblies affiliated by previous learning about stimuli (*Brains* 78). "Because of the contributions from past experience, [the AM patterns] are aspects of the meanings of the stimuli, holding in the animal that has constructed them" (78). They are the means "by which an animal 'in-forms' itself as to what to do with or about an odorant" (89) based on its history with it. In other words, AM patterns embody the past significance of the stimuli to the organism (*Brains* 78). As such, they are a different logical type, a means of interpreting the nose's coding of the odorant, of reviving, or "re-collecting" perceptual history as dynamic pattern in the presence of admitted difference.

A second function of the oscillating bulbar burst is to insure the coherence of the message sent to the next rung on the hierarchy—the olfactory cortex. As transpires ideally in any hierarchy, successive levels of neuronal assemblies along sensory pathways receive information broadly from numerous sources on a need-to-know basis. A single receiver is contacted by multiple senders, thousands in this case, at the same time a single sender targets multiple recipients (*Brains* 83–4). AM patterns are transmitted from the bulb to the olfactory cortex by means of such a divergence-convergence, or branching tactic that effectively eliminates the original aggregate pattern formed in the nose, which is "ironed out" so to speak, in what Freeman calls a "laundering operation" outlived only by the common waveform (*Societies* 60). The olfactory system thereby elevates signal from background noise, that is, it distinguishes a meaningful percept from a "recept" (*Societies* 58–61). The more expansive neuronal assemblies of the cortex will spin, or chaotically reorganize, input from the olfactory cortex where the individual's history with similar input, as written in the synaptic assemblies (the way that groups of neurons have learned to respond), will continue to give percepts form. The brain thereby reshapes itself, "making" sense of sense data by contextualizing them within the attractors encoding its history, thereby rendering the original sense datum unintelligible in and of itself. The organism's past experience dominates the classification of new input, constraining it from the top down. In other words, the brain's imposition of a new logical type replaces original input. To summarize, the brain must thoroughly decompose and reconstitute the raw sense data it collects before it can apprehend them. It formalizes meaning by bringing known, relevant information to bear on stimuli unknowable as they are (*Brains* 82) based on a pragmatic accountability to the history of the value of the stimuli (or those like it) and their consequences to the organism.

In quantifying changes in neural complexity, the neuroscientist Gerald Edelman arrives at the same conclusion as Freeman:

> Extrinsic signals convey information not so much in themselves, but by virtue of how they modulate the intrinsic signals exchanged within a previously experienced neural system. In other words, a stimulus acts not so much by adding large amounts of external information that need to be processed as it does by amplifying the intrinsic information resulting from neural interactions selected and destabilized by memory through previous encounters with the environment. (Edelman and Tononi 137)

Edelman, who also relies on the principles of nonlinearity in his information systems approach to the brain's dynamics,[37] hypothesizes a "dynamic core," a complex system of linkages integrating perception and action throughout the extensive network known as the thalamocortical system (Edelman and Tononi 42). This "dynamic core" is functional for precisely the reason that poetry is, because it is both highly integrated and highly differentiated into smaller "functional clusters" (146). As the preponderance of perceptual information is generated by the unique history of the organism, Edelman calls the scene of perceptual experience the "remembered present" (*Remembered* 78, 138).[38]

As perception attunes a single organism to its boundless surround, it enables interaction between disproportionate physicalities. Its workings are an effective means of embodying stimuli and endowing them with meaning that is delimited and personalized so that the individual organism may comprehend those aspects of the environment relevant to itself. The manner in which patterns emerge within perception allows for the classification of input in terms of preexisting categories and thus category maintenance (memory) as well as the categorical plasticity necessary to the productive confrontation with novelty (learning). The nonlinear dynamic described by complexity theory gives rise to patterns that are coherent, yet unpredictable: in amplifying initial uncertainties by means of a recursive dynamic, attractors can both regularize discrepant input and characterize novel response (Crutchfield et al. 50–3). When initial input cannot be absorbed into a preexisting attractor, the basin of attraction (the set of initial circumstances that will evolve to a particular attractor) "moves over," that is, modifies itself to make room for a new one[39] (Nicolis and Tsuda 216).

Complexity was a nascent science as Bateson went to press, its dynamics not yet verifiable within the brain. However, the advent of typological shift driving the emergence of "mind" that Bateson tags as essential may be attributed, retrospectively, to nonlinearity, a concept explicating the commonplace that the emergent whole is more than the sum of its parts. Each chaotic reorganization reinterprets input rather than merely aggregating it. As chaotic activity generates order from randomness, it is also a means of characterizing novelty born of the interaction with the larger, enveloping system that feeds into the subordinate mind, a commerce both dramatized within and offered by poems.

While a chaotic explanation of the cohesiveness and versatility of categories is, strictly speaking, not extendable to poetry, the processing of verse is recursive in the loose sense that it entails the feeding of units into larger units. Like the brain, the poem capacitates the ascension through a hierarchy that ranges from the sensory registration of particles of sound to the active assignment of meaning. Each level of the hierarchy is interpreted by higher levels, gaining significance within the context it informs, within a complex of meaning given by a linguistic memory. For instance, the word "rush" recurrent in Hopkins's octave informs, in ways beyond the syntactical, the line in which it appears ("The descending blue; that blue is all in a rush" (7)), enriching one's understanding of spring blue, and thus the octave, at the same time its meaning to the poem emerges as it is contextualized within line and octave. As argued, the word also informs the whole of the sestet (the overall message of which is to drink in spring's bounty quickly, before its imminent loss), a neural "net" of sorts that in turn categorizes the word "rush," adapts it to its own purposes, reinforcing itself while expanding the classification "spring." As in the brain, poetic interactions across scale may transpire in either a top-down or a bottom-up direction. At the same time units inform others, they are granted meaning within those units that absorb them. Since the poem is linguistic, the contexts into which new, unexpected units of language are integrated are also in a sense remembered contexts embodying the meanings of the language that have accumulated historically, both abstractly, with respect to language itself (i.e., within the poem as mind), and concretely, with respect to the reader who remembers while processing the poem.[40] Established meaningful networks of sense are reinforced by familiar input, refreshed by input that is vaguely familiar, and reformed when necessary to accommodate input to which they are unaccustomed, all with the end of enabling reference, the designation of an object by acting upon it. While the processing of lyric is not identical to the processing of perceptual information, the genre reserves for itself a similar means of making meaning and clearly recapitulates Bateson's abstraction of the epistemological mechanism he identifies as "mind." That said, a full account of the dynamics via which the units of lyric interact awaits another book.

As new order emerges in the ascension through logical types, the brain also generates firstness internally. Instances of secondness recurring at each level of scale are mediated by higher-level patterns interpreting them, local instances of thirdness, what Peirce defines as that which spans seconds by way of relating them ("Guess" 249). As Dickinson (whose use of disintegrative techniques is extreme) avers in Poem 320 excerpted in the epigraph to this chapter, embodied difference is the site at which meaning arises, taking the form of an indelible, mediating "scar," a remainder, or trace. Difference makes space for mediation and thus the reception of meaning. Thirdness is the means of interpreting the encoding of difference, what Bateson calls a new logical type (87). These manifestations of thirdness, transient but recallable, themselves exist in a relationship of *firstness* with respect to the higher-level interpretations they inform in a process that plays out at each rung of the hierarchy until the percept and the poem finally evolve to become a singular act of intercession between the absolute first and last, an ultimate third in the form of a mutation, an action, a poem, or an interpretation thereof. In its execution, thirdness is a mode of apprehension, of grasping in its literal and figurative senses—a bringing into the province of the understanding.[41] Within perception, action toward an object conciliates the polar tension between the percept and the perception of the self, between the object and the organism. In inscribing traumatic separation or in the threatening, or the foreboding of its inscription, the poem as a whole also becomes a mediating act. The poetic value of unity and the poetic presence of identifiable pronominal constructs correlate with one another because their relationship is one of bidirectional cause and effect. The poem is unified as the action that intercedes between the "I" and the "you," solidifying them as such: action in its singular form is necessarily unified, whether or not it takes on the quality a dancer would call "connected."

In positing their ultimate, common origin in the natural world, Bateson's theory secures a homologous rather than simply an analogous relationship between minds. Reading his linking of the mind proper and the nature in which it is integrated through the lens of Peirce, one might say that the homologous nature of their connection secures a new external source of firstness for the former, one inherent in its relation to the larger, encasing "mind" of nature. As each system is itself emergent, it replenishes the font of firstness that will inform the system it embeds, thereby deriving it. The mind proper will renew firstness through its substrate's own active mediation of internal seconds, generating the potential that will accost the system it embeds (in the present theory the poem).[42] Inspired by fresh perception, this poetic successor mind is embedded in a creative mental act in this most basic, perceptual sense. As the poem taps a source of firstness in the brain it then realizes through the internal regeneration of secondness, it gives rise to an emergent mediation of its own. As such, it functions as an authentic source of firstness for the reader it implies and lodges. The poem thus postulates a new mind confronting the fountainhead of potential it offers, the figure that is Eliot's third.

Throughout the concatenation of "minds" nesting within nature—the hypothetical or actual perceiving mind, the poem, and its interpretation—ultimate thirdness infuses the lower-level event with firstness at the site of their connection, recapitulating the opportunity to select significant difference. A mediation manifest as a phenotype is an interpretation of the coding of genetic difference that enables the refreshing of the environment as a source of firstness with respect to perception. The percept inspirational to the writing of the poem and implied by it, whether real or hypothetical, sees the mediation of the poet and his environment in the action of writing the poem. As the poem is linguistic, it supplies its own environment (the material poem) and source of firstness for the speaker as well as its own mediation of difference in an actual and/or a codified linguistic utterance. The material poem inclusive of such mediation in turn serves as an environment for the reader: the interpretative action performed on the part of the reader mediates herself and the poem. While Peirce conceives of firstness as a semantic source and names it first, it is as much a product of meaning-making within a system deriving minds.

Within the forging of this homologic chain, the poem's origination in the bewildering confrontation with firstness that prompts a perceptually based poetic is reflected in the topos of singing within a radically new environs. The mythic recurrence of the regression of the poet-figure to bird form, his verse to bird song, points also to the emergence of new mind, to the fact that the mind that sings is qualitatively different—a new logical type within a new locale. The sudden removal of the Kaluli boy into the afterlife and Philomela Nightingale's sentence to a treetop niche as sudden events punctuating the ordinary give rise to the circumstances in which new mind emerges and thereby establish the poem as a mind. All lyric poetry is, in this sense, "occasional," that is, referable to a specific, prompting occasion of *ecstasis*, or a moving out of from the dormancy that is one's status and into the new embodiment a different "type" of mind demands. Lyric, in contradistinction to other art forms, displaces the singer in acknowledgment of the intrinsic typological difference of the song.

Lyric as a mind in the act of finding might then be said to be the medium of medium formation, an ur-medium, if you will. Bateson's mandate that minds be understood within the broader systems with which they interact serves not merely to secure an epistemological bond between neurology and the workings of lyric—it explicates the way that perception subsumes the lyric operation that recapitulates it.

The chart below schematizes the nesting of the minds in question, beginning with nature and ending with the reader's interpretation of the poem, particularly the way that firstness, secondness, and thirdness arise within and between each.

1. Mind of Nature

    Firstness = Potential generated at interface of organism and environment
    Secondness = Genetic encoding of difference, *emerges to*
    New phenotypes set in relation to environment
    Thirdness = Action within environment by new phenotype, altering environment *becomes*
    NEW ENVIRONMENT FOR MIND 2

2. Mind as Perceptual Event, Hypothetical or Actual, of Poet

    Firstness = Potential generated at interface of poet and environment
    Secondness = Selection and encoding of stimuli and their effects through contrast mechanisms, *emerges to*
    Poet in relation to environment perceived
    Thirdness = The generated utterance of the poem as a physical action, *becomes*
    NEW ENVIRONMENT FOR MIND 3

3. Mind of the Poem

    Firstness = Potential generated at interface of the "I," speaker, or voice of the poem and the materiality of the poem
    Secondness = Selection and processing of stimuli (as senses of words) through disjunctive lyric techniques, *emerges to*
    "I" in relation to perceived "you"
    Thirdness = The poem itself, as a linguistic action, *becomes*
    NEW ENVIRONMENT FOR MIND 4

4. Mind of the Receiver

    Firstness = Potential generated at interface of the receiver of the poem and the poem as linguistic environment
    Secondness = Selection and processing of stimuli in the form of semantic difference in process of interpretation, *emerges to*

Mind of reader in relation to poem perceived
Thirdness = The interpretive action assigning meaning

One key takeaway from this concatenation of nested minds in which the lyric sits (apart from the revelation that the brain may be regarded as inherently poetic) is that the reader is clearly situated beyond the I/You relationship delivered by the poem. In effect, the verbal action that mediates this poetically codified relationship serves as an environment for the reader, who is thus not conflatable with the "you," but rather the third point of a triangle situated opposite these pronominal constructs. Though the reader dwells beyond the poem that is her textual environment in overhearing or "overlooking" it, she is compelled to engage with it according to a co-constructive perceptual dynamic, and is therefore embedded in it. The mediation of the "you" and its complementary "I" gestures out to initiate yet another instance, another level of perception, not only because it is literally perceived in the course of its reading or hearing but also because it is packaged to insure its processing in the manner that environments are perceived. As such, the poem positions an incidental reader beyond and before it, enframing her as she engages with it. The poem perceived at length becomes a "you" constructed by the reader. It is not enough to say that the reader enters into or even constructs the text, or, conversely, that the text enters the reader. The operations figured in these expressions transpire in the reading of nonpoetic texts—those abstracted from their embeddedness—and can refer solely to the qualitative experience of reading. The poetic text a reader integrates exposes the ways and means of its "minding" in order to prompt a homologous act on her part. For present purposes, the process of lodging minds one within the other concludes as the final interpretant the reader constructs. The interpretation of poetry is in most cases a terminal event in the chain of lyric reading as it does not offer an environment to be newly perceived. One might, of course, interpret an interpretation, a process assuming its analysis. Critical work may and often does require glossing: it may feature lyrical islands, archipelagoes even, but critical response takes the characteristic form of a Batesonian mind only in the rarest of cases.

The positioning of the reader as a mind exterior to the poem's dynamic but fitted to it explains the insight that the lyric is "overheard." For Jahan Ramazani, the possibility of its overhearing renders it social, as even within the most private of its manifestations, for instance, as prayer: "the circuit of speech is never closed; at the very least, a fissure is opened for the … eavesdropping other" (Ramazani 129). Yet, despite the poem's subtle invitation to enter, it remains the most personal or private of genres, the one least likely to divulge its meaning, because the reader assimilates and reconstructs the poem in "perceiving" it. What becomes impossible to access and to replicate is the experience articulated by the poet or by the poem itself, depending on one's critical sensibility, which becomes a choice of "mind" in the hierarchy. The reader's experience with the poem is qualitatively different from that of the "I" or the poet because the reader is situated differently from either figure, including in a historical sense, and because she is embedded in the poem of the mind in a way readers of other kinds of texts ultimately are not. We are here closing in on the problem of other minds: one has access to the actions, verbal and otherwise, arising from minds and not minds themselves. Yet, a door remains ajar, first because the genre's features make possible the embedding of the reader's experience in that of its source minds (the dynamics giving rise to private experience are available, reduplicated), and second because the active poem, the poem as action that is the environment for the reader is also the record of a perception of the mind that is "of" the poem. The poem is an action, an experience, a material artifact. Gianni Vattimo interprets Heidegger to say that poetry is not "subjective self-reference," but rather a trace of one's self offered as a "monument" affording access to others (Vattimo 73). Perhaps this is one reason lyric prompts such aggrandizing claims for its role as a purveyor of truth. The closest we can come to entering the mind of another is through the assimilation of another's *cognitive* situatedness to our own, the "minding" that poetry permits, a term that brings with it connotations of care and, in turn, responsibility.

In stressing the poem's correlation with, indeed, its status as, an environment with which another mind might interact, a new basis for the materiality of lyric language may be cultivated. Understanding it as such accounts for the alternate conceptions of poetic language as imagistic, expressive, and material, while lending support to the inevitability of the copresence of these modes: the dividing of these concepts and the allying of them with theoretical stances, a partitioning of camps that hearkens back at least to the French symbolists, is a matter of preference and emphasis that in no way loosens their entwinement. Each aspect of the perceptual transaction has always been of the poem, if theorized only belatedly.

Perceptual and Poetic Iconicity

The manner in which a percept signifies objects in the world is complex, engaging all three of the types of signs Peirce delineated. While the relationship of a stimulus to an object of perception is strictly metonymic (the scent molecule indexes the decomposing corpse), the relationship of the *percept* to the object it signifies is manifold in nature. In one sense, the percept is a symbol, a "learned" construct of the material being of the perceiver that represents a reality from which it itself differs substantively. In subsuming action, the percept is indexical, as action engages causally with objects. The sign is finally iconic in maintaining the structure of an environment. Uexküll observed early on that what are preserved from *Umwelt* to *Umwelt* as acts of meaning-making unfold—and as a result possess objective consistency—are the structures of meaning carriers (31), objects whose potential meaning to percipients is actualized as they are perceived and acted upon (36)). To explain the way that perception aligns embodied, transduced, and reorganized sensory input with the environment, Joaquín Fuster revivifies the psychological concept of a gestalt. Discarding the term's nativist baggage, he adopts it to account for the isomorphism of referent and percept that is conserved despite the isolation and transduction of stimuli and the radical dissimilarities between a physical object and the perceptual medium in which it is represented. "What defines a gestalt or the percept of an object is [*sic*] the relationships between its elements (and between them and the background), not the absolute values of those elements in terms of frequency, length, pitch, hue, or what not" (90). What he calls "cognits" are posterior cortical networks activated within perception, internal gestalts that mirror the structures of objects in the environment (91). In a theory influenced by Freeman, Fuster posits that cognits are activated when a match is detected between their internal relationships and those of the object (91–2), which match in effect categorizes the object. Visual cognits, especially, "retain topological relations with the objects they represent"[43] (97) because vision confers relative spatial information via the parallel (i.e., simultaneous) processing of input. (The other sensory systems tend rather to process information serially (92): Freeman's account of olfaction is not concerned with the necessity of preserving structure in part because the modality imparts little such information.[44]) The complexity of the relations vision registers and reveals may be among the reasons it is conceived in its metaphorical tenor to be emblematic of poetry. It is Stevens once again who characterizes the iconic nature of poetic representation: "The accuracy of accurate letters is an accuracy with respect to the structure of reality" (*Angel* 71), where "reality" is both internal and external.

What perception chiefly retains of the environment is its configuration.[45] Indeed, a neurological mechanism that altered the structural attributes of objects, such as their shape, size, and relative location, would prove maladaptive in hindering interaction with them. Access to structural attributes grants functionality.[46] While there is a sense in which physical reality is obscured in its construal, a formal accuracy of representation is necessary to facilitate the negotiation of an environment, the grasping of significance, literally and figuratively, through symbolic processes such as thought. A structural iconicity, if you will, is based on perception's preservation of the junctures at which features are segmented from other features, and objects from other objects, information that permits both the internal distinctions upon which object recognition depends and the bringing of figure into relief against ground (Fuster 88). In his seminal work relocating the study of perception to the natural setting in which organisms act and perceive, J. J. Gibson lays emphasis on those features of the environment with which perception is most concerned, the disjunctions providing the organism "affordances." Affordances are those aspects of the environment available for the organism's use (39–40, 127–8). For example, the discernment of an object's boundary affords its handling, the discernment of the features of a face affords the recognition of friend or foe, the discernment of a brink affords not falling off a cliff (127–8). The axiom that "perception is the perception of difference" is based on the fact that the faculty places inordinate stress on distinction making, precisely because it enables successful action.

It is finally the poem's structural replication of objective delineations that justifies conceiving of it as an environment with respect to the mind of the poem and the mind of the reader.[47] Edges and brinks in the natural environment are analogous to the breaks and borders of the poem that themselves afford "grasping"; the environment the poem offers is elegant, streamlined in its tendency to self-shatter, and thereby to render the disjunction with which the mind is adaptively coupled. The reader may enjoy a personal, qualitative experience of poetic sound and sense, but she experiences the breaks as they are, making use of them as she will. The lyric poem has been exposed as a "mind" mirroring the divisions of an environment it negotiates; chiastically, the poem is also an environs affording opportunities for the registration of difference to be processed "perceptually." The recognition of the coupling that leaves the poem both a perceptual record of a mind and the environment that mind has perceived then permits a sequent mind to regard the poem as an environment and to align itself with it. In lyric one might access, in however fictive a sense, if not other minds, the structural residue of their affairs.

In the end, one need resort to neither a scientific nor a semiotic justification of the nesting propensity of what Bateson calls minds in order to understand that the lyric assumes such nesting as a ramification of its vatic identity. The "illustrations" spun by St. John in Stevens's poem are mediating gestures whose primary purpose, as the prophet tells us, is not to represent objects, but to "help us face the dumbfoundering abyss/between us" and them (27). Yet, by virtue of negation and figurative substitution, they contribute to the "effect," if you will, of a firstness residing beyond the grasp of the crustacean mind (13–14). Revelation, by its nature, reveals nothing because the interpretation of the whole, necessarily obscured by the embedded mind delivering it, requires a fresh interpreting mind in a series configured as God, prophet, member of the laity. Rather than initiate us into the secret of the whole, vatic utterance reconceals it, and in so doing defers initiation in necessitating a new semiotic act. The nature of poetic mediation is revealed to be tenuous, gossamer in its proclivity to dissipate into a firstness framing and informing the ensuing "mind" the lyric tradition acknowledges.

Emerson's brand of idealism also understands that firstness is conserved through its regeneration as mind embeds mind. As he notes, a mind that does not avail itself of the nourishment accessible at points of communion with nature stalls at the dead end of unambiguous representation—of unqualified duality—in consequence of which, human fate is put into contest, rather than concert, with other fates, leading to the dead end of "parrying and defence"[48] ("Fate" 954). To circumnavigate this impasse and to generate novelty, Emerson not only puts himself back into nature but also conceives of his participation in nature as a thinking, a freedom (953) that embeds mind within mind. "It is not in us," he writes of mind, "but we are in it" (955): "truth come[s] to our mind" as "air to our lungs" and light "to our eyes" (955). Individual man is the part of Nature that thinks Nature, thinks on behalf of Nature, and his thought, as such, is inseparable from Nature's divinity (955, 956). Emerson's expansive view of cognition, "It is not mine or thine, but the will of all mind" (956), will be picked up and naturalized by Bateson, whom he anticipates, if in broad strokes.

It is in its embodiment of the acts of a mind embedded in the "like-minded" system of nature that the enduring, time-tested threads of lyric are knotted. By instigating thinking it acknowledges as embedded, lyric reenacts original creation, however one understands it, and is not itself subordinate to it, merely result or exemplar. Coleridge's creative secondary imagination indeed "echoes" the perceiving primary imagination ("the living Power and prime Agent of all human Perception"), "a repetition in the finite mind of the eternal act of creation in the infinite I AM," a repetition in "kind"[49] ("Biographia" 263).

The Inexhaustibility of Firstness

As the condition of firstness may be restored within perceptual acts in the search for alternative meanings, in this sense lyrical reading strategies are self-renewing, even within single interpretive acts. In theory firstness is depletable, but in practice it is rarely depleted. The claim that a poem must resist the intelligence only "almost successfully" does not entail the consequence that the intelligence drains it. Mourning is forbidden in Donne's "Valediction" because the condition inhering in the attachment of the lovers like a compass joined is constant, as it is within the poem. Firstness is not fully transcendable no matter how productive of duality in the form of their separation it becomes, but is ever refreshed, giving rise to the novel creation of distinction and remaining as a constitutional principle. Whitehead writes of the prehension:

> The definite ingression into a particular actual entity … is the evocation of determination out of indetermination. Potentiality becomes reality; and yet retains its *message of alternatives* which the actual entity has avoided. (Sherburne 22) (emphasis added)

We may choose to dismiss potential, but it remains as the options rejected in the execution of each creative act. This replenishment of the well of firstness serves to forestall the co-opting of poetry as raw material for other purposes, especially those of a political or propagandistic nature. Peirce understood the necessary coextension of the three moods as pervasive undercurrents impeding and driving hermeneutic response. In the words of Frye, "There is still a residual sense that something inexhaustible lies behind the other world of lyric, that it is good not merely to be there, but, as Ferdinand says at the masque in *The Tempest*, to remain there" ("Approaching" 36). Within the genre, epistemological frustration is indelible, or nearly so, depending on one's perspective and willingness to suffer enchantment, which may as well be enjoyed.

Peirce's triad is, of course, operative within other processes and milieux and does not in itself justify a perceptual dynamic. However, the lyric poem can safely be said to inscribe the complex interrelations of perceptual stages, forcing semiosis to be reenacted, step-by-step, by means of his three modes. The lyric renditions of potentiality in the forms of obscurity, music, and emotion; the genre's creation of meaning through formal disjunction and deixis terminating, possibly, in the distinction of the "I" and the "you"; and the diverse mediations of the same instantiate the interdependent modes in which lyric invests. Every lyric poem inscribes itself as a participant within this process of emergence. A particular poem may gravitate toward one end of the process or the other. Some enjoy its full gamut, while others do not, but each positions itself within the spectrum and assumes its full extent. If poetry absenting an "I" enacts the preliminary phases of apprehension and immerses the reader in them, it does so by way of emphasizing the organism's embeddedness and the early phases of the emergence from it. (It may nevertheless gesture toward a subject and its complement object that remain amorphous, unnamed.) Although bewilderment is proposed as an end in and of itself in certain postmodern poetics, a poem cannot maintain utter unintelligibility in the confrontation of mind with mind, or mind with new environment, as it were, try as it may. Even lyrics of this sort cannot be caged as separate beasts because they fall on a continuum that constitutes a category.

On the other hand, a poem with a relatively coherent subject and/or object creates the features of these "uses," the means by which their identification is made, through distinction making and its mediation, processes that draw from a firstness evincing the subject's embeddedness and permitting selection and the delineation of an environment. If there are not lingering mists out of which secondness can emerge, the features distinguished risk ossification. At that point, the contingent emergence of the self and the other has been arrested, and we and are no longer within the sites of lyric. That the object is presented as continuous with the subject prevents the poem from cohering fully as a manifestation of a singular and separate, bounded ipseity. When a consciousness regards itself as such, perception has reached a terminus in characterological stability, defined as the self abstracted and simplified into a set of traits predicated for the sake of establishing identity, the maintenance of which stabilizes social praxis. It is ancillary to my thesis that, to flirt with the precipice of biography, in which the self is no longer emergent from an environment that physically composes it, but is rather determined, or, conversely, to verge upon its counterpart, an utter obscurity that does not yield a degree of coherence, is to risk tipping off the lyric plateau.

Endeavors to replace the term "speaker" with "voice" and subsequent efforts to disembody voice amount to critical moves to avoid such narrative or dramatic characterization as against its tendency to gel. Poetry recognizes that the human is of the earth, the *humus* with which it is cognate, and evinces this recognition in conceiving of "verse" as a ploughing, an insemination of the soil with difference, in order to effect the complex emergence of the human from it. It is this inexhaustible proposition that lyric poetry offers and accepts.

Notes

1 Very often, neurotypical functioning is inferred by observing the effects of injury or disease upon what is in consequence an atypical brain.

2 Figuration is a new way of regarding the term figured. Also, see Robert J. Zatorre's article "Neural Specializations for Tonal Processing" for a cogent explanation of pitch processing in the right hemisphere.

3 Every potential state does not presume preexisting randomness; however, as the physical capture of stimuli is not completely within the control of the organism, relational firstness does. Varela emphasizes this random quality of potential.

4 As mentioned in the Introduction, I assume with Gerald Edelman that a structural correlation obtains as between the neurological substrate and the contents of consciousness.

5 One assumes Skarda means the structure of light as structured by the environment and as further structured by the sense organ, which would involve, minimally, the compression and inversion of the structure impacting the lens. The idea of a phenomenal fabric derives from and assumes J. J. Gibson's "ambient optic array." Stressing a natural model of perception in which light is the raw material of perception and not its object, the ambient optic array refers to the physicality—the physics—of the arrangement of light as it is available to the eye. See J. J. Gibson's *The Ecological Approach to Visual Perception* for a detailed treatment of the structures of light the environment affords the perceiver.

6 Small wavelength, or S cones respond maximally to wavelengths of 420 nanometers, M cones, 530 nm, and L cones, 560 nm.

7 If our percepts varied as the physical world varied, we would, among other things, experience stable objects differently. For instance, the same bush would appear to us to be different shades of green. The result of such instability would be the need for further effort to ascertain object permanence and possibly the mistaken inference that stable objects shift. If we recognized objects as stable despite their being mediated differently, we might still be led to question their stability. Such complex processing would be inefficient and interfere with our profitable responses to objects.

8 See footnote 5 of the Introduction.

9 For Skarda, the problem becomes, then, not how the structure of light is bound, but how it is preserved. That said, there is no dearth of theories proffered to solve the binding problem, that of where and how the features of the percept are unified. The team of Gray, Singer, and Eckhorn argues that perceptual unity is preserved through the synchronous firing of ever-larger neuronal networks so that the pattern is preserved as it is integrated into a distributed whole. Optican and Richmond hypothesize that higher-level neurons convey information from their

subordinates by integrating it into the temporal pattern of their discharge, which becomes the informational medium. For Joachín Fuster, perceptual binding is the "joint activation of all of a network's neurons." Joint activation is the synchronous "increase in the firing frequency of the neurons that constitute the network" (99). For Fuster, "High Frequency activity does not encode a cognit in a time code, but is a manifestation of the activation of a network that encodes the cognit in cortical space" (100, 103). Walter Freeman was the first to make the connection between high-frequency firing and binding. Each theory proposes a mechanism for the preservation of initial structure and the inference of a phenomenal fabric, which must necessarily remain an inference within the perceptual process. To date, by what mechanism discrete information is reassembled remains officially unresolved, but it is generally agreed that percepts are not bound in a dedicated place within the brain.

10 Shifters are terms whose referents are vague. They include personal and demonstrative pronouns, vague definite articles, spatial and temporal adverbs, and designations of the non-timeless present.

11 See footnote 20 of Chapter 1.

12 This is, of course, Keats's rather imprecise definition of "negative capability," a concept that is perhaps too blurry to equate with firstness or secondness, but which seems to accord with them nonetheless.

13 "Tenor" and "vehicle" are I. A. Richards's terms. "Target" and "source" are from Lakoff and Johnson's cognitive linguistic account of metaphor.

14 Empson regards ambiguity as a representation of internal conflict. See *7 Types of Ambiguity*.

15 Longenbach notes that the earliest surviving Western poetry is lineated (18).

16 Examples of this technique abound, for example, George Gershwin's "The Man I Love" performed by Sarah Vaughn.

17 That said, it is not necessary to register the contrast in either a progressively top-down or bottom-up direction as opportunities abound for bidirectional play in perception, in the poem itself, and in its experience. The physical processing of perceptual information proceeds in a bottom-up direction, and incoming information is shaped from the top down. Explicit perception is, as per reverse hierarchy theory, experienced top-down, commencing at the completion of the bottom-up physical process. After the initial impression of the whole, one may observe details prior to larger units of the percept.

18 The line is from Wordsworth's sonnet of the same name.

19 From the *Holy Sonnet* "Batter my heart, three-person'd God."

20 Such freedom does not necessarily entail free will, as it is not necessarily consciously enacted. Selection implies alternatives that are unselected, and selection is enacted on an unconscious, physical level.

21 The other criteria Culler sets forth in *Theory of the Lyric* include: hyperbole, multiplying discourses, becoming itself an event; ritual, spell or chant, accorded by ring structure and repetition; an optative mode, imagining a response; and presence conferred by the "here and now" of the enunciation (16).
22 This may seem like an odd qualification; however, it is possible to differentiate between the self and the other on an unconscious level, as in the phenomenon of blindsight.
23 The gaze that is the subject of feminist political theory is thus pernicious because it objectifies: one does not gaze upon because one considers object—one renders object by gazing upon.
24 It should be noted that we have here moved beyond perception to the conceptual dynamic built upon it, a building that is one of the two tenets of Varela's enactionism.
25 The line is taken from "Ode: Intimations of Immortality from Recollections of Early Childhood."
26 In other words, we are not aware of every perception as a perception and do not consciously decide to carry out every action. Imagine how cumbersome and maladaptive, if not impossible, such a necessity would be.
27 It's not that the pronouns in question are absent from Olson's poetry. However, the "I" does not appear as a coherent, self-aware entity as it does elsewhere in the genre.
28 Among lyric forms, the ode is suited to its role as an occasional public medium as it offers a singular addressee for public tribute, and thus personalizes the relationship between the private citizen and the commonwealth the odic object represents.
29 See Culler's discussion of the lyric optative mode in *Theory of the Lyric*, page 16.
30 The line is from Shakespeare's Sonnet 15 (1193).
31 The line is from Wordsworth's "Ode: Intimations of Immortality from Recollections of Early Childhood" (35).
32 As Bateson's term "mind" refers to multiple systems, it is not meant to denote mind in the mental sense exclusively, but subsumes that meaning at the same time it is applicable to other systems. My use of the term in this section reflects the same understanding.
33 See footnote 14 within the Introduction for an explanation of neutral evolution. Although Bateson does not address the theory directly, his understanding of "mind" can be seen to absorb it.
34 That perception is initiated by difference and encodes difference is a long-standing though somewhat overgeneralized principle. It is implicit in Johannes Müller's Law of Specific Nerve Energies, which classifies the different receptors belonging to each sense modality, and in Helmholz's analysis of the possible sensory differences within each modality. The more basic difference triggering perception was first noted by Müller, who argued, with Thomas Hobbes, that a stimulus must affect

a receptor differently if it is to be perceived. Information arises at the point input changes. Consistent input results in the phenomenon of habituation, the gradual diminishment of sensory response as a result of repeated exposure.

35 Bateson's criterion of the coding of admitted difference is consistent with Susan Oyama's more or less contemporaneous claim that information comes into existence only through the process of ontogeny (3, 4) or as part of the organism's co-constructed development within an encompassing system. She is among the earliest theorists to defend the co-emergence of genetics and environment.

36 This tendency is expressed as the Hebb Rule, formulated by Donald Hebb. Three primary factors affect the gain: The first is the priming of the bulbar neurons by neuromodulators, the class of brain chemicals that alter neuronal sensitivity by inducing a state of arousal. A second form of priming is occasioned by the simple repetition of input: an already-excited neuron is excited further, exponentially increasing the ratio of output to input. Third, gain tends to increase at synapses that excite one another preferentially in a phenomenon called pair bonding. Learning creates affinities among neurons, which are then able to form cooperative assemblies. Input produces greater output at the favored synapses than it would otherwise, and the increased output is reentered as input. The elevated level induces the nerve assembly to prompt the pervasive AM pattern activity ("Physiology" 81–2). When the gain increases sufficiently, the bulb is destabilized and the oscillation "explodes" as the bulbar burst (*Brains* 74).

37 Although each author uses complexity theory to explain the integrative directionality of cognition, the objects of their measurements are different. Edelman locates complexity in the degree to which interconnected neural networks are differentiated and the amount of information processed relative to the information available from the environment. Freeman measures the chaotic activity of the wave oscillation of the synchronous firings of groups of neurons.

38 This idea, that an organism classifies input by integrating it into its neurological history, is now pervasive, evident, also, in Joachín Fuster's theory in which sensory input is matched to preexisting neural nets he calls "cognits" (91, 96).

39 Freeman writes, "Brains are drenched in chaos" (*Brains* 87): their activity, ranging from the firing of single neurons to the improvised choreography of an entire hemisphere, is nonlinear. The versatility of the brain's ability to integrate is also indebted to the divergence/convergence mechanisms that permit promiscuous relations across scale: a high-level cognit can pool attributes from widely distributed lower-level cognits, thereby forming a more general perceptual category (Fuster 95, 96).

40 As the memory of language is to a large extent collective, this is another means by which social import creeps into lyric.

41 In Whitehead's terms, this grasping is a "prehension," a "vector in that it bears along what is there, transforming it into what is here" (Sherburne 23).
42 The influence of system upon system is in fact bidirectional. Smaller systems also impact larger ones and indeed estrange them, though less significantly. The perceptually guided actions of the organism alter the environment whose potential in relation to the organism is thereby altered; a poem changes the linguistic landscape, to however minor a degree.
43 Fuster assumes that the mechanism of gestalt identification also accounts for isomorphism between qualitative perceptual (i.e., mental) and neural structures (89).
44 Information about the location of an odorant's source does in fact correlate with the intensity of the odor.
45 Such inner/outer correspondences are quantified arithmetically within the field of psychophysics, which traces, for instance, the relationship between the amplitude of informing electromagnetic radiation and visual intensity.
46 Nonstructural, qualitative aspects of perception are also functional in their consistency. They do not, however, assume iconic correspondence; for instance, the consistency of color qualia expedite the recognition of object consistency, as discussed above.
47 The presence of significant disjunction, of functional boundaries may also give rise to the metaphorical construal of perception and poems as houses.
48 One might think of this as the negative feedback of the point attractor, a system, like a pendulum, which ideally graphs as a limit cycle or circle, and which closes in upon itself. In reality, the pendulum's dwindling momentum, overcome by the resistance of friction, will eventually arrive at stasis and graph as a point.
49 In echoing perception, the imagination becomes in effect conceptual.

4

Acts of the Mind: Lyric Action and the Whole of Perception

Action hangs, as it were, dissolved in speech ...

—Thomas Carlyle

Nestled within *The Prelude*'s "Book the First," one finds the epic's celebrated "boat-stealing episode," the story of the boy Wordsworth's clandestine launch of an "elfin pinnace" chanced upon while on a twilight outing. In a display of youthful impetuosity, 10-year-old William pilots the skiff from its mooring at the foot of one Stybarrow Crag only to witness a contiguous ridge rise into view as he rows out into the center of the lake.

A rocky steep uprose
Above the cavern of the willow-tree,
And now, as suited one who proudly rowed
With his best skill, I fixed a steady view
Upon the top of that same craggy ridge,
The bound of the horizon—for behind
Was nothing but the stars and the grey sky.
She was an elfin pinnace; lustily
I dipped my oars into the silent lake,
And as I rose upon the stroke my boat
Went heaving through the water like a swan—
When from behind that craggy steep, till then
The bound of the horizon, a huge cliff,
As if with voluntary power instinct,
Upreared its head. I struck, and struck again,
And, growing still in stature, the huge cliff
Rose up between me and the stars, and still
With measured motion, like a living thing
Strode after me.[1] (394–412)

As his venture commences, it is unknown to the future poet that the more massive Black Crag lies beyond Stybarrow, and so, as his vantage point recedes, the hidden cliff becomes visible, appearing to him to advance of an animal volition. Wordsworth's use of the intransitive form of the verb "struck" to describe his reaction to his misperception affords the reader the temporary sense that he acts upon the crag directly, striking at it in a desperate act of self-defense. Presently, it becomes clear that he rather strokes the water with his oars, rowing away, frantically, from a looming mass that only appears to stride after him. As the past tense of both "strike" and the oarsman's term "stroke," the verb evokes, ambiguously, responses of fight *and* flight, instinctive reactions that prove equally inappropriate to his predicament. One can infer that, in confirming the fugitive's backward motion, the input of peripheral vision (the registration of that motion), audition (the sound of the "striking" oars and the lapping of water audible in the still night), and haptic perception (the sense of his hands on the oars) do not conform with the image swelling in the center of his visual field, and so the crag is misperceived to be a prideful, threatening animal. The boy's reaction is genuinely motivated by his perception, but his sequent perceptions fail to jibe with his actions, heightening his fear: rowing away from an inanimate mass does not yield the mass's diminishment in size as a result of his increased distance from it. The young Wordsworth's attribution of autonomous motion and even life to an inert geologic formation to account for his discrepant sensory experience is symptomatic of a fundamental disconnect between action and perception, in consequence of which the poet-in-training is plunged into a state of terror.

In this insightful passage, Wordsworth—perhaps wittingly, perhaps not—produces an archaeology of perception-action-emotion cycles, and a subtle one at that. In the process, he unearths a basis for the pathetic fallacy. A secondary meaning of "uprear" is to "exalt," to "elevate with joy, pride, or confidence," and by virtue of its denotative range, the verb imputes emotional force to the apparently volitional action of the cliff. By grounding the projection of feeling onto nature in an instance of unsuccessful action into the environment, Wordsworth roots the pathetic fallacy much more deeply in the perception-action-emotion cycle than does critic John Ruskin, who takes the figure to task as the irrational projection onto brute nature of a confused emotional state, one ungoverned by the reason (155). The discomfort produced by this weak-minded, "fallacious" practice is without a doubt far-reaching, as evidenced within the subsequent critical response. One could argue, following Ruskin, that the boy is simply confounded by his fear of the unknown, yet his emotion does not originate apart from—or prior to—his intentional participation in the landscape. Wordsworth does not "perceive … wrongly, because he feels" (Ruskin 158): he feels as he does because he perceives wrongly. The emotion projected onto the natural scene is neither frivolous nor indulgent, and it is certainly not unmotivated, arising, as it does, from the poet's misperception. Far from evincing a weakness of mind, Wordsworth's emotion is implicated as a player in the event in spurring the inappropriate action of flight.

This pregnant incident in a self-confessed "preparatory poem" to a full-fledged memoir resonates as a symbolic point of embarkation within a poetic career.[2] The displacement of secure knowledge it dramatizes constitutes for Wordsworth a partly biographical, partly fictionalized instance of conception made possible by the obsolescence of past categories. In a layered, Freudian reading of this passage, Joshua Wilner notes, by way of establishing its significance to authorial motivation, that the boat stealing scene is in fact a culminating dislocation in a series of the same:

> His ramble into the countryside is part of a succession of displacements to ever less familiar places of dwelling: having initially been transplanted from his birthplace to school and Hawkeshead, he now is on vacation from Hawkeshead, and lodged in the village inn in Patterdale, "a vale/Wherein I was a stranger" (375–6). His discovery of the boat is thus framed as an antipodal scene of maximal displacement and symbolic condensation. (39)

The rebellion staged as a joy ride caps off and intensifies a string of oustings, replaying and figuring them as an "outing" (a word cognate with "utterance") that terminates in the haunting of his consciousness. In the days following the incident, familiar thoughts and customary images are usurped by the residual impress of the encounter. The mature Wordsworth names the resulting psychic affliction "solitude/Or blank desertion":

> after I had seen
> That spectacle, for many days my brain
> Worked with a dim and undetermined sense
> Of unknown modes of being. In my thoughts
> There was a darkness—call it solitude
> Or blank desertion—no familiar shapes
> Of hourly objects, images of trees,
> Of sea or sky, no colours of green fields,
> But huge and mighty forms that do not live
> Like living men moved slowly through my mind
> By day, and were the trouble of my dreams. (417–26)

It is hardly surprising that the poetics of Romanticism naturalize the exile motif, realizing it in the figure of the poet as a solitary, errant consciousness spurred on to a less than voluntary confrontation with "unknown modes of being." Within this episode, the thwarting of expectation interrupts the child's seamless cruising through nature, giving rise to an almost solipsistic feeling of isolation, a state of estrangement that should inspire song. The event in a sense clears the perceptual slate: the eventual recovery of the cave is a symbolic reentry into a womb-like orifice, an original point of mooring. Wordsworth follows the more critically inclined Coleridge in understanding that original experience is available only perceptually or via a homologous act of conception (and I wish to emphasize the double meaning of the latter term) ("Biographia" 263). What Wordsworth stumbles upon and comes to understand for himself, if only implicitly, is that perception necessarily embroils action: the happy functioning of an organism depends upon the concerted operation of the two. Varela's enactionism both adopts this fundamental premise and embraces Coleridge's claim that the dynamic of creative agency is rooted in perception, enlarging it to include forms of cognition other than the imagination: "Cognitive structures emerge from the recurrent sensorimotor patterns that enable action to be perceptually guided" (173). The boy's aborted negotiation of the landscape is so imposing a failure of basic perceptual functioning that Wordsworth locates the impetus to *poiesis* in the drive to overcome it. He would turn to poetry to remedy the schism in basic cognition his *Bildungsroman* in verse marks as incipient with respect to a poetic career.

What is often under or even unacknowledged about Romantic utterance, conceived, as it is, as a casting out of mental content onto nature, is its recognition of the importance of sensory input to the creative process. In accordance with the idea that the secondary imagination builds upon perception, the outward projection of concepts is often preceded and informed by the internalizing of an external source. The importance of the "alliance," to use Wordsworth's word, between perceiver and object of perception is verbalized in "Book Second" of *The Prelude*:

His mind
Even as an agent of the one great mind,
Creates, creator and receiver both,
Working but in alliance with the works
Which it beholds.—Such, verily is the first
Poetic spirit of our human life. (1805, 257–61)

Wordsworth's Latinate terminology is unfalteringly precise: "alliance" suggests a contractual relationship, an agreement between peers to fulfill a joint obligation, that is, to act in a way motivated by the alliance, a term that in itself rejects the unidirectional engagement associated with the Romantic movement. The pattern common to the typical conversation poem is followed, by way of example, in Coleridge's "The Eolian Harp," which opens with due indulgence in the multisensory imagery offered up by the landscape. Reveling in "the clouds, that late were rich with light" (6), imbibing the "scents/Snatch'd from yon bean-field" (9–10), and attending to "the stilly murmur of the distant sea" (11) can be seen as attempts to acknowledge the role of environmental influence in perception and thereby to ground cognition in sensory experience, the echoing secondary imagination in the primary imagination. To the extent that Romanticism builds upon the genre of the romance and is, as Harold Bloom has suggested, the internalization of the quest motif ("Introduction" 3–4), it redirects the gaze of Eros trained upon a beloved to inanimate nature, recasting the venturing out of quest as perceptually inspired (often cognitive) action. In an earlier example of a recognition of the seminal status of perceptual input, Sir Philip Sidney's Muse's injunction to Astrophil to "*look* in thy heart and write" (14) (emphasis added) is often read as a prod to find inspiration in the beauty of Stella, the heart's inhabitant—in her image (and not in the innermost desires or truest feelings the organ is thought to house). To initiate an imaginative poetic process built on perception, to see one's self in nature, or, more accurately, to see one's self in relation to nature, one must first see nature. The sensorial is the wellspring of inspiration.

Coleridge's prescient understanding of imagination as a faculty derivative, in the non-pejorative sense, of perception marks the culmination of a long tradition of enquiry into the nature of its functioning, particularly his attempt to reconcile empirical psychology's basis in sensation with Sidney's notion of creative transcendence expressed in his "Defence." The perfection of the eighteenth-century dismissal of the idea of poetry as imitative and its mastery as a mere technical feat was indeed one of Romanticism's central accomplishments. Coleridge writes, famously and infamously, "The primary IMAGINATION I hold to be the living Power and prime Agent of all human Perception, and as a repetition in the finite mind of the eternal act of creation in the infinite I AM" (263). The secondary imagination responsible for the generation of poetry is identical in kind to the form of imagination that drives perception (263). The idea that Romanticism valorizes a consummate creativity whose matrix is lodged exclusively within a mind that suffuses reality with its product ignores the homology Coleridge strives to forge.

The importance of sensory influence to poetic creation was, as I have noted, by no means a Romantic epiphany. Yet, it is accorded a certain attention within the movement because, as the youthful Wordsworth comes to learn, successful integration with nature depends upon the successful apprehension of sensory input. His confrontation with "unfamiliar shapes" eventually leads to his recognition of perception's role in the imagination as well as the imagination's role in perception. Perhaps more significantly, the event engenders the insight that imaginative product is unsettling, barren if it not familiarized through appropriate action—whether behavioral or cognitive—upon what is perceived. (One might recall that the blending of the familiar and the unfamiliar was among the aspirations of Wordsworth's and Coleridge's joint volume "Lyrical Ballads.") The boy's maladaptive percepts ("huge and mighty forms that do not live" (424)) uncover the possibility of, if not a solipsism, a disconnect or misalignment that is at least partly the source of his terror. Walter Freeman's position with respect to an organism's relationship to objective reality, like that of Stevens and the phenomenologists who precede him, is one of epistemological solipsism, which he defines as the view that "all knowledge and experience is constructed by and within individuals" (*Brains* 9). However, such private knowledge is formed subsequent to perceptual input and is further pragmatic in guiding action, which is the transcendence of solipsism, indeed the transcendence of the individual in the forging of its alliance with an environment. Wordsworth's eventual comprehension of his experience as illusory ("constructed" is a better word as "illusion" maintains its complement, truth), rather than as either real or delusory, eventually forces the awareness that "truth" derives from perceiving efficaciously, prompting his quest to re-empower the senses to perceive aright, setting the young poet on his ambitious course.

The Perception of the Unfamiliar

It is important to note that the experience detailed in "Book Second" is aberrant: objects are most often not so blatantly misidentified giving rise to inappropriate response. The thalamocortical pacemaker's dynamic of expansion and contraction introduced in Chapter 3 may and often does facilitate the virtually instantaneous and unquestioned recognition of an object of perception and the appropriate action toward it. What happens neurologically when conventional strategies of identification fail, as they do for the young poet? Rather than attempt to broach the more complex workings of the visual system, I return to Freeman's explanation of olfaction to answer this question. When encountering a brand new stimulus, the olfactory bulb is so befuddled that it is unable to find an appropriate basin of attraction to capture it and flounders for a time, firing randomly. When the bulb fails to generate a burst, the organism undertakes an "orienting response," a stance of attention that maximizes the probability of reexposure to the odor by soliciting further context. Freeman maps the itinerancy of the AM patterns from the bulb to the olfactory cortex to the entorhinal cortex, whose function is to integrate the disparate information relayed from each of the sensory systems by merging their waveforms into a unified signal (*Brains* 101–2). Synchronous oscillating motion provides a common dynamic that overcomes the modular nature of perception and provides a basis for perceptual integrity, the experienced unity of consciousness. At the same time that a feedback flow generates the memory-attractors constraining input, a feedforward flow proceeds from the entorhinal cortex through the motor systems. In the absence of a bulbar burst, the organism reorients itself, acting into the environment in order to collect additional sense data, deploying a tactic analogous to reading further into the text to gather more information. In quotidian situations, the bodily mechanics of such actions are often quite simple: one might train the eyes toward a vista, or turn the head in the direction of a surmised location to pinpoint the origin of a sound. Wordsworth rows further away from what appears to be an emergent formation. At the same time, signals from the entorhinal cortex flow forward into the motor systems for the purpose of gathering proprioceptive information specifying the location and position of the body in space (101–2). The motor systems then feed this information (the muscle movement that is the boy's continued rowing) back into the entorhinal cortex and hippocampus where the space-time orientation critical to the planning of subsequent action is accessed (103). Proprioceptive feedback messages and space-time limitations amount to order parameters that bias the formation of attractor landscapes in the sensory cortices, constraining them based on physical reality, the body's motor capabilities, and its memory of past motor actions and their results (102). In most cases, the brain accumulates enough information to categorize the percept.

In the event that input remains unfamiliar, it becomes necessary to create a new attractor (or gestalt), an eventuality that transpires for Wordsworth. In this case, the existing attractors in the basin rearrange themselves to accommodate it (*Brains* 80; Nicolis and Tsuda 116). The integration of new sensory input into an experiential whole simultaneously reorganizes the whole of experience as novelty carves its niche within memory. The flexibility of chaotic organization allows for the continuous readjustment of the whole of memory: unless and until rigid habits set in and retard or even preclude the integration of new sensory material, the grand experiential gestalt is expanded and fine-tuned with every exposure to the novel.[3]

As confrontation with anomaly entails an upheaval in the attractor landscape, the window in which possibility is entertained is consequently lengthened, unduly so for the boat stealer. Poetry forces one to linger here in the interval of contention with the fresh, though not indefinitely.[4] As the boy's brain can neither locate an appropriate category to fit his experience on the lake nor make a proper new attractor, at least not for some time, his seeming betrayal by nature is disconcerting, profoundly so. No longer in concert with his native surroundings, he is thrust into the troubled condition of an isolate consciousness replete with vague, unidentifiable shapes. The elongation of this unrecognized resistant state, a state of extreme imbalance, forestalls imaginative categorization of the sort that adjusts one's alliance with nature, rendering the poet unable to give birth to fully formed inventions—to be a poet as it were. What is specifically dramatized in Wordsworth's formative adventure is the failure of perception to correlate with action. Perceptual input is assimilated by the imposition of a structure onto it, one that ensures appropriate response. The boy is haunted because new sensory information is sufficiently discordant as to prevent its proper classification. The misalignment of his perceptions and his movements, his failure to negotiate a landscape that becomes in consequence a "ladscape," gives rise to an impotent solitude that will at length come to inspire the pursuit of potent action and the successful integration into an environs Wordsworth understood to found the basis for the imagination—and thus poetic making—an insight he would reaffirm throughout his opus.

Prioritizing Action

It was Uexküll who first observed the cyclical interdependence of perception and action, the ways in which organisms move to adapt to environmental flux and in moving alter environments. Such alterations are detected through sensory feedback that informs further action, "harmonizing" an organism with its surroundings, to borrow his pet musical metaphor[5] (Uexküll 69). In Uexküll's wake, Joaquín Fuster coined the term "perception-action cycle" to denote the ongoing "interplay of perceptual and executive cognits" (108), an exchange that assumes their mutual co-construction, making their complete disentanglement impossible and muddling the priority of either.

The reconceiving of *truth* as active, as the result of action, is, of course, a revision of pragmatism. Not surprisingly, a critique of the priority granted perception was first mounted by John Dewey, who reconceived stimulus-response theory within a pragmatic framework:

> We begin not with a sensory stimulus, but with a sensori-motor co-ordination ... in a certain sense it is the movement which is primary, and the sensation which is secondary, the movement of body, head, and eye muscles, determining the quality of what is experienced. In other words, the real beginning is with the *act* of seeing; it is looking, and not a sensation of light. (358)

The understanding of action as precedent to perception and the two as overlapping is critical to the work of Freeman, who explicates the neurological mechanism by means of which action ushers in the perceptual activity that follows it. When, subsequent to perception, a motor plan is sent to the motor systems in preparation for the innervation of the spinal column, a copy of the plan (a "corollary discharge message") is simultaneously relayed to the sensory cortices to enable them to predict the sensory consequences of the intended action ("Consciousness" 151). The phenomenon of corollary discharge allows the process he renames "preafferance" to distinguish it from "reafferance"[6] and thereby to prioritize action with respect to the construction of perception. Preafferance is the means by which the organism imagines the changed relationship of its sensory organs to objects as a result of its movement (*Brains* 33). In mathematical terms, the corollary discharge message acts as a parameter constraining perceptual attractor landscapes by "enhancing" basins of attraction and thereby facilitating the identification of input (*Brains* 133). Within preafferance, global neuronal activity patterns instigating action simultaneously prepare the sensory cortices to anticipate the consequences of that action (*Brains* 33). The senses are primed, in other words, to expect specific stimuli, precisely the process that misfires during Wordsworth's outing, leaving his sensory cortices woefully unprepared. Settling into an expected perception should amount to a reduction in uncertainty (Edelman and Tononi 147–8) and not its amplification.

Empirical and rational approaches to cognition might concede the functional interdependence of perception and action. They may further espouse the claim that perception exists to enable motor action. However, the directionality assumed by this commonplace is at best partial and at worst artificial. It derives from the primacy granted to sensation by empiricist philosophy, a legacy influencing the cognitivist view that the brain accurately represents what it perceives, and action follows as a response to the world as it is. Yet, this assumption overlooks the organism's reformation of stimuli based upon its history and the coincident reformation of itself. "The body does not absorb stimuli, but changes its own form to become similar to aspects of stimuli that are relevant to the *intent* that emerged from within the brain" (Freeman, *Brains* 27) (emphasis added). What the body alters are the neurological substrates of remembered action plans, the organism's formation of which constitutes its intentionality.

In order to emphasize the active role played by the organism in constructing percepts, Freeman recuperates Saint Thomas Aquinas's Aristotelean position that perception results from action into the environment (*Brains* 26). Following Aquinas, Freeman reconstrues intentionality as "the directing of an action toward some future goal that is defined and chosen by the actor" (*Brains* 8). As he points out, the word "intention" means "to stretch forth." On a neurological level, intentionality is "the process by which goal-directed actions are generated in the brains of humans and other animals" (*Brains* 8) by incorporating past experience with an action in order to calculate its likely result in a present circumstance[7] (Freeman and Hosek 511). Aquinas's correction of medieval church doctrine distinguishes the intentional processes through which organisms self-realize as a result of their actions, from the fully self-conscious, willful ones by means of which they make ethical choices (from intentionality in the legal sense) (*Brains* 26). The Freeman-Aquinas model of intentionality also differs substantially from the analytic concept, which describes the relationship between mental states and the objects at which they are directed. In this view, intentionality is a psychological phenomenon, often conceived of as the relationship of a cognitive stance toward the world vis-à-vis the world itself (26). This understanding assumes the representational mode of cognition endorsed by cognitivism, the idea that objects in the world are re-presented to a passive consciousness that subsequently adopts an attitude toward them (Freeman and Hosek 512). The supposition that the mind interprets inert symbols of the external world and then acts on its interpretation runs counter to that of the present pragmatic model of cognition in which intent subsumes the actions of embedded, embodied organisms into the environment. Intentional action in this sense reconciles memory and perception because it is constructed both by perceptual input and the past results of the organism's actions responding to similar input. Intentionality, then, is the biological "process by which humans and other animals act in accordance with their own growth and maturation" (*Brains* 8). To engage in intentional behavior is to change the self through action.

The inversion of priority that underlies Freeman's notion of intentionality is critical: conceiving of action as a constraint upon perception recognizes their mutual co-construction. Perception, conversely, anticipates and constrains action: as Raymond Gibbs describes, the faculty is subjunctive because it comprehends objects by "imagining how they may be physically manipulated" (12). Francisco Varela's subsuming of action into perception recognizes this mutuality. The first of two criteria he establishes for what he dubs an "enactionist" view, "perception *consists in* perceptually guided action" (173) (emphasis added), formulates a now widespread belief. Freeman's view that action and perception are continuously formative with respect to one another, in an ultimate sense an indivisible process Varela chooses to name perception, may be folded into the latter's enactionism. It is by means of their mutual co-construction that perception and action are foundational to cognition, jointly primary in relation to "higher" cognitive functions. Given that action co-emerges with perception, sensation—the cornerstone of the empiricist project—can no longer be regarded as primary.

In fact, perception and action are at times neurologically equivalent.[8] "Recent work suggests that many aspects of visual and motor imagery share a common representational, and possibly neuropsychological, substrate" (Gibbs 7). As discussed in Chapter 3, an organism's participation in an environment involves the simultaneous extension of bottom-up and top-down operations. By means of recursive feedback loops, global attractors bias lower-level neuronal activity (sensory input) at the same time lower-level activity shapes global activity (memory and action) (Freeman, "Consciousness" 154). This process involves a highly enmeshed circular causality (itself a simplistic metaphor) from which linear vectors are abstracted for the sake of comprehensibility. We say, inspired by empiricist doctrine, that perception causes action or, if we are rationalists, that preexisting mental contents shape perception. But these are retrospective assignments of agency fitted to a particular worldview that simplify our understanding of cognition by abstracting cause-and-effect relations. As the construction of action and perception is ongoing and mutually effected,[9] and the dynamic enabling it is complex in the technical sense,[10] it is fundamentally impossible to isolate the functions neurologically. The number of individual components within the system, the connectedness of neurons physically remote from one another, the divergence and convergence mechanisms involved in hierarchical ascension, and nonlinearity all contribute to the impossibility of disentangling either perception or action to find the thread's end.[11] It is no wonder, then, that divinity should so easily become the explanation for what is in fact unknowable as a source of poetic utterance.

It is through acting, then, that the organism constructs percepts as part of the ongoing process of forming a pact with the environment, fulfilling its terms through intentional action. As a perceptual event embroils action, what a percept represents is not merely an object perceived "but also encodings of actions relevant to that object" (Gibbs 60). What becomes a presumptive necessity for the inclusion of action within the *lyric* event explains in part why discussions of its mimetic capacities are fraught and ultimately unsatisfying. If the genre imitates anything, it imitates the reciprocal processes by which perception and action co-construct one another. Thus far, I have contended with the poem as substance and the poem as "mind" in the Batesonian sense, as inclusive of neurological and mental activity. What awaits investigation is its coextensive ontology—action. To root poetic composition convincingly within perceptual processes and to account for the formative role action plays within perception, it is necessary to recognize the ways in which poetic words are also actors. That the irrepressibly self-assertive "I AM" is ever active on its own behalf is reflected in the conventions of versifying.

Intrinsic Lyric Actions

An implication of the foregrounding of action that bears noting is the embodiment it assumes. The new embodiment conferred by transmogrification within the myths stresses the significance of body in general, and the connection of new body to new perceiving mind. Acting, of course, implies a body that acts, a material generator of force. Embodiment is further necessary to the connection between the lyric "I" and "you," as the you, a stand-in for a percept, is defined as against the physical, perceptual limits of the "I":[12] in a sense, the percept begins where the perceiver ends. In addition, cognition is distributed: "Perception is not solely located in brain activity, but must always be situated in terms of more complex dynamic couplings involving the whole body in action" (Gibbs 49). As has been addressed, one might say that poetry evinces an awareness of its embodiment as tenuous: the courtly subject bemoans his corporeal response, for instance, his alternating registration of hot and cold and his wasting away, the beleaguered physicality Sappho chronicles in "In my eyes he matches the gods." Organismic presence in a poem is often reduced to a voice, a synecdoche that carries with it an implication of embodiment in tension with the sense of disembodiment the abstraction of the voice from the body confers within this medium ever in the process of transmuting its physicality (the lyric as decomposing corpse). The term that gained traction in the twentieth century has grown increasingly rarefied, regarded now by some as all but passé. But if one reconstrues a poem as creative of "effects of voicing" (Culler, *Theory* 35), one must concede that these effects index a voice and that voice in turn points to an embodied organism. The effect is to distill action to a vocalizing at the back of the poem.

Lyric implies an actor, however remotely that actor is situated, because it itself enacts. Emerson reminds us that it is in the nature of words to be active: "All language is vehicular and transitive, and is good, as ferries and horses are, for conveyance, not as farms and houses are, for homestead" ("Poet" 463). What it conveys is symbolic meaning, albeit in a non-fixed way within poetry, which discharges meaning as so many passengers are discharged upon their delivery to a terminal. Poetic language garners post-transcendentalist championship for its capacity for transport, but of energy. In rallying poets to circumvent what he calls "the lyrical interference of the ego," by which he means the rigid, bourgeois category of the self, Charles Olson urges the direct registration of perception through the transformation of that energy within the poem and its preservation in a form transducible by the reader (16). Olson captures the energetic quality of the poem by stressing its movement. Working at the speed of the nerves (lest the ego solidify and intervene), the poet must keep in mind that "always one perception must must must MOVE, INSTANTER, ON ANOTHER!" (17). Each of these poetics either proclaims or assumes poetry to be fueled by perceptual processes that are in some way active. In fact, it is a not an uncommon intuition that poetry restores the word to its holistic splendor by activating it, releasing its innate propensity to act, as it were. Evidence for the primacy of perception within poetic utterance, then, is not merely to be found in a preponderance of imagery, which is often thought to be a mediated record of perception, or in the aforementioned ways poetry recapitulates perceptual dynamics, but in its recurrent intuition that creative or imaginary processes are homologous to perceptual processes intricately intertwined with actions, in the medium's embrace of the threefold nature of language.

It is not insignificant that Olson and Coleridge lean rhetorically on capitalization to stress the urgent need to attend to the immediate juncture at which being in its most fundamental sense (the bundle of nerves that is the great I AM) is maintained. This juncture within the mythos and practice of the poetic enterprise embroils the breath, the aboriginal medium of poetry. It is not only throughout the brief tenure of modern and postmodern poetics that poetic being manifests as a voice. Voice is a literal poetic presence, one lost sight of in the modern period, carried on the breath. And here the ancient understanding of the breath as the site of divine influence—as *afflatus* or *inspiritus*—makes for neat formula. To imagine that the stimulus to creation enters on the breath is to wed the creative impulse to the life-sustaining ebb and flow of respiration, ensuring, in the process, that the "output" arm of the respiratory mechanism will be engaged. The word—the lyric word in particular—is an *utterance*: it emanates from a subject and is transported to a receiver on the exhalation. The vocal then implies the olfactory and is one with it, for to engage the breath is to stimulate the sense of smell automatically. Inhalation not only precedes exhalation and entails it, it is a stream on which the precursors to perception are transported. Stimuli in the form of olfactory chemicals are borne on the breath as sensory ingress surfs the current on which the divine and the mysterious sources of the creative are conceived to flow. Inspiration, in its distinctive Latin formulation, cannot but import collateral sense data. Olfaction—more broadly, perception—shadows poetic utterance. It is this the high Romantics realized in both senses of the word: the creative act transpires at the vital interchange between an organism and its environment. The breath is an overt and effectively uninterruptible mode of connection between the two, a primary event (exchanging oxygen and carbon dioxide) on which the mutuality of the terms hinges, the interdependence Wordsworth so eloquently characterizes.

It is in co-constructing perception and action, and organism and environment, that lyric inscribes the actions it performs or encodes diversely. *Poiesis* (*ποίησις*) is itself a making.[13] That "making" is active is reflected in the many languages in which a single verb serves to perform the tasks that English delegates to two—"making" and "doing"—among them the French *faire*, the Latin *facere*, the German *machen*, and the Greek *ποιεῖν*, to list only the language's principal constituent tongues. As J. L. Austin asks, "When we issue any utterance whatsoever, are we not 'doing something'?" (92). There is in addition a certain athleticism conferred by the primary orality of this medium conceived of as utterance, an impulse borne on the breath and shaped by the speaking or singing that survives the pervasive technologies of writing, if only in spirit. Of course, all spoken language emits sounds, but in identifying as an utterance, the lyric medium foregrounds linguistic mobility. This literal, outward, "*ex*-pressive" movement serves both to subtend and to reinforce any senses of movement the utterance may reference or evoke. The sheer power of lyric language is highlighted within the poetics of a Whitman, whose operatic tone and topical scope conjure a vocal force that is extreme, *and* that of an Olson, whose mandate urging that poetic perceptions "move instanter" one upon the next validates their irrepressibly active quality while hinting at the overlap of perception and action, their intermittent simultaneity. Action is intrinsic to poetry as the means of mediating pronominal constructs, as a go-between traversing the space between an elicited "I" and "you" in a manner appropriate (i.e., satisfying) to their relationship. Love poems woo, odes praise, the poetry of Romanticism projects a co-constructed concept onto nature. One recalls that Bloom's lyric hero is he who ventures out of his stasis, which presumes an acting in the form of courting adventure, itself a "coming to," an arrival at an unforeseen scene, internalized or not. Further, the deictics "I" and "you," as all deictics, are themselves born of an animating force, elicited by the physical movement of pointing, a gesture that is part linguistic, part grossly motor, and thereby mobilizing, as Keats dramatizes, penetrating *poiesis* when he extends to a "thou" his "grasping," "living hand" ("Hand" 2, 1). All lyric action harkens back to such elemental gesturing, even when the compulsion to act is unself-aware, as in Olson's muscular verse.

The lyric's active bent is also given by its proclivity toward performative language. The illocutionary force of poetic utterance in particular has been touted as a central if a problematic feature of the genre.[14] In initiating the study of performatives, J. L. Austin distinguishes illocutionary acts (those performed in the course of their speaking) from perlocutionary acts (those accomplished as a result of their speaking) (99–100, 129–30). Illocution is the "performance of an act *in* saying something as opposed to the performance of an act *of* saying something" (99–100). For example, the utterance "I promise" completes the action of promising. Illocutionary statements tend to be constructed in the first-person indicative mood and the noncontinuous present tense (47) and assume a "signatory of the action," here the lyric "I," who, as Culler notes, most often utilizes the present tense (*Theory* 277). Perlocutionary utterances, in contrast, encode the direct impact of an action on its recipient, as in the sentence "He annoyed me" (Austin 102). Austin stresses that perlocution severs an act from its consequences (the act of annoying from the state of annoyance) (112) to focus on the latter. Perlocution makes for an ill fit with lyric because it determines (rather than potentializes) an effect upon a receiver that is rarely of concern within representatives of the genre and is in theory beyond their ken. As within lyrics the consequences of actions are the subsequent perceptions of a single mind, the rupture that reveals the content of a new mind marks, in effect, a limit of the genre.

A number of contemporary critics have noted that illocutionary delivery is somehow intrinsic to lyric, if not always present within it. I agree with this assignation: the illocutionary act is central in animating poetic language, endowing it with a movement coextensive with its capacity to generate images, that then augments the way the lyric makes meaning.[15] Types of illocutionary statements that should resonate for the connoisseur as endemic to the genre include:

I pray ("This Morning I Pray for My Enemies"—Joy Harjo)
I praise ("I praise the dance"—St. Augustine)
I sing ("I sing the body electric"—Walt Whitman)
I complain, I lament ("I complain. I lament."—Emmanuel George Cefai)

The list continues: I laud, I endorse, I enchant, I esteem, I implore, I woo, I argue, I welcome, I vow, I pledge, I promise, I urge, I swear, I dedicate, I enact, I congratulate, I apologize, I thank. Illocutionary statements need not be directly articulated: for instance, riddles question though they do not often pronounce the words "I ask"; imperative statements implicitly demand. When poetic language is not strictly illocutionary, it tends to act nonetheless in referencing conative, that is, active mental states, for instance, those of desire, impulse, volition, and striving. What Austin designates "expositional performatives," a subclass embracing the shift from the descriptive to the illocutionary (85), also populate lyric, expressions such as I argue, I conclude, I testify, and I admit. Arguing, which characterizes much of the doings of sonnets in particular, utilizes epideixis, eloquent, persuasive discourse, a staple of ancient Greek lyric Culler wishes to understand as central (*Theory* 50, 130): "'performance' is doubtless the best translation of *epideixis*," discourse intended "to move" (*Theory* 130).

Roman Jakobson notes that conative language correlates naturally with the positioning of an addressee by vocative and imperative utterances (Jakobson 67, 68). Many such constructions express will and desire, especially the desire, fundamental to the genre, that the absent appear.[16] Invocation is itself a type of action, the action of calling forth, the issuance of an invitation to a compelled visit, or a visitation, as it were. It is a directed act, an extension of oneself that positions one to receive the perceptual input central to the genre because calling into being *makes visible*, as in Sappho's summoning of the goddess in "Artfully Adorned Aphrodite" into auditory and presumably visual range. A source of external stimuli (or stimulation) is courted through action in the form of address toward what is perceived, the only action a poet can accomplish in a literal manner. When Sappho sings the opening lines of her only intact, extant poem, it is her utterance that stations her to receive the blessing of the goddess she *looks to* based on her successful past experience with said action:

> Artfully Adorned Aphrodite, deathless
> child of Zeus and weaver of wiles I beg you
> please don't hurt me, don't overcome my spirit
> goddess, with longing,
> but come here. (Powell 1–5)

The poem's formality and forceful delivery, typical of the invocatory mode, serve to intensify the sense of physicality attending its practice. The calling into being of Aphrodite, the expressed wish that she linger, like Wordsworth's beholdings, as "*ally*" (*σύμμαχοσ*) is the wish to make palpable a presence that will inform the poem. This particular Sapphic invocation and the goddess's response to it are unusual in that together they constitute the whole of the poem, the subject matter of which is unrequited love and the search to assuage the vacancy it renders. The ritualistic calling forth of the muse is a peculiarly literary-poetic invention and inventive device, and its fitness for the poetic enterprise runs deeper than its personification of the inspiriting source. Though rarely observed in lyric poems, the convention is fundamentally lyrical in enacting a perception. It survives as the much more common, one might say diminished, figure of apostrophe, which, as a type of invocation, makes perceptible objects rather than deities. In constructing a perception from the action of invoking it, and subsequently attending to it, the figure acknowledges the twining of the two faculties, precipitating a dynamic in which subsequent actions emerge "instanter" with sequent perceptions as the poem is voiced. As an invocation, apostrophe both positions the poem to receive intake *and* is itself the inspired output, the poetic expression addressing object or god that correlates with its invoked presence. In marrying action and perception, the figure epitomizes poetic utterance.

The impossibility of the reception of an utterance by an elicited addressee is an acceptable fiction, then, because it is the nature of lyric that the poem as perceptual act does not concern itself with its object as a fellow percipient, with its receipt of the message. The impact of an action on the addressee, on an urn or a sleeping infant, an indifferent beloved or the wind, tends to be characterized as either nonexistent, undetectable, or of no interest: the perlocutionary is extralyrical. Jonathan Culler sees apostrophe as a wish that the object addressed *might* respond (*Theory* 223), the fictionality of the figure a license to indulge the optative mode (*Theory* 215). The point is rather that the addressee *does not* respond, is sentient within the fiction of address only by virtue of the fact that verbalizing posits it as a receiver. Access to the impact of the utterance upon it awaits another lyric, an "answer poem" that flips the directionality of the process and permits a kind of interchange at a distance. The exception that is exemplified by Aphrodite's response to Sappho within her poem may be argued to be rather an event of the poet's imagination, Sappho's perception of her exchange with the goddess and not an objective representation of the goddess's response, or one uttered from her own divine perspective. In fact, it is the linking of Sappho's action with her perception of Aphrodite's remonstration that is necessary to the poet's aborning awareness that she will repeat her behavior, to the seminal consciousness of a self Bruno Snell ascribes to her and to the genre of poetry (65).

Among the more pervasive forms of illocution within poetry is prayer, a quintessentially lyrical mode in its use of invocation, one that further implies the physical act of abasement that is kneeling. In his insightful chapter on crossings and barred access at the border between lyric and prayer in *Poetry and Its Others*, Jahan Ramazani attributes to the aestheticized prayers the genre compasses an especial ingenuity forced by the reality that God must, regardless of one's beliefs, be imagined (171). (That said, all invocation is a creative enterprise, creativity necessary to the imagining of any addressee, an entity to some degree fictional even when concrete.) Prayer is illocutionary in that it entreats, as Ramazani points out, by default: "[Prayer] does not exist to convey information, to which the hearer is already privy" (127). It is rather a type of wooing and propitiation that has in common with the courtly dynamic a petition to be admitted into the graces of an idealized being:[17] one might allege that the courtly love object already knows of her lover's desires. The ode and the elegy likewise engage this dynamic featuring allurement and appeasement. Among the functions of elegy is the courting of proper relationship with the deceased, the aligning of one's actions toward him, in the form of the lament and praise common to eulogizing, with his invoked presence, a setting right along the path to closure that imagines an approving response. Within the ode, it is of course the merely valorized and not the deceased with whom one aligns or allies one's self. In distinguishing the prayer poem from prayer proper, Ramazani notes that, unlike the former, the latter does not provide fresh insights (131). Though that is most often the case, there is no bar to originality in prayer, and prayer poems (those of Hopkins and Herbert serve as salient examples) certainly offer novelty to the speaker and the overhearer, if not to God. Even when it is liturgical or trite, prayer often *courts* fresh perception in requesting a reality different from the one abided for the time being, one it anticipates as a new object of perception positioned beyond the act of praying.

Prayer may fall under the aegis of ritual as does, per Culler, epideictic speech (*Theory* 350). Lyric as a whole has often been branded ritualistic, deriving through one line of descent, as it does, from Orphic rites. Its ritualistic quality inheres in part in its performativity. Austin stresses that illocutions are by nature conventional, dependent for their effect upon consensus as to the propriety of utterer and circumstance. Lest a performative misfire, "there must exist an accepted conventional procedure having a certain conventional effect, that procedure to include the uttering of certain words by certain persons in certain circumstances" (14). The saying of "I do," the performative that acts ritualistically to wed, does not consecrate a marriage in the absence of a proper, that is an ordained or civically appointed officiant. Ramazani claims that poetry approaches the ritualistic by means of an aestheticized suspension of illocutionary action: poetry is a "performative utterance aesthetically held in suspended animation. It is a ritual-like act that has been self-consciously aestheticized" (133). One can account for this aestheticizing elongation within the genre's recognition of the mutuality of perception and action. Needless to say, ritual is often communal; numerous social functions have been ascribed to it, theories holding that it either cements or disrupts social cohesion. En route to these ends, it prescribes precise, concerted alliances of perception and action (one looks upon the spouse-to-be when reciting nuptial vows). Rituals may appeal to any or all of the senses (of both observer and participant), and their incorporation of symbolism reinforces their basis in the sensory. They are also clearly enacted. That their performance is prescribed, often invariable, provides an exact structuring of perception and action, a formulaic integration of the two that ensures the efficacy of the rite and confers its ritualistic quality. For ritualistic action to be effective, it must accord with perceptions, enfold them appropriately. Rituals elapse: they form a narrative, if you will, of acting and perceiving, and their theatricality derives in part from the meaningful sequencing of the same. However, the suspension of the performative of which Ramazani speaks is conferred by the poem's simultaneous status as a percept and an action. Lyric aestheticizes ritual in the sense Ramazani intends not only in its treatment of novel content, which commands an expanse of time to process, but through its coextensive presentation of perception and action, the "both at once" quality of poetic language that serves to compress what might transpire in part sequentially and thereby to render, paradoxically, the impression of stalled time, the suspending of action in the inscribing of the percept.

The active quality of lyric language is finally necessary for the conveying of fresh perception. It is via its intimate ties to action that perception is a creative mechanism, as its primary function is not to represent the world as it is, but rather to govern action back into a world it constructs and is constructed by. Regardless of whether or not it arises at the conscious level at which the will intercedes, intentionality, acting into an environment, initiates perception in a sense, calling it into being. Whether performative or otherwise suggestive of action, and whether that action is cognitive or behavioral, lyric language summons, and in summoning creates, rather than reflects, a reality. It is pragmatic in the sense that its "truth" resides in what happens to an idea, when "idea" is also conceived of in the basic sense of *thea*—a seeing, as well as in the "idea" generated by the action. In the pragmatic model of cognition, meaning inheres in action and the way it changes an organism, an understanding prevalent within a genre that sharply curtails the expository, evolving a subject instead through emergent perceptual processes.

Perception-Action as Inspiration

As poetry is mythologized at the site of the breath, theories that pertain to the creative agency giving it birth likewise implicate this literal form of inspiration and its entailments as originary to poetic invention. Western poetics is heir to contradictory accounts of the nature of creative conception that tend to align themselves with either the perception or the action this representative poetic vehicle makes possible. The first, which imagines the poet to be a divinely inspired vatic or prophetic figure is given seminal philosophic defense by Plato. The argument mounted within the "Ion" that the poet, like the prophet, is a ministrant of divinity serves to relegate him to a mere mouthpiece whose performance is devoid of both personal artistry and authentic knowledge. To compose, the rhapsodist must be out of his senses, possessed but not self-possessed ("Ion" 533d–534e), a conduit "like a fountain which gives free course to the rush of its waters" ("Laws" 719c). The view that the poet is "inspirited" by divine breath and poetry a balanced transaction in which output equals input is persistent in its appeal, even in the unlikely hands of that advocate of the god-like poet-maker, Sir Philip Sidney. Within the seventy-fourth sonnet of his Astrophil and Stella sequence, Astrophil dubs himself a "layman" and then coyly inquires,

> How falls it then that with so smooth an ease
> My thoughts I speak, and what I speak doth flow
> In verse, and that my verse best wits doth please? (9–11)

The answer divulged at the poem's climax is that his lips are "inspired with Stella's kiss" (14). Although his muse is flesh and blood and his process humanized, the poem recapitulates, even as it spoofs, the occasion of Caedmon's versifying as from the mouths of the unschooled and the inarticulate spews the miracle of finely honed verse. (It is precisely the lowly stations of the neophyte and the smitten that serve to underscore the divine source of their artistry.) The most extreme versions of vaticism may be said to inhere in the visionary poetics of Blake, who claimed to transcribe metered passages as long as thirty lines in spite of himself (115–16) and in Yeats's siphoning of the poetic metaphors channeled, conveniently, by his wife (*Vision* 8).

Vying with the vatic conception of poetic praxis is the superficially less glamorous idea, inherent in the English word "poetry," that the poet himself acts in making or doing something. In an implicit quarrel with the Platonic sentence to madness, Horace's *Ars Poetica* marks an initial attempt to formalize and to impose standards for greatness designed to facilitate such activity, one echoed in the robust revival of the Renaissance treatise as technical manual. The trend would produce ample fodder for the parodic pen of Edgar Allan Poe, who, in "The Philosophy of Composition," purveys formulae for the calculus of poem-making, an enterprise realizable through what he describes as "the precision and rigid consequence of a mathematical problem" (1081). His search for terms prescriptive of superlative poetry culminates in the determination that "o" is "the most sonorous vowel" and "r" "the most producible consonant" (1083).

If Sidney is as delightfully arch in his depiction of the vatic as Poe is when prescribing rules for poetry, he is also quick to embrace the mode as evidence of the poet's proximity to the divine ("Defence" 214–15). At the same time he divests the pejorative sense of imitation, he secures for the poet a divine lineage by installing him as a competing maker, one who "doth grow in effect another nature" (216). Poetic creation is an echo of divine creation because the poet is the supreme work of the Almighty in whose image he himself was made (217). If Sidney's is not quite a syncretic view, it is through the marriage of the divine and the human he arranges that "The Defence" both apotheosizes the poet and organicizes the poetic act, giving us imagination as the preferred synonym for invention, a faculty that synthesizes action and perception.

From a vantage point posterior to the advent of psychological interpretation, these historical and polemical shifts in emphasis seem to make for quaint taxonomy. In isolation, each view at worst rejects and at best sublimates talent and genius, the first to a godhead and the second to the tradition-driven expectations of audience. Yet the twentieth century neither escaped their influence nor transcended the dichotomy as such. The Beat poets—and Alan Ginsberg in particular, after Jack Kerouac—recuperate the visionary poetics of Blake and Whitman in an attempt to distance themselves from various formalisms, most notoriously New Criticism's quasi-mathematical reduction of the well-wrought artifact to a singular thematic value distilled by its centripetal architectonics. The Beats' carte blanche eschewal of editing follows Blake's dictum that "First thought is best in Art, second in other matters." In a conversation with Robert Duncan, Ginsberg muses that composition is believed to flow from "an absolute, almost Zen-like, complete absorption, *attention* to your own consciousness, to the act of writing" (147). The notion that poetry emanates from a source below or beyond the level of conscious control serves to preserve a mystique for the form. Even the prevailing, temperate view that allows the obfuscation of genesis—the superstition that Eurydice, as inspirational principle, must not be looked upon—to exist in tandem with a conscious command of technique separates the two as processes, for example, inspiration and execution, or pure creation and editing. Following Coleridge's observation that to distinguish is not necessarily to divide, I would like to suggest that the two attitudes—one involving attention, mystification, surrender and by some accounts genius, the other long apprenticeship, painstaking mastery, experience, and by some accounts genius—figure a single process within which they constrain, inform, and create one another. The dynamic unifying the two may itself be explained by recourse to the dynamic co-emergence of perception and action. It is incumbent upon a discussion of these notions of creative agency to recognize that their divergent etiologies abstract the early phases of perception driven by environmental influence, and its memory and action-infused latter phases, from what is a unified process. As we have seen, perception is both receptive to stimuli and actively creative in its reformulation of stimuli as percepts. Within poetic lore, the conceit of inspiration is complemented by the idea of *poeisis* as craft or making (always a doing); the shaping of sensory input by perception allows acting into an environment to court sensation. Evidence for the aforementioned primacy of action within the compositional process is found in the gesture by means of which one courts inspiration: the convention of invoking a muse formalizes the poet's active receptivity to the sensory input that elicits invention.[18]

The necessary interdependence of making and inspiration finds an inchoate expression within the Romantic revision. It is precisely because Romanticism negotiates what might be considered a definitive turn to internalization, because it naturalizes but does not fully divest its mythic inheritance, that the classical dyad is given full formulation within its lore and theory. The figure of the Eolian harp, promulgated by Coleridge especially, maintains the inspiriting source as the wind, an afflatus divinized or mystified on occasion, but natural nonetheless. At the same time, it refigures the poet, reshaping the vessel as a tuned, that is meticulously prepared, instrument capable of a virtuoso recital sensitively responsive to the provocations of the wind. The conceit suggests the adaptation of player to environment that allows the creative source to be relocated within a kind of receptiveness inclusive of action.

According to Bruno Snell, this marriage of divine input and personal response is first locatable within Sappho's poem "Artlessly Adorned Aphrodite." In his book charting the evolution of self-consciousness, *The Discovery of the Mind*, Snell sets the scene for her innovation, noting that textual evidence dating to preclassical Greece suggests that the motive force for all human agency, including the generation of mental contents and actions, was believed to have been external. "According to [Homer's] view—and there could be no other for him—a man's action or perception is determined by the divine forces operative in the world; it is a reaction of his physical organs to a stimulus, and this stimulus is itself grasped as a personal act" (43). In a notion of human animation that is paradoxically ennobling and humbling, one was driven solely by external powers; whether battling or poeticizing, one never felt, thought, or acted but at the behest of the gods. Snell goes so far as to credit lyric poetry, and particularly Sappho's practice of it, as the medium through which the recognition of a consistent self-agency first evolved within Western thinking. He interprets her speaker's self-deprecating realization that she will once more love unrequitedly to indicate that she conceives her reaction to her predicament to be within her own power (53, 57, 65). Love is still administered by injection: the well-aimed dart of Eros causes the speaker to love, but the emotional response to the condition it inflicts is entirely her own, motivating "a steady course towards a concrete goal dictated by desire or ambition" (65). Through the practice of a derivatively perceptual art, Sappho has discovered her personal agency, a development within lyric poetry, per Snell, that constitutes the first extant instance of the emergence of self-consciousness (65). The attribution of an active response to a lyric being fleshes out the vatic view of the poet as passive vessel and gives rise to an inchoate awareness of the self. To this I would add that the poet's recognition of an aborning self is enabled by the poem's generation of an action and a perception that give rise to such a construct. It is precisely the culmination of perception in the ownership of personal response that is frustrated for the boy Wordsworth: when his perception fails to accord with its precipitating action, it fails to confirm the action, and thus the agency of the *actor*.

If the dawn of self-awareness in the West can be localized in Sappho's poem, it is because it recognizes multiple fonts of creative agency. Ultimately, muse and maker, perception and action are coextensive. The creative act that is lyric is situated at the site of their interaction and is therefore derivative of organism-environment interactions.[19] At bottom, the poem's composing, its existence, and its experience are integrated perception-action events in which the dual nature of creativity, the constant subtle shifts and adjustments between self and environment, are effected through perception and action, which themselves underlie the images of *vates* and maker.

What is finally granted the poet given the capriciously bestowed favor of the gods and his own consummate skill is the activation of a perceptual dynamic within the imagination. The theories of enactionism and preafferance reprised below each preliminarily confirm that the composing imagination is "an echo" of perception as Coleridge conceived it to be, a truncated repetition in which its beginning in sensation is lopped off and its latter stages reiterated:

> The secondary Imagination I consider as an echo of the former, co-existing with the conscious will, yet still as identical with the primary in the *kind* of its agency, and differing only in *degree*, and in the *mode* of its operation. It dissolves, diffuses, dissipates, in order to re-create; or where this process is rendered impossible, yet still at all events it struggles to idealize and to unify. ("Biographia" 263)

The secondary, creative imagination that produces poetry does not necessarily engage in original perception as part of the act of creation (which, again, may be hypothetical or implied), but is a faculty built upon its processes. It is an active endeavor whose agency differs in that it gives rise to imagined products—perception in the broader, secondary sense—rather than percepts. The imagination differs in mode in that it must independently disintegrate, perform the work perception performs in tandem with the environment, so that it may integrate uniquely. As mentioned, it is a precept of enactionism that other forms of cognition, including concepts and imagined images, arise from embodied perceptual experience and are neurologically and mentally similar in kind (Varela et al. 177–9). When expectation is thwarted, the imagination *in fact* enters into the perception-action process. Within preafferance, the failure of a stimulus anticipated through action to materialize as a percept activates the imagination of the stimulus. As Freeman phrases it, "When an expected stimulus is present, we experience it. When it is not, we imagine it" (*Brains* 108). It is possible, then, to infer that action plays a role in the generation of both percepts *and* imagined images, which are themselves necessitated by the erasure of the familiar.

What Plato interprets as the poet's passivity is in part attributable to the drug-induced ecstasis that was the preferred state for composing within the Orphic tradition. Yet, ecstasis is a going out of one's self that presumes a moving into something else (an environment) that is the prerequisite for knowledge in the pragmatic sense. Plato overlooks the crux of invocative praxis, the critical, active role the poet plays in summoning images into being and the fact that his gesture toward this goal overrides mere passive attending. In the end, the expositional performative "to prophesy" is a definitive action within the genre not only because it follows upon the processing of input but also because all action is prophetic in that it is a forecast, an imagining of consequences enabled by preafferance. The intentionality of the organism is predictive, a calculus of an action's potential outcomes. As the immediate repercussions of acting are in part perceptual, to act reintroduces the obscurity in which percepts and prophecies originate. As this process is continuous while awake given sentience, action is overlain by subsequent perceptual events, compelling their interpretation through the processes of selection and distinction making. Prophesying, as an overtly predictive action, gives rise to perceptions that must be deciphered: it is thus representative of all action, an ur-action intrinsic to the lyric in suggesting the perception-action cycle.

Emotion in Perception-Action Cycles

An understanding of the interconnections of perception and action is not complete without a nod to emotion, a gesture that returns us to an old lyric knot, the difficulty of associating the genre with feeling-based experience in spite of indications that it should be so associated. Emotion is in fact a multifunctional faculty, but I am here concerned specifically with its role as an integral player in the complex of perception and action, the theory that it performs an evaluative function, registering its evaluation as an experiential sign of what to do. William James first tied emotion to action and located it in the body. Evoking the Eolian Harp, he writes of emotional experience, "*The* [physiological] *changes are so indefinitely numerous and subtle that the entire organism may be called a sounding-board*" ("Emotions" 450). "Our whole cubic capacity is sensibly alive" (451). His phrasing captures a tension between the "subtle" and the "indefinitely numerous" qualities of the changes inherent in the bodily registration of emotion that would prove key. As noted in Chapter 2, emotion is a vaguely or virtually differentiated form of experienced potential.

In this early theory, James positions emotion as an after-the-fact assessment of an action. While one can certainly cognize emotion retrospectively by reflecting on it, its experience is now believed to precede the action that realizes it. The prevailing contemporary theory of the faculty as it relates to perception and action is the somatic marker hypothesis, Antonio Damasio's neurological grounding and expansion of the appraisal theory of emotion first proposed in a full-fledged form by Magda Arnold in the 1950s. For Arnold, appraisal is the emotionally driven process by which an organism determines the significance of an object to itself, making a crude distinction between likely harmful and likely helpful objects based upon its past experience with them (I.54–6). Emotion in this view is the felt tendency to act in an appropriate direction, either toward or away from a provocative object as it behooves the organism (Arnold II.94), based on its cognitive evaluation—or prediction—of said action's likely outcome.

The study of emotion has subsequently seen camps divide on the question of whether cognition, in the form of cortical activity (the thought-enabling wisdom), is necessary to emotional experience —the cognitivist position, or whether emotion-action cycles may play out subcortically (instinctually, as venom)—the basic emotion position.[20] The former understanding permits the analysis of complex situations and the latter life-saving speed and efficiency. Each position is grounded and complicated by the recent work of Joseph LeDoux, who identifies discrete neurological systems supporting the unconscious and conscious processing of specific emotions. Seeking to rescue emotion from its reduction to a cognitive function, LeDoux assumes the two systems to be interactive while demonstrating that they may also function independently (69), accepting an evaluative role for emotion while stressing its unconscious aspects. In his work on the fear system, he distinguishes the role the hippocampus plays in the formation of explicit emotional memories by virtue of its intricate connections to the rhinal cortex, from that of the subcortical thalamo-amygdala pathway, which processes emotions unconsciously (163–4). Because the thalamo-amygdala pathway is implicated in implicit or unconscious memory (such as muscle memory), it prompts autonomic responses associated with emotions, such as an increase in the rate of breathing (202). Unconscious processing through the amygdala is activated first; as the more expeditious of the two systems, it allows one to react quickly in emergency situations as prompted by the feeling in one's gut[21] (285). Cognitive input may or may not intervene between the perception of the significant stimulus and the action taken in response to it.[22] Conceding that there is not yet an adequate understanding of the role of the bodily experience of emotion (295), LeDoux establishes the indispensability of the thalamo-amygdala pathway and its activation of arousal systems together with feedback from the periphery to emotional experience while remaining doubtful as to whether cortical input to the amygdala is absolutely necessary to such experience (298). In the wake of a century of inquiry, the question of whether there is, in fact, a completely subcortical, noncognized version of emotional experience, or whether the two levels are so intimately related as to preclude the independence of either, remains. Valerie Hardcastle distills the situation:

> There are now two views of emotion on the table. Cognitive appraisal theories claim that cognitive interpretations are an integral part of emotion and either precede or co-occur with physiological responses. In contrast, the basic emotion theorists propose that physiological arousal precedes cognitive appraisal and is the more fundamental process. (243)

In an attempt to soften the divide between cognitive appraisal and basic emotion theorists, Hardcastle accepts LeDoux's claim that the amygdala marks incoming data with a "valence" of potential meanings (238) but takes to task his extrication of cognition from noncognitive emotion. She argues that the amygdala does not and could not possibly generate potential meaning prior to cognitive input and that cognitive activity is not, as James had proposed, a post hoc amplification of the experience of emotion, but rather a determining factor within it (239). She challenges LeDoux's claim that the independence of the subcortical processing mechanism is a time-saving development (242), pointing out that the assumption of the functional specificity of subsystems does not entail the assumption of their functional isolation (244). The two, she reasons, must be highly cooperative in order to ensure a coherent response on the part of the organism,[23] proposing that recursive feedback loops generated by nonlinear dynamics enable their virtually simultaneous engagement (245).

When the brain receives an emotion-provoking stimulus, it seeks to interpret it as it would any other stimulus. Amygdala activation is part of the interpretation; so is cortical activation. Both are implicated in the circuit that resonates in the presence of an emotion. The two systems work together to establish a coherent and cohesive response to input, to maintain the circuit's trajectory in an established attractor basin (245). Hardcastle thus makes the co-constructivism of the two systems that was originally proposed by Stanley Schacter and Jerome Singer bidirectional. The use of nonlinear dynamic systems theory to characterize the interplay of systems one might affiliate with venom and wisdom explains both the stable, integrated response to various input and the novel response that emerges when appropriate. The mutual systemic construction of the cognitive and bodily representation of emotion Hardcastle posits accords with and is, I believe, a necessary precondition enabling Antonio Damasio's claim that emotion is a complex appraisal mechanism. Damasio argues that emotion is evaluative in distilling the possible repercussions of one's actions into the environment into a "somatic marker," a physical feeling that amounts to a judgment about the best course of action in a given situation. Far from being a gratuitous and irrational vestige of our animal past to be reined in and mastered by the advanced human forebrain, emotion is a shorthand representation of the brain's evaluation of the effects projected from an anticipated action. Put simply, it is a goad and a guide to appropriate response (*Descartes* 173–5). Damasio's theory empowers the faculty to take into account the extensive set of possible repercussions (reactions that are irrational in their virtual simultaneity) that might follow from gestures more freighted than the basic survival tactics of seek or avoid.[24] Peirce is perhaps correct in arguing that all mental states are emotionally tinged, however subtly. All feelings are in a sense, although perhaps not in the sense he intended, feelings of the *toute ensemble* in that they register an intricate calculation of the consequences of a selected course of action, including its possible repercussions to the organism, representing them as an action tendency. Emotion experienced bodily is vague, obscure, because it points to the organism's situatedness in the form of future contingency. This is true of even a simple, instinctual, fear-based appraisal that leads to the release of venom. On a neurological level and as *experienced*, emotion is as-yet-undifferentiated heterogeneity, a sign of future action and its consequences to the organism of which it is not necessarily consciously aware. Cognitive participation is necessary to account for the complexity of the projected outcome versions. If there is in fact a strictly noncognitive form of emotion, potential must inhere within it simply, as a minimal set: the dyad of survival-demise that is negotiated by venom. However, human outcomes may rarely be compartmentalized so neatly.

Perception-emotion-action cycles then recapitulate the dynamic of prophecy in projecting the tendency of the whole, the set of potential versions of the organism's situatedness, forward. In effect, emotion signifies an action plan and its hypothetical consequences; it is an experiential version of preafferance. The referent of the emotion—best action and its consequences—is to some extent obscured, because the perceiving organism has neither perfect predictive powers nor perfect control over the environment. Reading one's gut is an inexact science: surmise is necessary due not only to the singularity of consciousness but also to the fact that the whole constantly undergoes a flux born of the ongoing readjustment of its mutually co-constructed parts. Apocalypse, the revealing of what is hidden, demands the ascension to the bird's-eye view that extricates the one from its dependence on other entities so that it may divine. The Shelleyean, Emersonian, and Stevensian poet strives to envision this perspective, but the latter figure especially understands that access to the ramifications emotion evaluates, the whole of the repercussions of the organism's potential actions to its own situatedness, is limited. That poetry is never really revelatory of such fundaments is further explained by Hardcastle's comment articulating a technically complex, perceptual version of Heideggerian thrownness: "The stimulus drops in, so to speak, onto ongoing interpretive efforts against a background of experiences, onto an activity pattern sensitive to initial conditions" (245). Analogously, the totality of the effects of the organism's actions is fundamentally unpredictable, and therefore not clearly representable, because the parameters constraining the formation of the projected trajectories are generated in a complex fashion as they emerge. Emotion is always at best a guess, an essay, the complexity of which is distilled into a vague expression, a sign that must be interpreted in action because its vagueness lingers, even when it is abstracted and tagged.

How cognized emotion is operative in the lyric dynamic is to some extent obvious: love drives the lover to woo, awe the supplicant to pray, grief the bereaved to lament. The poem also rouses emotion in a basic sense, mainly through its sounds, registering its presence bodily on poetically rendered and human sounding boards, producing uncategorized feeling that prompts response, informs interpretations unconsciously. The poetry that is not subject-centered, that is, as I have characterized it, less fully emerged from its embeddedness, may be less emotional, and/or less receptive to the labeling of the emotion it does generate, because the actor in the poem (the action of the poem) is less self-aware. Yet this kind of poetry generates emotion nonetheless, often through the manner in which it tunes its lyre. There is no thought, in the broadest sense of the word, without feeling.

What is naive, then, about Carnap's equation of lyric with primal utterance is not its charge of primitiveness, but rather its utter neglect of the contexts (neurological and environmental) emotion entrains, contexts recognized in Stevens's modifying epigram, "The poem is the cry of its occasion/Part of the *res* itself and not about it"

(XII.1–2).[25] As lyric renders the process of decision making in which all options, or at least all best options, are entertained in their totality so that potential may be felt and realized appropriately, the genre integrates emotion, both basically and cognitively. Venom and wisdom are feeling driven forms of knowledge about the best thing to do. This is what the many attempts to affiliate the genre with private, emotionally colored experience miss. Emotion in poetry accords with its objects in responding to them and driving the action intrinsic to the poem, integrating it with the perception it realizes. As feeling is registered bodily, it fleshes out a vocal presence, however indistinctly, implying the poem's embodiment. In this sense also, the poetry announces, foregrounds its materiality, which is also its phenomenal existence, which is also its activity. The dancer is by her nature indistinguishable from the dance and is by virtue of this fact mesmerizing.

An Afterword

We have arrived at the view that poetry takes on ecological significance when it is understood to be at once material, phenomenal, and active, and when its diverse instantiations are seen to form a continuum of cognitive emergence. What, then, is one to do with the judgment that lyric poetry fits under a single umbrella, that it is all, in some sense, "eco"? It is tempting to concede that, given the breadth of its application, the prefix becomes meaninglessness when applied to a poetics or to a poetry. Following Emerson and a common-sense line of thinking, all that organisms do is "ecological." But lyric poetry is so in a specific, perceptual sense, and it is creative, *enactive* in this sense. This recognition serves to deepen critical insight, which, as Culler reminds us, is an end worthy in itself. If there is something to be done with such a comprehensive view, perhaps it is not to alter the way in which we interpret individual utterances (though one may from time to time do exactly that), but rather to find one's own brand of poetry—the lyrics that occasion a presence to what embeds one, to the nature of one's choice—and to read it with the end of renewing a health.

Notes

1 The text is that of the 1805 version of *The Prelude*.

2 Wordsworth intended to compose a follow-up epic-length poem, *The Recluse*, which was to chart his career as a mature poet.

3 Although the use of dynamical systems theory to describe brain dynamics is to some degree controversial, its viability is defended by Raymond Gibbs:

> Although there is debate over whether dynamical approaches can "scale up" to explain higher-order aspects of cognition, including language use and consciousness, I am enthusiastic about this perspective because it directly acknowledges the interaction of an agent's physical body (including its brain and nervous system), its experience of its body, and the structure of the environment and social context to produce meaningful adaptive behavior. (11)

4 In his seminal work "Art as Technique," Viktor Shklovsky makes the point that poetic language defamiliarizes, thus lengthening perception.

5 See, also, Ulrich Neisser's *Cognition and Reality* for an early linking of perception and action.

6 "Reafferance" refers to the feedback the brain receives subsequent to motor action.

7 Maurice Merleau-Ponty, John Dewey, and Jean Piaget also prioritize action in relation to perception in their respective works *The Phenomenology of Perception*, "Psychological Doctrine in Philosophical Teaching," and *The Child's Conception of Physical Causality*.

8 Evidence that sensory and motor information are, in fact, indistinguishable within the cortex continues to accumulate. Indeed, a rather neat way that the irresolvability of the two is exemplified is in the relatively recent discovery of "mirror neurons," neurons in the postparietal cortex that fire both when an action is undertaken and when the same action is observed.

9 Perception is not the only influence on action, which also depends on "the internal conditions of the organism, including the drives and motives prevailing at the time," and "the behavioral, cognitive, and emotional associations of the percept" (Fuster 107).

10 According to Raymond Gibbs, conceptualizing action from a dynamical system perspective explains why people need not explicitly decide something each time they act (75).

11 Joaquín Fuster also notes that the intricate and continuous shaping of perception and action is enabled by the bridging of sensory and motor structures at each level of their respective hierarchies, which are themselves connected heterarchically by "reciprocal polysynaptic pathways" forming what one might think of as the rungs of a ladder (107).

12 I make this argument in my essay "'A Music Numerous as Space': Cognitive Environment and the House that Lyric Builds" published in *The Oxford Handbook of Ecocriticism*

13 Concededly, "fiction," from the Latin *fingere*, "to form," is a making as well; however, the word lacks the overtone of "doing."

14 Culler remarks that defining lyric language as performative is problematic because the statement can be made of all literary discourse as literature is not propositional (*Theory* 127). Austin christened the performative category to distinguish it from truth-dependent constative language, and Culler here observes Austin's distinction (128). While performative language is indeed a means of achieving fictionality, other types of fictive language are not as frequently performative or active, nor is their action intimately intertwined with the dynamics of perception, in the manner of lyric language.

15 Austin distinguishes the force of performative language from its meaning (which equals the combination of sense and reference) (Austin 100). However, in this understanding of perception, action contributes to reference and thus meaning.

16 Imperatives of course have other functions besides issuing commands. They may also give directives, express wishes, grant permission, extend invitations, and offer disinterested advice.

17 This is, it goes without saying, far from an original thought. I defer to the theories that Occitan courtly love poems functioned as coded versions of religious speech within Manichaeism in particular. See, especially, Denis de Rougemont's *Love in the Western World.*

18 Neither is the action that inaugurates the creative act merely figurative. For Wordsworth, Stevens, and Verlaine, the simple, pedestrian act of walking was inspirational, invocatory. That invocation is an active, pre-compositional process is affirmed by the superficially tautological folk wisdom that in order to write one must show up at the page. The sheer act of coming to write is often the prompt to further writing.

19 As neurodynamics exemplifies, the relationship between these co-implicated sources of perception is one of a mutual co-construction derivative of a larger relationship between organism and environment. Susan Oyama meticulously dismantles the logic of giving priority or discrete status to either nature or nurture in her landmark text *The Ontogeny of Information*. She further exposes the grounding of this dichotomy in the Western separation of form and matter. As she points out, even the term "interdependence" assumes two separate entities that "inter" act (14). The holistic, ecological thinking she clarifies has only recently been taken to heart within the hard sciences, due in part to the diversion of resources funneled into the development of cognitivism's computer model of the mind.

20 This question is related to that of when emotion arose phylogenetically, for if emotional activity can transpire in the absence of cortical involvement, it is in theory present in species lacking neocortices.

21 LeDoux also establishes that the separate processes of the perception of an emotionally significant object and its appraisal may overlap: evaluative mechanisms

may be activated before perceptual processes reach their conclusion, decreasing response time (69).)

22 Cognitive input provides the nuanced variety of somatic responses necessary to correlate the peripheral registration of stimuli with the feelings experienced. LeDoux is here resolving a debate between Stanley Schacter and Jerome Singer on the one hand, whose work, with that of James, depends on the specificity of somatic response, and Arnold and Walter Cannon on the other, who claim that qualia (the qualitative experiences of emotion) are too indistinct to correspond to the extensive array of human emotions cognized. Drawing on an understanding of autonomic nervous system functioning not available to Cannon and Arnold, LeDoux demonstrates that the autonomic nervous system can respond selectively *to some extent* (292) (emphasis added).

23 The intuition that emotion must be integrated with concept formation recurs within twentieth-century literary criticism. In fact, it was the vagueness of interpretations based solely in the emotional responses of the critic that was at the center of the case Wimsatt and Beardsley made against the Affective Fallacy (21–40). Inspired by, among other things, Eliot's objective correlative, they deemed emotion to be problematically obscure if it was not clearly correlated with an objective idea. Eliot himself had granted emotion a role in conception in recuperating the poet's ability to "feel [his] thought as immediately as the odour of a rose" ("Metaphysical" 64).

24 Damasio's theory is that this complex processing ability avails the human organism in social situations especially, as they are among the most complex of environments we encounter.

25 Stevens's line may be found in "An Ordinary Evening in New Haven" (473).

Works Cited

Adorno, Theodor W. "Cultural Criticism and Society." *Prisms*. Cambridge: MIT P, 1983, 17–34.

Adorno, Theodor W. "On Lyric Poetry and Society." *Notes to Literature*. Vol. 1. Ed. Rolf Tiedemann. Trans. Shierry Weber Nicholsen. New York: Columbia UP, 1991.

Anon. "Western Wind." *The Norton Anthology of Poetry*. 4th ed. Ed. Margaret Ferguson, Mary Jo Salter, and Jon Stallworthy. New York: W. W. Norton, 1996.

Arbib, Michael A. "The Evolving Mirror System: A Neural Basis for Language Readiness." *Language Evolution*. Ed. Morten H. Christiansen and Simon Kirby. Oxford: Oxford UP, 2003. 182–200.

Aristotle. "Categories." *The Basic Works of Aristotle*. Ed. Richard McKeon. New York: Modern Library, 2001. 7–39.

Aristotle. *The Rhetoric and Poetics of Aristotle*. Trans. Ingram Bywater. New York: Random House. 1954.

Arnold, Magda. *Emotion and Personality: Volume I Psychological Aspects*. New York: Columbia UP, 1960.

Arnold, Magda. *Emotion and Personality: Volume 2 Neurological and Physiological Aspects*. New York: Columbia UP, 1960.

Augustine, St. "In Praise of Dancing." *Englewood Review of Books*. N.p. n.d. Web. March 14, 2019.

Austin, J. L. *How to Do Things with Words*. Cambridge: Harvard UP, 1975.

Bachelard, Gaston. *The Poetics of Space*. Trans. Maria Jolas. Boston, MA: Beacon, [1958] 1994.

Bate, Jonathan. *The Song of the Earth*. Cambridge: Harvard UP, 2000.

Bateson, Gregory. *Mind and Nature: A Necessary Unity*. Cresskill, NJ: Hampton P, [1979] 2002.

Batteux, Charles. *Les Principes de la littérature*. Lyon: A. Leroy, 1800.

Behrens, Irene. "Die Lehre von der Einteilung der Dichtkunst, vornehmlich vom 16. Bis 19." *Jahrhundert: Studien zur Gerschichte der poetischen Gattungen*. Halle: Niemeyer, 1940.

Blake, William. *The Letters of William Blake*. Ed. Archibald G. Russell and Frederick Tatham. London: Methuen, 1906.

Bloom, Harold. "Introduction." *Romantic Poetry and Prose*. Ed. Harold Bloom and Lionel Trilling. New York: Oxford UP, 1973. 3–9.

Bloom, Harold. *The Poems of Our Climate*. Ithaca, NY: Cornell UP, 1976.

Bovet, Ernest. *Lyrisme, Épopée, Drame: Une Loi de Histoire Littéraire Expliquée par L'Évolution Générale*. Paris: Colin, 1911.

Bradley, S. A. J., ed. and trans. *Anglo-Saxon Poetry*. London: J. M. Dent, 1982.

Bragg, Lois. *The Lyric Speakers of Old English Poetry*. Rutherford, NJ: Fairleigh Dickinson UP, 1991.

Brogan, T. V. F. "Line." *The New Princeton Encyclopedia of Poetry and Poetics*. Ed. Alex Preminger and T. V. F. Brogan. Princeton, NJ: Princeton UP, 1993. 694–7.

Brown, Stephen. "The 'Musilanguage' Model of Human Evolution." *The Origins of Music*. Ed. N. Wallin et al. Cambridge: MIT P, 271–300.

Buber, Martin. *I and Thou*. Trans. Walter Kaufmann. New York: Scribner, 1970.

Cameron, Sharon. *Lyric Time: Dickinson and the Limits of Genre*. Baltimore: Johns Hopkins UP, 1979.

Cannon, Walter B. *Bodily Changes in Pain, Hunger, Fear and Rage: An Account of Recent Researches into the Function of Emotional Excitement*. 2nd ed. Boston, MA: Charles T. Brandford, 1929.

Cannon, Walter B. "The James-Lange Theory of Emotions: A Critical Examination and an Alternative Theory." *American Journal of Psychology* 39 (1927): 106–24.

Cannon, Walter B. *The Wisdom of the Body*. New York: Norton, 1932.

Carnap, Rudolf. *Philosophy and Logical Syntax*. New York: AMS P, 1978.

Cascales, Francisco. *Tablas Poéticas*. Madrid: Espasa Calpe, [1617] 1975.

Cefai, Emmanuel George. "I Complain I Lament." *Poemhunter.com*. N.p. n.d. Web. March 14, 2019.

Clare, John. "I Am." *John Clare: Major Works*. Oxford: Oxford UP, 1984.

Coleridge, Samuel Taylor. "Biographia Literaria." *The Selected Poetry and Prose of Samuel Taylor Coleridge*. Ed. Donald A. Stauffer. New York: Random House, 1951. 109–428.

Coleridge, Samuel Taylor. "The Eolian Harp." *The Selected Poetry and Prose of Samuel Taylor Coleridge*. Ed. Donald A. Stauffer. New York: Random House, 1951. 57–8.

Congreve, William. *The Mourning Bride*. London: J. Dicks, 1883.

Craik, Kenneth. *The Nature of Explanation*. Cambridge: Cambridge UP, 1943.

Crane, Hart. "General Aims and Theories." *The Complete Poems and Selected Letters and Prose of Hart Crane*. New York: Liveright, 1933. 217–33.

Croce, Benedetto. *Aesthetic: As Science of Expression and General Linguistic*. 2nd ed. Trans. Douglas Ainslie. London: MacMillan, 1922.

Crutchfield, James P., J. Doyne Farmer, Norman H. Packard, and Robert S. Shaw. "Chaos." *Scientific American* 255 (1986): 46–57.

Culler, Jonathan. "The Poetics of the Lyric." *The Pursuit of Signs: Semiotics, Literature, Deconstruction*. Ithaca: Cornell UP, 1981. 161–88.

Culler, Jonathan. "Reading Lyric." *Yale French Studies* 69 (1985): 98–106.

Culler, Jonathan. *Structuralist Poetics: Structuralism, Linguistics, and the Study of Literature*. London: Routledge and Kegan Paul, 1975.

Culler, Jonathan. *Theory of the Lyric*. Cambridge: Harvard UP, 2015.

Damasio, Antonio. *Descartes' Error: Emotion, Reason, and the Human Brain*. New York: Grosset-Putnam, 1994.

Damasio, Antonio. *The Feeling of What Happens*. New York: Harcourt Brace, 1999.

Day Lewis, C. *The Lyric Impulse*. Cambridge: Harvard UP, 1965.

de Man, Paul. *Allegories of Reading: Figural Language in Rousseau, Nietzsche, Rilke, and Proust*. New Haven, CT: Yale UP, 1979.

de Man, Paul. "Anthropomorphism and Trope in Lyric." *The Rhetoric of Romanticism*. New York: Columbia UP, 1984. 239–62.

de Man, Paul. "Hypogram and Inscription: Michael Riffaterre's Poetics of Reading." *Diacritics* 11, No. 4 (Winter 1981): 32.

de Man, Paul. "Lyric and Modernity." *Blindness and Insight: Essays in the Rhetoric of Contemporary Criticism*. 2nd ed. Minneapolis: U of Minnesota P, 1971. 166–86.

de Man, Paul. "Lyrical Voice in Contemporary Theory: Riffaterre and Jauss." *Lyric Poetry: Beyond New Criticism*. Ed. Patricia Parker and Chavia Hosek. Ithaca, NY: Cornell UP, 1985. 55–72.

de Man, Paul. "Wordsworth and the Victorians." *The Rhetoric of Romanticism*. New York: Columbia UP, 1984. 83–92.

de Saussure, Ferdinand. *Course in General Linguistics*. La Salle, IL: Open Court, 1972.

Deacon, Terrence W. *The Symbolic Species: The Co-Evolution of Language and the Brain*. New York: W. W. Norton, 1997.

Derrida, Jacques. "*Che cos'è la poesia?*" Trans. Peggy Kamuf. *The Lyric Theory Reader: A Critical Anthology*. Ed. Virginia Jackson and Yopie Prins. Baltimore: Johns Hopkins UP, 2014. 287–91.

Derrida, Jacques. "Plato's Pharmacy." *Dissemination*. Trans. Barbara Johnson. Chicago: U of Chicago P, 1981.

Derrida, Jacques. "Structure, Sign, and Play in the Discourse of the Human Sciences." *Criticism: Major Statements*. 3rd ed. Ed. Charles Kaplan and William Anderson. New York: St. Martin's, 1991.

Dewey, John. "Psychological Doctrine in Philosophical Teaching." *Journal of Philosophy* 11 (1914): 505–12.

Dewey, John. "The Reflex Arc Concept in Psychology." *Psychological Review* 3 (1896): 357–70.

Dickinson, Emily. "After great pain, a formal feeling comes—." *The Poems of Emily Dickinson*. Ed. R. W. Franklin. Cambridge: Harvard UP, 1999.

Dickinson, Emily. "Best Things dwell out of Sight." *The Poems of Emily Dickinson*. Ed. R. W. Franklin. Cambridge: Harvard UP, 1999.

Dickinson, Emily. "I dwell in Possibility—." *The Poems of Emily Dickinson*. Ed. R. W. Franklin. Cambridge: Harvard UP, 1999.

Dickinson, Emily. "I felt a funeral, in my Brain." *The Poems of Emily Dickinson*. Ed. R. W. Franklin. Cambridge: Harvard UP, 1999.

Donne, John. "A Valediction Forbidding Mourning." *The Norton Anthology of Poetry*. Ed. Margaret Ferguson et al. New York: Norton, 1970. 306.

Donne, John. "Holy Sonnet 14." *The Norton Anthology of Poetry*. Ed. Margaret Ferguson et al. New York: Norton, 1970. 289.

Eckhorn, R. et al. "Coherent Oscillations: A Mechanism for Feature Linking in the Visual Cortex." *Biology of Cybernetics* 60 (1988): 121–30.

Edelman, Gerald M. *Bright Air, Brilliant Fire: On the Matter of Mind*. New York: Basic Books, 1992.

Edelman, Gerald M. *The Remembered Present: A Biological Theory of Consciousness*. New York: Basic Books, 1989.

Edelman, Gerald M. *Wider than the Sky: The Phenomenal Gift of Consciousness*. New Haven, CT: Yale UP, 2004.

Edelman, Gerald M., and Giulio Tononi. *A Universe of Consciousness: How Matter Becomes Imagination*. New York: Basic Books, 2000.

Eliot, T. S. "The Metaphysical Poets." *Selected Prose of T. S. Eliot*. Ed. Frank Kermode. New York: Harcourt Brace Jovanovich, 1975. 59–67.

Eliot, T. S. "Tradition and the Individual Talent." *Selected Prose of T. S. Eliot*. Ed. Frank Kermode. New York: Harcourt Brace Jovanovich, 1975. 37–44.

Eliot, T. S . "The Waste Land." *The Waste Land and Other Poems*. San Diego, CA: Harcourt Brace, 1930.

Emerson, Ralph Waldo. "Experience." *Ralph Waldo Emerson: Essays and Lectures*. Ed. Joel Porte. New York: Library of America, 1983. 469–92.

Emerson, Ralph Waldo. "Fate." *Ralph Waldo Emerson: Essays and Lectures*. Ed. Joel Porte. New York: Library of America, 1983. 941–68.

Emerson, Ralph Waldo. "Nature" 1836. *Ralph Waldo Emerson: Essays and Lectures*. Ed. Joel Porte. New York: Library of America, 1983. 5–49.

Emerson, Ralph Waldo. "Nature" 1844. *Ralph Waldo Emerson: Essays and Lectures*. Ed. Joel Porte. New York: Library of America, 1983. 541–55.

Emerson, Ralph Waldo. "The Poet." *Ralph Waldo Emerson: Essays and Lectures*. Ed. Joel Porte. New York: Library of America, 1983. 445–68.

Empson, William. *7 Types of Ambiguity*. New York: New Directions, 1947.

Favareau, Donald. "Introduction and Commentary: Jakob von Uexküll." *Essential Readings in Biosemiotics: Anthology and Commentary*. Ed. Donald Favareau. Dordrecht: Springer, 2010.

Feld, Steven. *Sound and Sentiment: Birds, Weeping, Poetics, and Song in Kaluli Expression*. Philadelphia: U of Pennsylvania P, 1982.

Felstiner, John. *Can Poetry Save the Earth?: A Field Guide to Nature Poems*. New Haven, CT: Yale UP, 2009.

Feuerbach, Ludwig A. "Toward a Critique of Hegel's Philosophy." *The Fiery Brook: The Selected Writings of Ludwig Feuerbach*. Trans. Zawar Hanfi. Garden City, NY: Doubleday, 1972. 53–97.

Fineman, Joel. *Shakespeare's Perjured Eye: The Invention of Poetic Subjectivity in the Sonnets*. Berkeley, CA: U of California P, 1986.

Freeman, Walter J. "Consciousness, Intentionality, and Causality." *Reclaiming Cognition: The Primacy of Action, Perception, and Emotion*. Ed. Rafael Nunez and Walter J. Freeman. Exeter: Imprint Academic, 1999. 143–72.

Freeman, Walter J. *How Brains Make Up Their Minds*. New York: Columbia UP, 2000.

Freeman, Walter J. "The Physiology of Perception." *Scientific American* 264 (February 1991): 78–85.

Freeman, Walter J. *Societies of Brains: A Study in the Neuroscience of Love and Hate*. Mahwah, NJ: Lawrence, Erlbaum, 1995.

Freeman, Walter J., and Jennifer Hosek. "Osmetic Ontogenesis, or Olfaction Becomes You: The Neurodynamic, Intentional Self and Its Affinities with the Foucaultian/Butlerian Subject." *Configurations* 9 (2001): 509–41.

Freud, Sigmund. *The Interpretation of Dreams*. New York: Random House, 1996.

Friedrich, Hugo. *Die Struktur der Modernen Lyrik von Baudelaire bis zur Gegen wart*. Hamburg: Rowohlt, 1958.

Frost, Robert. "The Death of the Hired Man." *The Poetry of Robert Frost*. Ed. Edward Connery Latham. New York: Henry Holt, 1969.

Frye, Northrop. *Anatomy of Criticism*. Princeton, NJ: Princeton UP, 1957.

Frye, Northrop. "Approaching the Lyric." *Lyric Poetry: Beyond New Criticism*. Ed. Chaviva Hosek and Patricia Parker. Ithaca, NY: Cornell UP, 1985. 31–7.

Frye, Northrop. "Charms and Riddles." *Spiritus Mundi: Essays on Literature, Myth, and Society*. Bloomington: Indiana UP, 1976. 123–47.

Fuster, Joaquín M. *Cortex and Mind: Unifying Cognition*. Oxford: Oxford UP, 2003.

Genette, Gérard. *The Architext: An Introduction*. Trans. Jane E. Lewin. Berkeley: U of California P, [1979] 1992.

Gibbs, Raymond W., Jr. *Embodiment and Cognitive Science*. Cambridge: Cambridge UP, 2006.

Gibson, James J. *The Ecological Approach to Visual Perception*. Hillsdale, NJ: Lawrence Erlbaum, [1979] 1986.

Gifford, Terry. *Green Voices: Understanding Contemporary Nature Poetry*. Nottingham: CCC Press, 2011.

Ginsberg, Allen. *Allen Verbatim: Lectures on Poetry, Politics, Consciousness*. Ed. Gordon Hill. New York: McGraw-Hill, 1974.

Goethe, Johann Wolfgang von. *Note to West-östlicher Divan*. 1819. Trans. Henri Lichtenberger. Paris: Aubier, 1940.

Gould, Stephen Jay, and Elisabeth S. Vrba. "Exaptation—a Missing Term in the Science of Form." *Paleobiology* 8, No. 1 (Winter 1982): 4–15.

Greene, Roland. "The Lyric." *Cambridge History of Literary Criticism: Vol. 3, the Renaissance*. Ed. Glyn P. Norton. Cambridge: Cambridge UP, 1999. 216–28.

Greenfield, Stanley B. "The Old English Elegies." *Continuations and Beginnings: Studies in Old English Literature*. London: Thomas Nelson, 1966. 142–75.

Greenfield, Stanley B. "Sylf, Seasons, Structure and Genre in The Seafarer." *Old English Shorter Poems: Basic Readings*. Ed. Katherine O'Brien O'Keefe. New York: Garland, 1994. 231–49.

Hamburger, Käte. *The Logic of Literature*. 2nd ed. Trans. Marilynn J. Rose. Bloomington: Indiana UP, 1973.

Hamer, Richard, trans. "The Seafarer." *The Norton Anthology of Poetry*. Ed. Margaret Ferguson, et al. New York: W. W. Norton, 1970. 10–12.

Hardcastle, Valerie Gray. "It's O.K. to Be Complicated: The Case of Emotion." *Reclaiming Cognition: The Primacy of Action, Intention, and Emotion*. Ed. Rafael Nunez and Walter J. Freeman. Thorverton: Imprint Academic, 1999. 237–50.

Harjo, Joy. "This Morning I Pray for My Enemies." *Conflict Resolution for Holy Beings: Poems*. New York: W. W. Norton, 2015. 75.

Havelock, Eric. *Preface to Plato*. Cambridge: Harvard UP, Belknap, 1963.

Hebb, Donald O. *Organization of Behavior: A Neuropsychological Theory*. New York: Wiley, 1949.

Hegel, G. W. F. *Encyclopedia of the Philosophical Sciences in Outline and Critical Writings*. Ed. Ernst Behler. Trans. Steven A. Taubeneck. New York: Continuum, 1990.

Hegel, G. W. F. *Hegel's Aesthetics: Lectures on Fine Arts*. Vol. II. Trans. T. M. Knox. Oxford: Clarendon, 1975.

Hegel, G. W. F. *The Phenomenology of Mind*. Trans. J. B. Baillie. London: George Allen & Unwin, 1910.

Hegel, G. W. F. *The Philosophy of Right*. Trans. T. M. Knox. Oxford: Clarendon, 1952.

Heidegger, Martin. *Being and Time*. Trans. Joan Stambaugh. Albany: State U of New York P, [1953] 1996.

Heidegger, Martin. "... Poetically Man Dwells . . . ." *Poetry, Language, Thought*. Trans. Albert Hofstadter. New York: Harper & Row, 1971. 213–29.

Heidegger, Martin. "The Origin of the Work of Art." *Poetry, Language, Thought*. New York: Harper & Row, 1971. 17–87.

Heidegger, Martin. "What Are Poets For?" *Poetry, Language, Thought*. Trans. Albert Hofstadter. New York: Harper & Row, 1971. 89–142.

Heidegger, Martin. "*Wozu Dichtung?*" *Holzwege*. Frankfurt am Main: Vittorio Klostermann, 1950. 248–95.

Helmholz, H. L. F. Von. *Handbuch der physiologischen Optick. Vol. II*. Trans. J. P. C. Southall. *Helmholzs Treatise of Physiological Optics, Vol. II*. Rochester, NY: Optical Society of America, [1860] 1924.

Helmholz, H. L. F. Von. *On the Sensation of Tone*. 1863. Trans. A. J. Ellis. New York: Dover, 1959.

Herder, Johann Gottfried. "Essay on the Origin of Language." *On the Origin of Language: Two Essays*. Trans. John H. Moran and Alexander Gode. Chicago: U of Chicago P, 1966.

Hillis Miller, J. "Heart of Darkness Revisited." *Tropes, Parables, Performatives*. Durham, NC: Duke UP, 1991. 181–94.

Hirsch, E. D. *Validity in Interpretation*. New Haven, CT: Yale UP, 1967.

Hobbes, Thomas. *Leviathan*. Baltimore: Penguin Classics, [1651] 1974.

Hochstein, Shaul, and Merav Ahissar. "View from the Top: Hierarchies and Reverse Hierarchies in the Visual System." *Neuron* 36 (2002): 791–804.

Hölderlein, Friedrich. *Friedrich Hölderlin: Essay and Letters on Theory*. Trans. and ed. Thomas Pfau. Albany, NY: SUNY P, 1988.

Hölderlein, Friedrich. *Samtliche Werke*. Ed. Friedrich Beissner. Stuttgart: Kohlhammer, 1946.

Hopkins, Gerard Manley. "Spring." *Poems and Prose*. London: Penguin Books, 1953. 28.

Irving, E. B. "Image and Meaning in the Elegies." *Old English Poetry: Fifteen Essays*. Ed. Robert P. Creed. Providence, RI: Brown UP, 1967. 153–67.

Izenberg, Oren. *Being Numerous: Poetry and the Ground of Social Life*. Princeton, NJ: Princeton UP, 2011.

Jakobson, Roman. "Linguistics and Poetics." *Language in Literature*. Ed. Krystyna Pomorska and Stephen Rudy. Cambridge: Belknap-Harvard UP, 1987.

James, William. "The Emotions." *The Principles of Psychology*. Vol. 2. New York: Dover, [1890] 1980. 442–85.

James, William. "The Stream of Thought." *The Principles of Psychology*. Vol. 1. New York: Dover, [1890] 1980. 224–90.

Jauss, Hans Robert. "Zur Frage der Struktureinheit alterer und modernern Lyrik." *GRM* XLI (1960). 231–66.

Johnson, James William. "Lyric." *The New Princeton Encyclopedia of Poetry and Poetics*. Ed. Alex Preminger and T. V. F. Brogan. Princeton, NJ: Princeton UP, 1993. 713–37.

Johnson, W. R. *The Idea of Lyric: Lyric Modes in Ancient and Modern Poetry*. Berkeley: U of Cal P, 1982.

Jonson, Ben. "Ode to Himself." *The Norton Anthology of Poetry*. 4th ed. Ed. Margaret Ferguson, Mary Jo Slater, and Jon Stallworthy. New York: Norton, 1996. 304–5.

Keats, John. *The Letters of John Keats*. Ed. Maurice Buxton Forman. Oxford: Oxford UP, 1935.

Keats, John. "On First Looking into Chapman's Homer." *John Keats: A New Selection*. Ed. John Barnard. London: Penguin, 1988. 1.

Keats, John. "This Living Hand, Now Warm and Capable." *John Keats: A New Selection*. Ed. John Barnard. London: Penguin, 1988. 215.

Keller, Lynn. *Recomposing Ecopoetics: North American Poetry of the Self-Conscious Anthropocene*. Charlottesville: U of Virginia P, 2017.

Kingsland, Sharon E. *Modeling Nature: Episodes in the History of Population Ecology*. 2nd ed. Chicago: U of Chicago P, 1985.

Knapp, Bettina L. *Exile and the Writer: Exoteric and Esoteric Experiences: A Jungian Approach*. University Park: Penn State UP, 1991.

Knickerbocker, Scott. *Ecopoetics: The Language of Nature, the Nature of Language*. Amherst: U of Massachusetts P, 2012.

Kroeber, Karl. *Ecological Literary Criticism: Romantic Imagining and the Biology of Mind*. New York: Columbia UP, 1994.

Lakoff, George. *Women Fire, and Dangerous Things: What Categories Reveal about the Mind*. Chicago: U of Chicago P, 1987.

Lakoff, George, and Mark Johnson. *Metaphors We Live By*. Chicago: U of Chicago P, 1980.

Land, Edward. "The Retinex Theory of Color Vision." *Scientific American* 237 (1977): 108–28.

Lange, Carl. *Über Gemuthsbewegungen, webersetzt von H. Kurella*. Leipzig: Thomas, 1887.

Lattig, Sharon. "A Music Numerous as Space: Cognitive Environment and the House That Lyric Builds." *The Oxford Handbook of Ecocriticism*. Ed. Greg Garrard. Oxford: Oxford UP, 2014. 440–58.

LeDoux, Joseph. *The Emotional Brain*. New York: Simon & Schuster, 1996.

Lewis, C. S. *The Allegory of Love: A Study in Medieval Tradition*. New York: Oxford UP, 1958.

Locke, John. *An Essay Concerning Human Understanding*. Ed. A. D. Woozley. Chicago: Meridien, 1964.

Longenbach, James. *The Art of the Poetic Line*. Saint Paul, MN: Graywolf P, 2008.

Longenbach, James. *The Resistance to Poetry*. Chicago: U of Chicago P, 2004.

Mackey, Nathaniel. "Sound and Sentiment, Sound and Symbol." *The Politics of Poetic Form*. Ed. Charles Bernstein. New York: Roof Books, 1990. 87–118.

Marsh, Robert, and T. V. F. Brogan. "Invention." *The Princeton Encyclopedia of Poetics*. Ed. Alex Preminger and T. V. F. Brogan. Princeton, NJ: Princeton UP, 1993. 628–9.

Marvell, Andrew. "The Mower to the Glowworms." *Andrew Marvell: The Complete Poems*. London: Penguin Books, 1972. 109.

Mayer, Bernadette. "The Obfuscated Poem." *Postmodern American Poetry: A Norton Anthology*. Ed. Paul Hoover. New York: Norton, 1994. 658–9.

McLane, Maureen. *Romanticism and the Human Sciences*. Cambridge: Cambridge UP, 2000.

Merleau-Ponty, Maurice. 1945. *Phenomenology of Perception*. Trans. Colin Smith. London: Routledge, 2002.

Mill, John Stuart. "Thoughts on Poetry and Its Varieties." *The Crayon* 7, No. 4 (April 1860): 93–7.

Milton, John. *Paradise Lost*. New York: New American Library, 1961.

Miner, Earl. "Why Lyric?" *The Lyric Theory Reader: A Critical Anthology*. Ed. Virginia Jackson and Yopie Prins. 577–89.

Mithin, Steven. *The Singing Neanderthals: The Origins of Music, Language, Mind, and Body*. Cambridge: Harvard UP, 2006.

Müller, Johannes. *Handbuch der physiologie des Menschen, V.* Trans. W. Baly. *Elements of Physiology, Vol. 11*. London: Taylor & Walton, 1838.

Neisser, Ulrich. *Cognition and Reality*. San Francisco, CA: W. H. Freeman, 1976.

Nicolis, J. S., and I. Tsuda. "Mathematical Description of Brain Dynamics in Perception and Action." *Journal of Consciousness Studies* 6, Nos. 11–12 (1999): 215–28.

Nowell Smith, David. *On Voice in Poetry: The Work of Animation*. London: Palgrave Macmillan, 2015.

O'Hara, Frank. "Personism: A Manifesto." *Postmodern American Poetry: A Norton Anthology*. Ed. Paul Hoover. New York: W. W. Norton, 1994. 633–4.

Olson, Charles. "Projective Verse." *Charles Olson: Selected Writings*. Ed. Robert Creeley. New York: New Directions, 1951. 15–26.

Optican, L. M., and B. J. Richmond. "Temporal Encoding of Two-Dimensional Patterns by Single Units in Primate Inferior Temporal Cortex: III Information Theoretic Analysis. *Journal of Neurophysiology* 57 (1987): 1779–1805.

Ovid. Metamorphoses. *Book X*. Cambridge: Harvard UP, 1984.

Oyama, Susan. 1985. *The Ontogeny of Information: Developmental Systems and Evolution*. 2nd ed. Durham, NC: Duke UP, 2000.

Patterson, Annabel. "Lyric and Society in Johnson's *Under-Wood*." *Lyric Poetry: Beyond New Criticism*. Ed. Chaviva Hosek and Patricia Parker. Ithaca, NY: Cornell UP, 1985.

Peirce, Charles S. "A Guess at the Riddle." *The Essential Peirce: Selected Philosophical Writings (1867–1893)*. Vol. 1. Ed. Nathan Houser and Christian Kloesel. Bloomington: Indiana UP, 1992. 245–79.

Peirce, Charles S. "The Logic of Relatives." *Monist* 7 (1897): 161–217.

Peirce, Charles S . "The Nature of Meaning (Lecture VI)." *The Essential Peirce: Selected Philosophical Writings. Vol 2. (1893–1913)*. Ed. The Peirce Edition Project. Bloomington: Indiana UP, 1998. 208–25.

Peirce, Charles S. "On a New List of Categories." *The Essential Peirce: Selected Philosophical Writings (1867–1893)*. Ed. Nathan Houser and Christian Kloesel. Bloomington: Indiana UP, 1992. 1–10.

Peirce, Charles S. "The Principles of Phenomenology." *Philosophical Writings of Peirce*. New York: Dover, 1955. 74–97.

Perloff, Marjorie. *Poetic License: Essays on Modernist and Postmodernist Lyric*. Evanston, IL: Northwestern UP, 1990.

Piaget, Jean. *The Child's Conception of Physical Causality*. New York: Harcourt Brace, 1930.

Plato. "Ion." Trans. Lane Cooper. *The Collected Dialogues of Plato*. Ed. Edith Hamilton and Huntington Cairns. Princeton, NJ: Princeton UP, 1961. 215–8.

Plato. "Laws." Trans. A. E. Taylor. *The Collected Dialogues of Plato*. Ed. Edith Hamilton and Huntington Cairns. Princeton, NJ: Princeton UP, 1961. 1225–513.

Plato. "Phaedrus." Trans. R. Hackforth. *The Collected Dialogues of Plato*. Ed. Edith Hamilton and Huntington Cairns. Princeton, NJ: Princeton UP, 1961. 475–525.

Plato. "Republic." Trans. Paul Shorey. *The Collected Dialogues of Plato*. Ed. Edith Hamilton and Huntington Cairns. Princeton, NJ: Princeton UP, 1961. 575–844.

Plato. "Republic." Trans. Benjamin Jowett. *Plato: Six Great Dialogues*. Mineola, NY: Dover, 2007. 183–460.

Plato. "Symposium." Trans. Michael Joyce. *The Collected Dialogues of Plato*. Ed. Edith Hamilton and Huntington Cairns. Princeton, NJ: Princeton UP, 1961. 526–74.

Poe, Edgar Allan. "The Philosophy of Composition." *The Unabridged Edgar Allan Poe*. Ed. Tam Mossman. Philadelphia, PA: Runnings P, 1983.

Pope, John C. "Second Thoughts on the Interpretation of *The Seafarer*." *Anglo-Saxon England* 3 (1974): 75–86.

Popper, Karl. "Three Worlds: The Tanner Lecture on Human Values." University of Michigan. April 7, 1978. Lecture.

Pound, Ezra. *The ABC's of Reading*. New York: New Direction, 1934.

Pound, Ezra. "In a Station of the Metro." *Personae*. New York: New Directions, 1990.

Ramachandran, V. S., and Sandra Blakeslee. *Phantoms in the Brain: Probing the Mysteries of the Human Mind*. New York: HarperCollins, 1998.

Ramazani, Jahan. *Poetry and Its Others: News, Prayer, Song, and the Dialogue of Genres*. Chicago: U of Chicago P, 2014.

Reilly, Evelyn. "Eco-Noise and the Flux of Lux." *The Eco Language Reader*. Brooklyn, NY: Portable Press at Yo-Yo Labs, 2010. 255–74.

Richards I. A. *The Philosophy of Rhetoric*. London: Oxford UP, 1936.

Rogers, William Ellford. *The Three Genres and the Interpretation of Lyric*. Princeton, NJ: Princeton UP, 1983.

Rosch, Eleanor. "Principles of Categorization." *Cognition and Categorization*. Ed. Eleanor Rosch and Barbara B. Lloyd. Hillsdale, NJ: Lawrence Erlbaum, 1978. 27–48.

Rosch, Eleanor. "Prototype Classification and Logical Classification: The Two Systems." *New Trends in Cognitive Representation: Challenges to Piaget's Theory*. Ed. Ellin Kofsky Scholnick. Hillsdale, NJ: Lawrence Erlbaum, 1983. 73–86.

Rousseau, Jean-Jacques. "Essay on the Origin of Languages Which Treats of Melody and Musical Imitation." Trans. John H. Moran. *On the Origin of Language: Two Essays*. Chicago: Chicago UP, 1966.

Ruskin, John. *Modern Painters*. Vol. 3. New York: Merrill and Baker, 1900.

Said, Edward. "Reflections on Exile." *Reflections on Exile and Other Essays*. Cambridge: Harvard UP, 2000.

Sappho. "Artfully Adorned Aphrodite, Deathless." *Sappho: A Garland: The Poems and Fragments of Sappho*. Trans. Jim Powell. New York: Noonday P, 1993. 3–4.

Sappho. "In My Eyes He Matches the Gods, That Man Who." *Sappho: A Garland: The Poems and Fragments of Sappho*. Trans. Jim Powell. New York: Noonday P, 1993. 23–4.

Schacter, Stanley. "The Interaction of Cognitive and Physiological Determinants of Emotional State." *Advances in Experimental Social Psychology*. Ed. L. Berkowitz, New York: Academic, 1964. 49–60.

Schacter, Stanley, and Jerome Singer. "Cognitive, Social, and Physiological Determinants of Emotional State." *Psychological Review* 69 (1962): 379–99.

Schelling, Friedrich. *Philosophie der Kunst*. Darmstadt: Wissennschaftliche Buchgesellschaft, [1802] 1960.

Schiller, Friedrich. *On the Aesthetic Education of Man, in a Series of Letters*. Trans. Reginald Snell. Mineola, NY: Dover, 2004.

Schopenhauer, Arthur. *The World as Will and Representation*. Vol. 1. Trans. E. F. J. Payne. New York: Dover, 1969.

Scigaj, Leonard. *Sustainable Poetry: Four American Ecopoets*. Lexington: UP of Kentucky, 1999.

Searle, John R. *The Rediscovery of the Mind*. Cambridge: MIT UP, 1992.

Sebeok, Thomas. "Biosemiotics: Its Roots, Proliferation and Prospects." *Essential Readings in Biosemiotics: Anthology and Commentary*. Ed. Donald Favareau. Dordrecht: Springer, 2010. 217–36.

Sebeok, Thomas. *Signs: An Introduction to Semiotics*. Toronto: U of Toronto P, 2001.

Segal, Charles. *Orpheus: The Myth of the Poet*. Baltimore: Johns Hopkins UP, 1989.

Shakespeare, William. "MacBeth." *Norton Shakespeare*. Ed. Stephen Greenblatt et al. New York: W. W. Norton, 1997. 2555–618.

Shakespeare, William. "Sonnet 15." *Norton Shakespeare*. Ed. Stephen Greenblatt et al. New York: W. W. Norton, [1928] 1997.

Shelley, Percy Bysshe. "A Defense of Poetry." *Criticism: Major Statements*. 3rd ed. Ed. Charles Kaplan and William Anderson. New York: St. Martin's, 1991.

Sherburne, Donald W. *A Key to Whitehead's Process and Reality*. Chicago: U of Chicago P, 1966.

Sherrington, Sir Charles. *The Integrative Action of the Nervous System*. Cambridge: Cambridge UP, 1948.

Shklovsky, Viktor. "Art as Technique." *Russian Formalist Criticism: Four Essays*. Trans. Lee T. Lemon and Marion J. Reis. Lincoln: U of Nebraska P, 1965. 3–24.

Sidney, Philip. "Astrophil and Stella." *Sir Philip Sidney: The Major Works*. Ed. Katherine Duncan-Jones. Oxford: Oxford UP, 1989. 153–211.

Sidney, Philip. "The Defence of Poetry." *Sir Philip Sidney: The Major Works*. Ed. Katherine Duncan-Jones. Oxford: Oxford UP, 1989. 212–50.

Singer, W., and C. M. Gray. "Visual Feature Integration and the Temporal Correlation Hypothesis." *Annual Review of Neuroscience* 18 (1995): 555–86.

Skarda, Christine. "The Perceptual Form of Life." *Reclaiming Cognition: The Primacy of Action, Intention, and Emotion*. Ed. Rafael Nunez and Walter J. Freeman. Thorverton: Imprint Academic, 1999. 79–93.

Skinner, Jonathan. "Editor's Introduction." *Ecopoetics* No. 1 (Winter 2001): 5–8. https://ecopoetics.files.wordpress.com/2008/06/eco1.pdf.

Skinner, Jonathan. "Thoughts on Things: Poetics of the Third Landscape." *The Eco Language Reader*. Brooklyn, NY: Portable Press at Yo-Yo Labs, 2010. 9–51.

Snell, Bruno. *The Discovery of the Mind in Greek Philosophy and Literature*. New York: Dover. 1953.

Steiner, George. *Real Presences*. Chicago: U of Chicago P, 1989.

Stevens, Wallace. "An Ordinary Evening in New Haven." *The Collected Poems of Wallace Stevens*. New York: Vintage Books, [1954] 1990. 465–89.

Stevens, Wallace. "Connoisseur of Chaos." *The Collected Poems of Wallace Stevens*. New York: Vintage Books, [1954] 1990. 215–16.

Stevens, Wallace. "The Doctor of Geneva." *The Collected Poems of Wallace Stevens*. New York: Vintage Books, [1954] 1990. 24.

Stevens, Wallace. *Letters of Wallace Stevens*. Ed. Holly Stevens. Berkeley: U of California P, 1966.

Stevens, Wallace. *The Necessary Angel: Essays on Reality and the Imagination*. New York: Vintage, 1942.

Stevens, Wallace. "Notes toward a Supreme Fiction." *The Collected Poems of Wallace Stevens*. New York: Vintage Books, [1954] 1990. 380–408.

Stevens, Wallace. "Of Modern Poetry." *The Collected Poems of Wallace Stevens*. New York: Vintage Books, [1954] 1990. 239–40.

Stevens, Wallace. *Opus Posthumous*. New York: Vintage Books, [1957] 1990.

Stevens, Wallace. "The Rock." *The Collected Poems of Wallace Stevens*. New York: Vintage Books, [1954] 1990. 525–8.

Stevens, Wallace. "Saint John and the Back-Ache." *The Collected Poems of Wallace Stevens*. New York: Vintage Books, [1954] 1990. 436–7.

Stevens, Wallace. "Sunday Morning." *The Collected Poems of Wallace Stevens*. New York: Vintage Books, [1954] 1990. 66–70.

Stevens, Wallace. "The Well-Dressed Man with a Beard." *The Collected Poems of Wallace Stevens*. New York: Vintage Books, [1954] 1990. 247.

Stierle, Karlheinz. "Moglichkeiten des dunklen Stils in den Anfangen moderner Lyrik in Frankreich." *Lyric als Paradigma der Moderne*. München: W. Fink, 1991.

Tiffany, Daniel. "Lyric Substance: On Riddles, Materialism, and Poetic Obscurity." *Critical Inquiry* 29 (Autumn 2001): 72–98.

Tiffany, Daniel. *Toy Medium: Materialism and Modern Lyric*. Berkeley: University of California P, 2000.

Turing, Alan. "Computing Machinery and Intelligence." *Mind* (October 1960): 433–60.

Turner, Frederick, and Ernst Pöppel. "The Neural Lyre: Poetic Meter, The Brain, and Time." *Poetry* 142, No. 5 (August 1983): 277–309.

Uexküll, Jakob von. "The Theory of Meaning." *Semiotica* 42-1 (1982): 25–82.

Varela, Francisco, Evan Thompson, and Eleanor Rosch. *The Embodied Mind: Cognitive Science and Human Experience*. Cambridge: MIT Press, 1989.

Vattimo, Gianni. *The End of Modernity*. Baltimore: Johns Hopkins UP, 1988.

Vico, Giambatttista. *The New Science*. 3rd ed. Trans. David Marsh. London: Penguin, 1999.

Virgil. "Georgics." *Ecloques, Georgics, Aeneid 1–6*. Trans. H. R. Fairclough. Cambridge: Harvard UP, 1999. 97–259.

Walker, Jeffrey. *Rhetoric and Poetics in Antiquity*. Oxford: Oxford UP, 2000.

Weil, Simone. *Gravity and Grace*. Trans. Arthur Wills. Lincoln: U of Nebraska P, 1952.

Wellek, René. *Discriminations: Further Concepts of Criticism*. New Haven, CT: Yale UP, 1970.

Whitehead, Alfred North. *Process and Reality*. New York: Free P, 1978.

Whitman, Walt. "I Sing the Body Electric." *Leaves of Grass*. Ed. Sculley Bradley and Harold W. Blodgett. New York: W. W. Norton, 1973. 93–101.

Whitman, Walt. "Song of Myself." *Leaves of Grass*. Ed. Sculley Bradley and Harold W. Blodgett. New York: W. W. Norton, 1973. 28–89.

Wilner, Joshua. *Feeding on Infinity: Readings in the Romantic Rhetoric of Internalization*. Baltimore: Johns Hopkins UP, 2000.

Wimsatt, William, and Monroe C. Beardsley. "The Affective Fallacy." *The Verbal Icon: Studies in the Meaning of Poetry*. Lexington: U of Kentucky P, 1954. 21–40.

Woolf, Rosemary. "The Wanderer, The Seafarer, and the Genre of Planctus." *Anglo-Saxon Poetry: Essays in Appreciation for John C. McGalliard*. Ed. Lewis E. Nicholson et al. Notre Dame: U of Notre Dame P, 1975. 192–207.

Wordsworth William. "It is a Beauteous Evening." *Romantic Poetry and Prose*. Ed. Harold Bloom and Lionel Trilling. Oxford: Oxford UP, 1973. 173.

Wordsworth William. "Ode: Intimations of Immortality from Recollections of Early Childhood." *Romantic Poetry and Prose*. Ed. Harold Bloom and Lionel Trilling. Oxford: Oxford UP, 1973. 176–81.

Wordsworth William. "Preface to Lyrical Ballads." *Criticism: Major Statements*. 3rd ed. Ed. Charles Kaplan and William Anderson. New York: St. Martin's, 1991. 256–75.

Wordsworth William. *The Prelude: 1799, 1805, 1850*. Ed. Jonathan Wordsworth, M. H. Abrams, and Stephen Gill. New York: W. W. Norton, 1979.

Wray, Allison. "Protolanguage as a Holistic System for Social Interaction." *Language and Communication* 18 (1998): 47–67.

Yeats, W. B. "Leda and the Swan." poetryfoundation.org. Web. 1 February 2020.

Yeats, W. B. *A Vision*. London: Macmillan, 1937.

Zatorre, Robert J. "Neural Specializations for Tonal Processing." *Annual of the New York Academy of Sciences* 930 (June 2001): 193–210.

Zukofsky, Louis. "An Objective." *Prepositions +: The Collected Critical Essays*. Hanover, NH: Wesleyan UP, 2000. 12–18.

Index

CPSIA information can be obtained
at www.ICGtesting.com
Printed in the USA
LVHW081924111122
732936LV00004B/220